THE ROUND

THE ROUND

In Bob Graham's Footsteps

Steve Chilton

SANDSTONEPRESS
HIGHLAND | SCOTLAND

First published in Great Britain by
Sandstone Press Ltd
Dochcarty Road
Dingwall
Ross-shire
IV15 9UG
Scotland.

www.sandstonepress.com

Commissioning Editor: Robert Davidson
Editor: Roger Smith
Index: Roger Smith

The publisher acknowledges subsidy from
Creative Scotland towards publication of this volume.

ISBN: 978-1-910124-68-0
ISBNe: 978-1-910124-69-7

Cover design and picture layout by Raspberryhmac Creative Type, Edinburgh
Typeset by Iolaire Typesetting, Newtonmore
Printed and bound by Ozgraf, Poland

To Martyn, Josh and Liam, who inherited some of my character traits, but are not (yet) 'following in my footsteps'.

"The record [17:45] was likely to go, Billy having dawdled round in 18:50 back in 1976. He told us pacers that 16 hours was the target, but it was the amount under the target that stopped the world turning . . . Having run (and won) the Ennerdale the previous weekend as a depreciation run our Willie had most of Keswick AC and more dotted round the region . . . The day was still and mild but low cloud obscured the tops all day . . . Broad Stand was the riot it commonly is. Stuart was shoved up to pull up Billy then Jon. I was last and nearly had me and Stuart down Mickledore Chimney . . . Our time off Scafell was ridiculous and a small group was assembled at Wasdale Head. Billy only stopped a very short while, but I recall him with a butty and bottle of Mackeson as I stood croaking behind Joss's car. Only Joss continued with Billy on up Yewbarrow . . ."

From a report by Tony Cresswell, one of Billy Bland's pacers when he set the record of 13 hours 53 minutes (from 'Bob Graham – the Bland Way' in The Fellrunner, *July 1983).* Before researching this book, this was the only first-hand account I had ever come across of the record round. Billy's own account is included later.

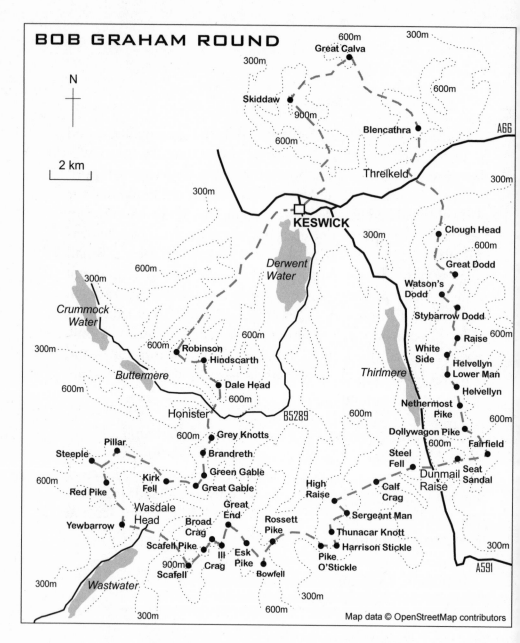

The peaks, route and crossing points

Contents

List of illustrations

1 – Phil Davidson, Bob Graham and Martin Rylands at Dunmail Raise, 13 June 1932
2 – Lizzie Graham (sister), Gordon Graham (nephew) and Bob Graham
3 – Bob Graham, with friends Ruth and Alfred Taylor in 1959
4 – Balmoral House, Lake Road, Keswick – Bob Graham's guesthouse in the late 1930s
5 – Barrow House, which Bob Graham ran as a hotel in the 1940s and 1950s
6 – Derwentwater Independent Hostel (formerly Barrow House) as it is now
7 – Ken Heaton, Alan Heaton and Stan Bradshaw
8 – Joss Naylor on his 60 @ 60 round, 1997
9 – Billy Bland and his support on the run-in through Newlands Valley, 1982 (?, David Bland, Martin Stone, Stuart Bland, Billy, Pete Barron)
10 – Billy Bland, flanked by Pete Barron and Stuart Bland, at the Moot Hall after his 13:53 record round, 1982
11 – Billy Bland and support, (incl Fred Rogerson, Jon Broxap and Joss Naylor) after his record round, 1982
12 – Billy Bland at the Langdale race, 1990
13 – Helene Diamantides/Whitaker at Dunmail on her 1987 round
14 – Helene Diamantides/Whitaker at the end of her solo round in 1988

Photo credits

1 – Abraham Photographic
2 – Gordon Graham
3 – David Taylor
4 – Dickson Barron
5 – Derwentwater Independent
    Hostel archive
6 – Steve Chilton
7 – Copyright unknown
8 – Colin Dulson
9 – Billy Bland
10 – Billy Bland
11 – Billy Bland
12 – Pete Hartley
13 – Helene Whitaker
14 – Helene Whitaker
15 – Anne Johnson
16 – Nicky Spinks

17 – Nicky Spinks
18 – Lee Procter/www.inov-8.com
19 – Mark Hartell
20 – Mark Palmer
21 – Mark McDermott
22 – Mark McDermott
23 – Scottish Hill Runners
24 – Steve Birkinshaw
25 – Jonny Muir
26 – Martin Stone
27 – Patrick Bonnett
28 – Patrick Bonnett
29 – Brian Covell
30 – Patrick Bonnett
31 – Steve Chilton
32 – Steve Chilton

Map

The map of the round was compiled and drawn by the author. Map data is derived from the OpenStreetMap dataset which is available under an ODBL licence (http://www.openstreetmap.org/copyright). The contour data is derived from Andy Allan's reworking of the public domain SRTM data (http://open cyclemap.org/).

Acknowledgements

There are many people to thank for their support, encourage-ment and contributions in the production of this book. Firstly, massive thanks go to Moira for understanding why I wanted to spend so much of my time in researching and writing another book. This was in the full knowledge that it was as unlikely as the first one to contribute any significant finances to possible new lifestyle choices. But I do hope she feels that the pleasure I have got out of the research and interviewing process, and the pain of the writing process, have been worth any sacrifices on the way.

I would like to acknowledge help with research given by several library teams. A number of productive days were spent in Kendal public library, and I really appreciated the support of staff there, particularly Jackie Faye. Middlesex University provided an efficient inter-library loan service. A lead from Middlesex took me to the Leeds University library. Staff in the Brotherton Library (Special Collections team) were fantastic – and what a brilliant building to work in.

The range of sources has been very wide, and every effort has been made to contact copyright owners, authors and publishers so that appropriate attribution of original sources could be made. In particular I would like to acknowledge two particular sources I have gone back to repeatedly. First, the Fell Runners Association (FRA) archive of digital copies of *The Fellrunner* magazine, which goes up to 2006 and is now available to read via their website. The following individual authors from that source have agreed to allow me to reproduce information from reports or articles they wrote for that publication: Des Oliver, Billy Bland, Tony Cresswell, Martin Stone, Mark Palmer and Alison Crabb.

Secondly, much valuable material was compiled by Fred Rogerson in his loose-leaf 'publication' entitled *History and Records of Notable Fell Walks, 1864–1972, Within the Lake District* (henceforth *Notable Walks . . .*). This is hard to get hold of, and I am immensely grateful that Cumbria Libraries hold a copy of it. Jeff Ford (of the Mountain Heritage Trust) tried valiantly, but ultimately unsuccessfully, to obtain a copy of the booklet for me, but he came up trumps by securing for me a DVD copy of a programme shown on Border TV *It's Bob's Round* (directed by Jannicke Wallace). Thirdly, Roger Smith and Paddy Buckley agreed for short quotes from the editions of *42 Peaks* that they edited to be used. Paddy also supplied copies of a couple of early photos from his own collection.

Bob Wightman kindly agreed to let me reproduce his findings on the early proto-rounds, and the differences in routes taken. He had compiled this information for the website he runs about the Bob Graham Round, and has generously allowed me to quote extensively from it. Staff at the Derwentwater Independent Hostel, Nicola and Kathy in particular, provided useful information on Graham's time running it as a hotel, plus a couple of photos from their archive. Through them I was able to make contact with a member of Bob Graham's family, who now lives in Scotland, but does occasionally call in to the hostel for old times' sake. Gordon Graham (Bob's nephew) provided some fascinating material about Bob's early life, plus a photo used in the book.

Massive thanks are due to the fell running community. Its members unfailingly managed to provide me with contacts, links, and information when asked, often via the lively FRA Forum. These contacts allowed me to conduct a series of crucial interviews with some of the main players in this story. For so generously agreeing to meet with me, give up their time, and share their stories I am owe a debt to the following: Adrian Belton, Steve Birkinshaw, Billy Bland, Colin Donnelly, Mark Hartell, Anne Johnson, Jim Mann, Mark McDermott, Jonny Muir, Mark Palmer, Nicky Spinks, Martin Stone, and Helene Whitaker. In most cases we may not have met before, but it is great to have met and shared memories with you. I hope I have done you all justice, and that I haven't misrepresented any of you.

Many people have provided photos from their own collections, although by its nature trying to traverse so many peaks as fast as one is able doesn't actually allow too many photo stops, so it wasn't always possible to use ones from actual Bob Graham Rounds. Individual photos are credited as appropriate.

I had real trouble deciding on a title for this book. The title for the previous one – *It's a hill, get over it* – just fell into my hands, and worked so well in so many ways. This time I had several ideas, which riffed on slightly different themes. I sought advice from Moira, and also from three members of my athletic club, Ed Price, Michael Martin and Jamie March, who I thought might help. We did a bit of 'title bouncing', and the feedback from them all was instrumental in me deciding on the result you see on the cover.

Celia Cozens was that vital critical friend that authors need to give a dispassionate view on the manuscript as it develops. Her advice on structuring the narrative around the interviews was absolutely crucial to the style adopted, and she later carried out an initial proof read for me. Alan Durant was my second critical friend and he once again offered constructive comments involving changes that I hope have improved my writing.

I would like to express my grateful thanks to all at Sandstone Press, especially Bob Davidson – who has again guided me patiently through the process of bringing my second book to press.

Prologue

Bob Graham started his Lake District round at Keswick Town Hall at 1am on Sunday 13 June 1932. Skiddaw was climbed by the standard route. He continued on to Great Calva and then to Blencathra, and so down to Threlkeld. Then began the long stretch over the Dodds to Helvellyn, and then via Fairfield and Seat Sandal to Dunmail Raise. For all of this period Graham was paced by Martin Rylands, who was a skilled and experienced mountain walker. George Abrahams was at Dunmail Raise to take photographs.

After a short break he tackled the central Lakeland fells, taking the Scafells by way of Mickledore and Broad Stand, and so down to Wasdale, where he had another short break. Graham was accompanied by Phil Davidson, from Keswick, over this tough section. Up over Yewbarrow and the peaks through the Gables to Honister with Robin Dean, from Aspatria, as pacer. Darkness was now coming in for the final section as Bill Hewitson paced Graham over Dale Head, Hindscarth and Robinson. They passed near Mill Dam Inn in the Newlands Valley at 11.52pm. They were re-joined by Rylands and Davidson, and the remaining run-in to Keswick was covered in good time, and at 12.39am they reached Keswick Town Hall.

Davidson had left Graham at Wasdale and gone over Sty Head to Keswick. He went home for a bath and some food, then trotted out to Newlands. Small groups of people, including companions on the fells, were gathered at several points along the road from Newlands and at the finish to cheer and congratulate him. After finishing, Bob and the pacers retired to Bob's guest house for a meal and much needed rest. Graham was up at 6am to cook his pacers breakfast, and they all went off to their respective jobs.

Introduction

Few sports are less competitive than mountaineering and none of us would like to see the Lake District hills turned into a race track, but for a century able mountaineers have now and again accepted the challenge of so many mountains grouped closely together and used them to test out their stamina and endurance. At first there was no record as such, for men accustomed to long days in the Alps simply wanted to see how hard a day they could manage in the Lakeland hills. But gradually the walks, without ever achieving proper rules, began to be slightly regularized, and the main aim became the ascent of as many mountains as possible within the 24 hours, the walker always returning to his starting point.

One might ask why people should bother to tear their hearts out on these sorts of tests. Unlike some record breakers in other fields they achieve little or no fame – sometimes the attempts have been kept very secret indeed – and, of course, they make no money out of it, nor would wish to do so. I believe that most of these fit, and often very distinguished, mountaineers have taken part in these exceptionally strenuous feats simply in order to test themselves to the very limit. Physical fitness is as worthwhile an aim as many others and it does man good to know just what he can do. He is not so much trying to beat a record as to beat himself. Although the physical effort must be tremendous, the mental effort – the determination to carry on despite increasing bodily fatigue – is even greater, and this necessary discipline of mind and body is undoubtedly a good thing. Some people might look down their noses at record breakers, and I must confess to an abhorrence of speed records on rock climbs, but I see nothing wrong in a man trying out his strength and courage, unwatched and probably almost alone, in the Lakeland hills. In a way, that's why they are there.

And the requirements are not merely stamina and willpower, for the fell record contender must also know the hills intimately and be a mountaineer in the broad sense of the word. The average harrier, although equipped with wonderful lungs and superb leg muscles, is not likely to be capable of ascending or descending, unroped and wearing his running shoes, the greasy slabs of Broad Stand in heavy rain or perhaps even in darkness, which, as often as not, is the lot of the would-be fell record breaker. And the traverse of the roughest ground in England at speed in darkness or mist, or a combination of the two, is the sort of test that only a mountaineer can successfully tackle. A sound knowledge of map and compass work under the most difficult conditions is, of course, essential and to have even a chance of success a contender must be more familiar with the lie of the land than the average fell walker. The whole project, too, must be most thoroughly planned with timings, feeding stations and resting points arranged in advance, tested companions carefully chosen, and food and clothing requirements catered for.

Perhaps it would be misleading to suggest that the appreciation of mountain scenery comes into the picture at all, since the contender is less concerned with the view than the more leisured walker or climber, but, at the same time, all these tough record breakers have at least noticed the beauty around them and been properly impressed by the changing glories and drama of a long, full day in the hills.

The words in those four paragraphs are not mine. They are from a chapter entitled 'The Long Walk' in Harry Griffin's long out of print book, *In Mountain Lakeland,* and are chosen because I think they neatly sum up what the Bob Graham Round (as it became known) is about, and also give a real feel for the mores of the time. The book was published in 1963, just after Alan Heaton had been the first to repeat Bob Graham's Lakeland feat of traversing 42 peaks, over 62 miles, with 27,000 feet of ascent, all within 24 hours. As the story of the Bob Graham Round unfolds it is an interesting yardstick against which to compare the later efforts of the highly competitive 'athletes' whose stories form the backbone of this book.

I come to this subject with no particular personal insights to give. I have not completed the Bob Graham Round myself. However, I have competed in fell races over much of the ground covered, and have certainly walked nearly all the peaks over the years. In fact I once set out to walk the whole round, over several days with a friend. For reasons lost in the mists of time we had a small disagreement on the approach being taken, and I lost the plot around Calf Crag, going across to Steel Fell on leg 3 (anticlockwise). The fleshpots of Grasmere were calling, and I wandered down Easedale instead of carrying on with the last two legs of the round.

This is also not a 'how to do it' book, although I suspect that some of the experiences of others will certainly be either motivators, or reality checks, for any Bob Graham Round (BGR) aspirant. The book tells both the story of the early endeavours that led to the round by Bob Graham in 1932, and something of Bob Graham's life, some of which may be new in the telling – this latter being in part thanks to a chance connection to a cousin of Bob Graham, who provided some early details that I believe have not been published elsewhere. A large part of the story is told through the eyes of men and women who completed early rounds, set record times or were innovators in tackling solo, winter or unsupported attempts. The times I have spent interviewing some of the main players have been some of the most enjoyable interludes in my recent life. Their generosity of time and thought has been invaluable and I hope will give a feel for what it means to be part of this iconic event.

There has been more than one occasion recently when I have had to say to myself 'remain calm and professional, it is just another person you are talking to'. I have had to try to ignore the fact that I might be shooting the breeze with someone whom I have admired from afar for years for their achievements. This was never more so than in the case of Billy Bland. However, the absolute bonus from talking with Billy is that I feel I am now able to throw new light on his motives, in particular for doing his record round when he did – sandwiched as it was between him winning two Lakeland Classics in one five-week spell.

I have not especially looked at extended rounds, except where they are relevant to a person's Bob Graham Round. As in any historical work, I have relied to a considerable extent on those who have gone before me, standing on giants' shoulders where necessary. I would like to thank all those in the fell running community with whom I have networked, and talked, for their input in to this journey in Bob Graham's footsteps. My debt to the all these individuals is detailed in the acknowledgements section.

But first let's consider the time before Bob Graham's 'long walk' and some of the events that were precursors to it.

Chapter 1

Origins of the challenge

It has always been a human characteristic to want to challenge oneself, from exploring new territories to setting athletic records. As I noted in my more general history and discussion of fell running, *It's a hill, get over it*,[1] 'the exploits of 19th century 'pedestrians' such as Robert Barclay Allardice, Corky Gentleman and the Flying Pieman provide some of the earliest formal endurance records'. I have tried in this book to bring together the various reports and analyses of these early events. That material also leans heavily on the work of Bob Wightman (the indented paragraphs in this chapter). Other material is based on the writing of Harry Griffin (particularly his book *In Mountain Lakeland*).

By the 1860s there were adventurous individuals, and sometimes groups, testing themselves in the Lake District fells and achieving ever more impressive 'walking rounds'. Possibly the first significant round of the fells was by Rev. J. M. Elliott of Cambridge, who in 1864 (or thereabouts, sources vary) departed from Wasdale Head and returned there eight and a half hours later after going over nine of the highest mountains in the Lakes. These were Scafell, Scafell Pike, Great End, Great Gable, Kirk Fell, Pillar, Steeple, Red Pike and Stirrup Crag,[2] making a distance of about 15 miles which involved some 6,500 feet of ascent. This round was eventually to become the basis

---

1 *It's a hill, get over it*, Steve Chilton, Sandstone Press (Inverness, 2013).
2 Griffin listed it as Yewbarrow in '*In Mountain Lakeland*'.

of the Lake District 24-hour Fell Record. Unfortunately, Elliott was killed on the Schreckhorn in the Bernese Oberland in 1869.

Six years later Thomas Watson from Darlington, together with Thomas Wilson (a Borrowdale guide) walked for 20 hours and covered 48 miles, with 10,000-plus feet of ascent. Starting from Keswick they walked to Scafell Pike and then cut across to traverse the Helvellyn range, followed by Blencathra and Skiddaw, finishing in Keswick. They did all this in nailed boots, several times losing their way in thick mist. They also had snow showers on Scafell Pike and gales that forced them to crawl to the summit of Blencathra.

An uncredited article in *The Manchester Guardian*[1] noted another five rounds in this period that are not included in either Wightman's or Baddeley's list, but were later repeated in the Fell and Rock Climbing Club Journal (the details are as per the newspaper article):

1869 – Pilkington and Bennett: Keswick, Scafell, Helvellyn, Skiddaw, Keswick. Time, 20h. (The details of the exact route have not been given)

187? – An Alpine Club man[2] *and Mackereth:* Bowfell, Scafell Pike, Helvellyn, and Skiddaw. Time, within the day. Ascent 9,000ft. Distance 41 miles; equivalent to nearly 60. (As yet full particulars of this walk have not been forthcoming)

1871 (the "Cornhill Magazine" of April, 1899, gives the date of this walk as 1876). – Jenkinson: Keswick, Great Gable, Scafell Pikes, Bowfell, Langdale Combe Head, Wythburn, Helvellyn, Saddleback, Skiddaw, Keswick. Much delay caused by mist. Time, 25h. Ascent, 12,250ft. Distance, 53 miles; equivalent of more than 80. (High Raise apparently included in this round)

---

1   'Notable fell walks' – in the edition dated 2 Mar 1906

2   The Cornhill Magazine article (noted in next entry) also does not identify Mackereth's companion, describing him just as 'a well-known member of the Alpine Club'. The article, by William T Palmer, gives considerable detail of the various rounds.

1871 – Pilkington and Bennett: Dungeon Ghyll, Bowfell, Scafell Pikes, Great Gable, Skiddaw, Saddleback, Helvellyn, Fairfield, Dungeon Ghyll. Time 21h 10min. Ascent, 12,900ft. Distance, 60 miles; equivalent to nearly 80

1878 – The brothers Tucker: Elterwater, Bowfell, Scafell Pikes, Skiddaw (via Borrowdale), Helvellyn, Grasmere, Elterwater (via Rydal and Ambleside, some 10 miles extra). Time, 19h 38min. Ascent, 9,000ft. Distance, 50 miles; equivalent to more than 60

Baddeley's 1964 Lake District guidebook[1] gave details of the following early 'rounds' (the editor doesn't acknowledge any of the earlier rounds noted above, except Elliott's, simply saying 'subjoined is a list of some of the most notable fell walks'):

1883 Charles and Lawrence Pilkington and Matthew Barnes.

Lodore – Great Gable – Scafell Pike – Great End – Bowfell – Fairfield – Helvellyn (via Dollywagon Pike) – Blencathra – Skiddaw – Lodore. 24 hours 25 minutes.

Lawrence Pilkington was a well-known mountaineer, his brother Charles was President of the Alpine Club, and Barnes was reported to be 'the guide'. They left Lodore at 11pm, were held up by thick mist on Great Gable, and were reckoned to have climbed around 13,000 feet and covered an estimated 60 miles (although these early estimated values are notably unreliable).

Getting from Bowfell to Fairfield without including intervening tops such as the Langdale Pikes or High Raise seems odd. However the description of the 1902 round of Johnson and Strong (see below) indicates that the preferred way at the time was to ascend/descend Bowfell via The Band and Stool End Farm, follow the road down Langdale, then go via Red Bank to Grasmere, thus avoiding the tops altogether.

---

1 *Baddeley's Lake District*, edited by R.J.W. Hammond [23rd Edition], Ward, Lock & Co (London, 1964).

1893 Robinson and Gibbs. Keswick – Great Gable – Scafell Pike – Great End – Bowfell – Langdale Combe Head – Wythburn – Helvellyn – Blencathra – Skiddaw (abandoned on Skiddaw). 23 hours 25 minutes.

John Wilson Robinson was a climber from Lorton, his companion being from Sunderland. Griffin reports this October round in detail in *In Mountain Lakeland*:[1] 'They carried alpenstocks and found plenty of use for them in the snow and ice on Scafell, while Gibbs had to be let down the slippery ledges of Broad Stand by means of the rucksack, kicking the ice off the holds as they precariously descended.' They later encountered storms, gales and deep darkness, but made good use of Robinson's local knowledge, because he knew the mountains better than most and commented in a letter to a friend: 'I am slow and should never dream of attempting a record, but have always felt that if I had any slight advantage over some others it was merely knowing the Scafell range pretty well.' This suggests that records were already in his, and others', thoughts.

> This round is interesting in that the descent into Langdale is now avoided, hence the references to Langdale Combe and Wythburn. However getting to Wythburn from there without traversing at least one top (a guess would be High Raise) and not mentioning it is somewhat strange. This round was also unusual in that it was attempted towards the end of October.

1895 Dawson, Poole and Palmer. Elterwater – Bowfell – Scafell Pike – Skiddaw – Helvellyn – Grasmere – Elterwater (via Rydal and Ambleside). 19 hours 18 minutes.

This took place in August, but they had to struggle through thick mists which lingered over the summits all day.

> Palmer apparently was the only one of the three who knew the route between the central fells and Helvellyn and he retired with an injured knee on Scafell.

---

1 *In Mountain Lakeland*, A H Griffin, 1963

1898 Broadrick Windermere – Bowfell – Great End – Scafell Pike – Scafell – Great Gable – Skiddaw – Helvellyn – Windermere. 20 hours 30 minutes (the 12 miles from Windermere to Stool End in Langdale were done on a bike).

The account of this round mentions ascending Bowfell via Hell Gill, which lies just to the south of The Band, rather than The Band itself.

1899 Westmorland, Strong, Johnson and Beaty. Seathwaite – Great Gable – Pillar – Scafell – Scafell Pike – Bowfell – Wythburn (via Langdale Combe and High Raise) – Helvellyn – Blencathra – Skiddaw – Keswick. 19 hours 25 minutes.

The first round (though note the different start and finish) to include any of the fells to the west of Great Gable. The omission of Kirk Fell suggests that the trod used by the Wasdale fell race around the northern flank of Kirk Fell was taken. Also note that High Raise is now explicitly mentioned.

1899 Westmorland and Beaty same fells from Threlkeld to Threlkeld in 23 hours 30 minutes.

These two must have enjoyed the earlier attempt, because they had another go at a complete round only a month or so after their previous effort.

1901 Broadrick. Rosthwaite – Great Gable – Pillar – Scafell – Scafell Pike – Bowfell – Fairfield – Helvellyn – Blencathra – Skiddaw – Rosthwaite. 23 hours 30 minutes.

Broadrick wrote a detailed report of his efforts for the Yorkshire Ramblers' Club Journal.[1] It contains some classic understatements about how they went about this sort of activity at the time. On one occasion he went alone and his account was accused of exaggeration. His opinion was that flannel clothing

1   Available at: http://www.yrc.org.uk/yrcweb/index.php/journal/vols1-5/45-vol1-cat/no4/87-v1n4p309

was best, and that knickerbockers were inappropriate. For his big round he hoped for a 'civilised meal about every five hours', and noted they spent 15 minutes dining inside the Dungeon Ghyll Hotel. His companion, identified as Mr Dawson (*possibly the participant in the 1895 round*), bathed in Grisedale Tarn, one of 5 swims he had on the round. On the section in the dark they had problems with their candle-powered lantern, the wind playing havoc with it.[1]

1902 Johnson and Strong. Threlkeld – Helvellyn – Fairfield – Bowfell – Great End – Scafell Pike – Scafell – Pillar – Great Gable – Skiddaw – Blencathra – Threlkeld. 22 hours 7 minutes.

Jones and Milburn noted: 'About 1902, Mr. S. B. Johnson of Carlisle accompanied by M. Strong set off from Threlkeld at 5am. By 7.20 they were on the summit of Helvellyn, by 8.19 Fairfield. They passed through the village of Grasmere at 9.12 thence over Red Bank to Langdale, arriving at Stool End Farm at 10.15. Mr. Westmorland joined them as guide. The summit of Bowfell was reached at 12 noon. Wasdale Head at 3.20 having traversed the Scafell range. Then, via Dore Head to Pillar at 4.33. Seathwaite via Gable at 7.25. They stayed 45 minutes at Seathwaite resting and refreshing themselves. With Mr Beaty now leading they reached Keswick in under 2 hours, the summit of Skiddaw at midnight. They marked out a course by the stars to reach Blencathra at 2.10 The descent down Hall's Ridge to the Lead Mines took some 45 minutes, Threlkeld, the starting point, was reached at 3.07, the round trip taking 22 hours 7 minutes.'[2]

The comment 'Then, via Dore Head to Pillar' indicates that Red Pike was traversed but perhaps not visited. Dore Head is the col at the northern end of Yewbarrow and for many years

---

1 According to an article in *The Manchester Guardian* on 15 May 1903, 'they both finished well and seemed in no way over-fatigued, and next morning were as fresh as any of their friends, one going up Scawfell for a stroll and the other a 28-mile ride on his cycle as a change'.

2 Jones T. and Milburn G. *Cumbrian Rock* ISBN 0-9511114-2-6.

had a well-known scree run down to the valley floor which would be useful on an anti-clockwise round using this route.

1904 Wakefield. Keswick – Great Gable – Kirk Fell – Pillar – Scafell – Scafell Pike – Bowfell – Fairfield – Helvellyn – Blencathra – Skiddaw – Keswick. 19 hours 53 minutes.

It is believed, because of their omission, that the northern Helvellyn tops were not traversed. In which case, the most likely descent would be to the public house at Thirlspot and then by road through St John's Vale to Threlkeld.[1] The roads in the district weren't paved at that time. The surface of many country roads was probably closer to that of modern forest access roads or rougher – hardly any better than keeping to the tops. The time of the Johnson and Strong team getting from Threlkeld to Helvellyn in 2 hours 20 minutes is not too dissimilar to that of a modern round going over the tops. It is possible that certain areas of the fells or fell approaches were simply 'off-limits' with landowners or estates preventing access, hence the avoidance of lines of fells such as the northern Helvellyn section.

1905 Wakefield Keswick – Robinson – Hindscarth – Dale Head – Brandreth – Green Gable – Great Gable – Kirk Fell – Pillar – Steeple – Red Pike – Yewbarrow – Scafell – Scafell Pike – Great End – Hanging Knott – Bowfell – Fairfield – Dollywagon Pike – Helvellyn – Blencathra – Skiddaw – Keswick. 22 hours 7 minutes.

This was the first round to include the Dale Head group. Also Kirk Fell and the remainder of the tops around the head of Wasdale are now included. In fact, with the exception of the section between Bowfell and Fairfield, as previously noted, and the omission of the northern Helvellyn section, this is a prototype 'Bob Graham Round'.

---

1 A report of the round in *The Manchester Guardian* of 1 Aug 1904 seems to confirm this, noting as it does 'a fifteen minute stop at Fisher Place for tea'. Fisher Place is in the valley, near Thirlmere.

A report on the round in *The Sedberghian* (Wakefield's old school magazine) explained in detail some of the low level alternative routes that he took between some of the peaks, for example coming down from Helvellyn to Thirlspot and using St John's in the Vale to get to Threlkeld before tackling Blencathra. Also Bowfell to Fairfield was accomplished by coming down the Band, then going over Red Bank to Grasmere and on. Wakefield did establish the tradition of the record holder assisting the contender to break his own record, helping Eustace Thomas on his effort in 1920.

An academic paper by Jonathan Westaway in *Sport in History*[1] includes some fascinating detail of these rounds by Wakefield et al, including a note about a record that was never accepted:

[Cecil] Dawson's last effort on the 16 June 1916, was completely successful. His time of 22 hours 17 minutes was ten minutes longer than Wakefield's, but he included Stybarrow Dodd and Great Dodd, which meant an extra six miles. Despite this, Dawson's claim on the record was not accepted by many people, perhaps because of sensitivities about the appropriateness of undertaking sporting stunts during wartime.[2]

---

1 Men who can last: Mountaineering endurance, the Lake District Fell Records and the campaign for Everest, 1919–1924. Jonathan Westaway, *Sport in History*, Special Issue on climbing, Vol.33, issue 4, 2013

2 Westaway continues: "The Lake District based Fell and Rock Climbing Club 'refused to have anything to do with the dispute, disclaiming any authority in the matter' and this was to be the position it would maintain, Eustace Thomas also indicating that the FRCC committee 'had passed a resolution that they would not recognize anything in the nature of racing on the Fells' after his successful attempt. Class-based assumptions undoubtedly played a part. Dawson was in trade and from Manchester, whilst Wakefield was a professional, on active service and from an established Kendal family. The phrase 'racing on the Fells' implies more than a whiff of condescension and an implicit rejection of any hint of working-class foot racing."

Westaway includes some background to the next attempt by Eustace Thomas, and expands in great detail on the reason for the vegetarian diet and other aspects of what Thomas called 'Mountain Endurance: Notes on a System of Training':[1]

1920 (29 May) Eustace Thomas. Virtually as above but in 21 hours 25 minutes.

Eustace Thomas, a member of the Manchester-based Rucksack Club, set out to beat that record. Coached by Wakefield and on a strict vegetarian diet, the 54-year-old Thomas trained for seven weeks in Borrowdale, beating the record over the Wakefield course with a time of 21 hours 25 minutes, a full 42 minutes under Wakefield's time.

Thomas appears to have been remarkably fit and something of an outdoor polymath. He was the first Briton to climb all the 4000m peaks in the Alps and was also responsible for the route now taken by the High Peak marathon, as well as doing the first traverse of the Welsh 3000ft peaks.

Westaway's paper also notes that an earlier book by W. T. Palmer[2] had already commented on the increasingly 'professional' approach being employed on these attempts, including an acknowledgement of the use of pacers:

---

1 Eustace Thomas, 'Mountaineering Endurance: Notes on a System of Training', *The Rucksack Club Journal*, 4, No.3, Issue No. 15 (1921). His system: ". . . encompassed a thorough reconnoitring of the route, gymnastics and mountain-based training, the use of lightweight clothing and footwear, massage, spinal exercises and foot preparation. Sleep, rest and psychological disposition were all covered. Above all Thomas' approach sought to understand the problem of endurance from a systematic physiological perspective, incorporating analysis of the nervous system, the respiratory system and breathing technique, the biomechanics of movement, gait and pace. The critical factor in Thomas' system was his analysis of the 'source of energy, and nature of fatigue'."

2 W. T. Palmer, *In Lakeland Dells and Fells* (London: Chatto and Windus, 1903)

Reflecting on the previous 40 years of endeavour in mountain endurance pedestrianism in the Lake District, W. T. Palmer noted the increasingly systematic approach to the Twenty-four Hour Record: 'pacing and prearrangement of all kinds is considered necessary, and the record-maker is relieved of all impedimenta'.

1922 Eustace Thomas. Keswick – Robinson – Hindscarth – Dale Head – Brandreth – Green Gable – Great Gable – Kirk Fell – Pillar – Steeple – Red Pike – Yewbarrow – Scafell – Scafell Pike – Bowfell – Fairfield – Helvellyn – White Side – Raise – Stybarrow Dodd – Great Dodd – Clough Head – Blencathra – Great Calva – Skiddaw – Keswick – Grisedale Pike – Grasmoor – Wandope – Eel Crag – Sail – Causey Pike – Newlands. 28 hours 5 minutes.

Not satisfied with repeating Wakefield's route, two years later Thomas improved on it, adding Great Calva. This was also the first round to include (at least explicitly) the tops on the ridge to the north of Helvellyn, though not Watson's Dodd. No start or finish point is given in Baddeley. In fact, Thomas started in Keswick and after completing the round went on to add the Grasmoor group. Despite this, the list of peaks (omitting the Grasmoor group) looks remarkably similar to a modern round. Add in those tops that would be traversed or passed close by – Grey Knotts, Broad Crag, Ill Crag, Great End, Esk Pike, Dollywagon Pike, Nethermost Pike, Helvellyn Lower Man, and Watson's Dodd – and the only tops missing are those nine on the modern round between Bowfell and Fairfield.

There were several attempts to better Thomas's time. Then, in 1931, Bob Graham made a first attempt, which ended in failure thanks to a navigational error. He waited a year and tried again. This meant adding another peak to the list of tops, because he had decided he wanted one top for each of his 42 years. Bob

Graham took 21 minutes less than the 24 hours to complete his round in a clockwise direction. It was reported to be a distance of 130 miles with 32,000 ft of ascent, which is now recognised to be grossly exaggerated.

Baddeley reported that on June 13, 1932, **Robert Graham** created what is probably a world walking record. The route was: Keswick – Skiddaw – Great Calva – Saddleback – Wanthwaite Pike – Helvellyn – Dollywagon Pike – Fairfield – Seat Sandal – Steel Fell – Calf Crag – High White Stones – High Raise – Sergeant Man – Harrison Stickle – Pike o'Stickle – Rossett Pike – Hanging Knotts – Bowfell – Esk Pike – Great End – Scafell Pike – Scafell – Yewbarrow – Red Pike – Steeple – Pillar – Kirk Fell – Great and Green Gable – Brandreth – Honister Hause – Dale Head – Hindscarth –Robinson – High Snab – Keswick. The round was completed in 23 hours 39 minutes.

Bob Wightman noted the following irregularities:[1]

It is likely that Graham knew the details of Thomas's round, so there is a reasonable chance that Great Calva was part of his original plans. However, Phil Davidson (one of his pacers) stated that this was the extra peak added to tally with Graham's age.

1. I think that Wanthwaite Pike is the same as Clough Head – there is no summit of that name around Threlkeld. Wanthwaite Crags lie just to the west of the summit. The 1867 map of the area does not show any summit by this name.
2. Great Dodd – Watson's Dodd – Stybarrow Dodd – Raise – Whiteside are not listed but it is known from other sources that he traversed these.
3. High White Stones is 'a slightly marked elevation a little south of Greenup Edge'; this could be the prominence at

---

1 http://bobwightman.co.uk/run/bgr_history.php

282101, but is marked on modern maps as the summit area of High Raise so it is not clear why both are listed. One consideration is that fells often have two names: one is the name of the pasture used by farmers and shepherds, the other is for the summit itself.

4. Looking Stead, on the ridge down from Pillar to Black Sail Pass, is given as one of the original 42 but is missing from this list.

5. Rogerson (1979)[1] gives the current 42 rather than the original set. Also, High White Stones is named rather than High Raise.

6. Thus this list only gives 34 tops (39 if the northern Helvellyn ones are added) for Bob Graham's round, not the expected 42. He would have to have passed over Helvellyn Lower Man and would have passed over or close to Nethermost Pike, Thunacar Knott and Grey Knotts. These would take the total to 43.

The efforts noted in this chapter all happened in an era vastly different to the present day. In Westaway's research, noted above, he rather loftily proposed that in the late 19th century the 'normative codes of masculinity valued a "neo-Spartan virility as exemplified by stoicism, hardiness and endurance", which was personified by figures such as the soldier-hero or the imperial explorer', before going on to suggest that:

Divided by the Great War, Wakefield's 1905 Lake District Twenty-four Hour Fell Record and Eustace Thomas's 1920 and 1922 records enable us to evaluate changing cultural conceptions of values such as endurance, stamina, perseverance and stoicism and their relationship to the construction of masculinity. For roughly a decade after the Great War these endurance events took on a heightened symbolic importance, part of the wider post-War reconstruction of masculinity. In

1   Rogerson F. *History and Records of Notable Fell Walks, 1864 – 1978, within the Lake District,* 1979

the immediate post-war period, defining the limits of human physical and psychological performance offered some kind of hope that what could not be overcome by main force could be endured, that new forms of human physical cultivation were perhaps the only possible response to mechanized wars of attrition. These mountain trials formed part of a wider phenomenon within the British outdoor movement, where enactive repertoires of strenuous rambling attempted to create a communion of shared endurance between the Home Front and the Western Front, the post-War world and what had gone before. In the period 1919 to 1932, the Lake District Twenty-four Hour Fell Records became, in both senses of the word, monumental feats of endurance.

Various attempts to extend the range of the endurance feats in the Lake District took place in the six decades after the Rev J. M. Elliott's first recorded 'long walk'. Bob Graham's round in 1932 was the culmination of this series of efforts to test man's endurance in this arena.

So, what more detail do we know about Bob Graham and his eponymous round?

Chapter 2

Bob Graham and the 1932 Round

Although the round mentioned in these pages is usually referred to as the Bob Graham Round (often shortened to BGR), it does not take in the same tops as the original. Bob Wightman notes on his Bob Graham website that:

> Graham's round did not include Helvellyn Lower Man, Ill Crag or Broad Crag despite his route passing over the first and close to the other two. In their place were Hanging Knotts, Looking Stead and High Snab.[1] The first of these is on Bowfell, the second on Pillar and the last on the North Ridge of Robinson. In fact Hanging Knotts and Looking Stead are often included in attempts at a 50 at 50 or higher round.

Also on the website, Bob Wightman comments:

> Griffin notes that 'On Buttermere Red Pike it started to rain and there was mist on Robinson and Dale Head . . . but when they reached Newlands Hause they knew it was downhill all the way home and that they could not fail.' I think that there is confusion here between the Red Pikes of Buttermere and Wasdale – the latter is most certainly traversed whereas the Buttermere fell is not on any usual round being on an outlying ridge. Also it is mentioned that

---

1 Wightman acknowledges that this information originally came from Bill Smith's *Stud marks on the summits*

they took just 39 minutes for the seven miles from Newlands Hause back to Keswick – hardly likely at that stage in a round. Both Baddeley and Smith note that High Snab, not really a summit in any sense of the word, was traversed. If this was the case, and it makes more sense, then Graham would not have visited Newlands Hause. It is possible that Griffin confused Graham's round with that of Alan Heaton who did go via that route.

The distance has often been misrepresented as being anything up to 140 miles in the various accounts, which do however usually give a fairly accurate estimate of height climbed as around 30,000 feet (and for effect stating that is greater than the height of Everest). *42 Peaks* notes that 'the record attempt was originally planned for the previous weekend, but had been called off because of poor weather.'

Contemporary accounts suggest that they ate very little during the round. For food Graham had bread and butter, lightly boiled eggs, plenty of fruit, and sweets for energy. Further detail is provided in a contemporary report which records that:

> In the early part of the day he ate fruit pastilles. At 10am he had a boiled egg, two thin slices of bread and butter and some tea. At 5pm he had two lightly boiled eggs and milk and soda. At 9.45pm he had some hot milk, and at the last 4 miles some hot strong tea.[1]

Graham was by no means a natural athlete. He was short and stocky, but had an excellent knowledge of the fells and was a keen, teetotal, vegetarian, non-smoking fitness enthusiast. The round was done on a very warm day, and he wore tennis shoes, shorts and a pyjama jacket. His pacers carried a pair of boots for him, but he chose not to use them. He walked the uphills, and ran the downhill sections.

---

1   In the *Lancashire Evening Post* on Thursday 5 Dec 1935

The splits for Bob Graham's 1932 round are available,[1] apart from the fact that the individual times taken for legs 1 and 2 (Keswick to Threlkeld and Threlkeld to Dunmail) are given as a combined time:

Keswick – Dunmail	8 hrs 30 mins	inc 30 mins rest at Dunmail
Dunmail – Wasdale	7 hrs 45 mins	inc 30 mins rest at Wasdale
Wasdale – Honister	4 hrs 45 mins	inc 15 mins rest at Honister
Honister – Keswick	2 hrs 39 mins	No rest

In an article in the Autumn 1972 *Fellrunner* magazine, Des Oliver stated that Bob Graham regularly walked 50 miles over the fells whatever the weather.

As part of his 'preparation' for his attempt at the fell record he walked over every fell he intended to include in his BARE FEET (imagine walking over Scafell Pike in your bare feet). His reason for this was two-fold: to toughen the skin (he suffered no blisters when he eventually broke the record), and to save wear and tear on the footwear (gym shoes). His memories of the walk included picking up grouse chicks from the heather crossing Calva; meeting George Abraham for a time and foot check on Dunmail Raise (a photo taken here shows Bob and his two 'pacers' wearing shorts which were pulled on especially for photographs. The Skiddaw/Helvellyn section was done without wearing the heavy khaki drill shorts only available in those days – no worries about meeting maddening crowds in 1932; being given some Nestles milk by the quarrymen at Honister who lodged in the hut which is now the Youth Hostel.

Des Oliver knew Bob Graham, and had a go at the round in the 1950s. He was also a member of the original Bob Graham Club

---

1   In Rogerson's '*History and Records of Notable Fell Walks, 1864–1972, Within the Lake District*'

committee when it was set up in 1971. I queried some of the detail in his quote above with him, particularly the training in bare feet. Oliver expanded on some detail, although he did note that it was 'all so long ago'.

> He [Bob Graham] told me about the walking in bare feet – including Scafell Pike! When I was preparing to repeat his route I was walking bare foot above the Buttermere fells and stood on a broken fence post with resulting bad lacerations, and that was the end of that idea.

Oliver was less certain about other detail, saying he couldn't confirm whether it was to toughen his [Graham's] feet or to save footwear (there were no fell runners' shoes in those days). He didn't think they would have 'picked up' grouse chicks, but that they did see them as they crossed Great Calva. He confirmed that:

> Nestles milk, from a tube, was taken at Honister, but from whom I don't know. Regarding Bob 'regularly' walking 50 miles over the fells this may be true, but I can't confirm. But I can confirm that Bob Graham and Phil Davidson walked from Keswick over to High Street and back the week before the record walk.

Bob Graham Round 'guru' Fred Rogerson, made this comment in part explanation for his starting the Bob Graham Club, pointing out that Graham was the first to go in what is now considered the 'normal' direction:

> I wanted to get recognition for what Bob Graham did in 1932, because he never got it at the time. People wouldn't believe what he had done. But it was the epic of this century. And it was all the more remarkable because all other previous 24-hour records, of fewer peaks, had been done anti-clockwise so he had no yardstick.

There is some doubt as to Graham's age when he made the round in June 1932. However, Phil Davidson,[1] the last survivor of Graham's quartet of pacers, said that the 42 peaks represented one for each year of Bob's life. He is also the source of the information that the extra peak added after the unsuccessful attempt in 1931 was Great Calva.

After completing the round, Graham claimed that 'he felt almost as fresh at the end of his long day as he did at the beginning', although he had apparently lost about half a stone in weight. This is remarkably similar to the thoughts of Eustace Thomas, whose training for his own endurance challenges convinced him that he had 'approached more nearly to the condition of tirelessness than ever before.'[2]

Graham was not the first, or last, to have his feats doubted. In *42 Peaks* there is a comment that:

> Some doubts were raised, certainly in private, as to whether Bob Graham had actually covered the distance and peaks claimed. He was not that well known a fellsman compared to Eustace Thomas. Had he really done it? Such doubts seem small-minded to us today, but they were genuinely felt at the time.

Graham also told Harry Griffin after the event that 'anybody could do it – provided they are fit enough'. Griffin also acknowledged, as noted earlier, that 'some people turn up their noses at these fell records'. He then counters that 'nobody ever gets injured or seriously lost, despite the pace and the conditions which often prevail. This is because these people are first and foremost mountaineers, able to traverse difficult country speedily and safely'.

What of Bob Graham himself? Harry Griffin commented in

---

1 Phil Davidson was an architect, designing among other buildings Bawd Hall in Newlands Valley.

2 *A century of fell running*, A H Griffin, in *Notable Walks . . .*

his Foreword to the *42 Peaks* booklet, 'I knew Bob Graham, and he often expressed surprise that nobody had succeeded in improving on his round'. So, what was his life like, and how did he train?

Bob Graham was brought up in Houghton, near Carlisle and as a young man worked as a gardener, first in Carlisle and then in Keswick. Some sources state that at the time of his record attempt he was running a guest house called Balmoral House, at 31 Lake Road, Keswick, which was next door to the Abraham Brothers photographic studio.[1] However, a document passed to me by the owners of the Derwentwater Independent Hostel showing the various owners of 31 Lake Road clearly shows that the premises were taken on as a private hotel by Bob Graham in 1938, and that prior to that it was a confectioner's shop in the ownership of Mrs Margaret Crosthwaite.

Describing Bob Graham in *English Lake Country*, Dudley Hoys says 'he was powerfully built, modest, kindly, and as a sort of snack, after supper in the summer, he would skip up Skiddaw and back'. Hoys asked him what he ate on his eponymous round – greengages was apparently his reply – and what really kept him going during the last eight hours of the effort, to which his reply was simply 'will-power'.

Sometime after his round, in 1945, Bob Graham bought Barrow House, in Borrowdale, and ran it as a hotel until 1961, when the YHA took it over. Barrow House is now an Independent Hostel, and has a detailed archive of its history, to which I was given access on a visit in August 2014. Joseph Pocklington lived at Barrow Cascade House, as it used to be called, until his death in 1817. It was Pocklington who erected a 'crazy ladder' against the Bowder Stone, in Borrowdale, to allow travellers to stand on its summit, as you still can today. He owned the land the stone stands on.

Barrow House was included in the YHA Handbook of 1931.

---

1   The *Manchester Guardian*, when reporting his round (in the paper dated June 14 1932) describes Graham as 'a young Keswick fruiterer'.

But it has not been in continuous use as a youth hostel. Lord Rochdale leased it to the YHA from 1931 to 1939. Then, during the war Newcastle Central High School for Girls was evacuated there. The present manager explained to me that it has 12 bedrooms/dorms now, but that she can see why Graham struggled to run it as a profitable B&B concern during his time there.

Bill Smith wrote a fascinating account in *The Fellrunner* in 2004 of a meeting he had with Eric Walmsley, who knew Bob Graham well. Eric recalled several stories of their friendship and activities:

> It was Bob's habit to take his guests out fellwalking, if they were so inclined, and he took the [Anglo-German] Society members out several times. Also present on some of these walks was the noted Grasmere artist, W. Heaton Cooper, who was a close friend of Bob's. He would sometimes assist Heaton Cooper in choosing scenes for his paintings, as he also did for the Abrahams' photography.

Fred Rogerson put Graham's activities in a more formal setting than that, saying 'Bob Graham was a Lake District guide who took people out on guided walks.' In 1923, before his first round, there was also someone else offering guided mountain adventures in the area: Millican Dalton,[1] the self-styled 'Professor of Adventure' who lived as a hermit in a cave in Borrowdale. Like Graham, he was a vegetarian teetotaller, but also a pacifist who enjoyed his chain-smoking and gallons of black coffee. Try as I might, I can find no reference to Dalton and Graham knowing each other, but they surely must have done so in such a tight community as Borrowdale. Dalton was also friends with Ralph Mayson who had a photographic business on Lake Road in Keswick, near the Abrahams' photographic studio.

Eric Walmsley also recalled Bob's time running Barrow House as a guest house with his sister and her husband:

---

1 http://www.keswick.org/explore/history-culture/millican-dalton/

All the meals were served from a hatch and he made many friends by chatting away to guests while passing the plates out. The guests also became friendly with each other once the ice was broken and details of climbs were swopped. Bob was an excellent cook and a great lover of people. You couldn't help liking him. He was also a great lover of nature and could identify all the wild flowers.

Eric reckoned Bob had to work hard to make the guest house pay and didn't have a great deal of time for walking from there:

Water was fetched from a dam in the stream that flowed down from the waterfall behind the house and this had to be constantly checked to ensure it was clean and not blocked. He afterwards moved to another guest house at Lyzzick Hall near Bassenthwaite.

The current Derwentwater Independent Hostel wardens, Kathy Morris and Dave Piercy, have commented that the waterfall has a fascinating history, as it was partly created by the original owner Joseph Pocklington. He diverted a stream above the fall to ensure that the full cascade could be seen from the dining room. Around 1945, Bob Graham set up a hydro-electric scheme to run the electric lighting, but apparently the lights were constantly flickering or failing completely and the scheme was discontinued. The hydro-electric scheme was reinstated in 2006 and is going strong. The owners were able to use the original dam and the same line of descent for the pipework as the original scheme.

The hostel has had some pretty useful fell runners working there, including at various times Jackie Lee and Janet McIver, both of whom have set fell race records. Martin Mikkelson-Barron, the current record holder for the Grisedale Grind, was born at the hostel. He is the son of Peter Barron, who was hostel manager at the time. At one point in the 1980s there was an advert for Derwentwater House with the strap line: 'Why not carbo-load at Bob Graham's old house. It didn't do him any harm!' It advertised itself as 'run by runners' and the contact person was Peter Barron, who was a pacer on Billy Bland's record round in 1982.

In 2014 the hostel hosted a visit by American ultra-distance running legends Rickey Gates and Scott Jurek. Martin Cox, Ricky Lightfoot and Billy Bland joined them in participating in a commercially run trail running weekend that was being hosted there. Over the weekend Ricky Lightfoot led some of the training sessions for the participants, providing specific advice on downhill running and difficult terrain, and Billy joined in a Q&A session, turning the weekend into a gripping Bob Graham Round experience. In a report of the event one of the participants described it as 'like going to play football in the park with your mates and Pele coming along to join in'. With a good forecast for Sunday 13 April, the best wishes of Billy Bland, and the promise of support from Ricky, Scott Jurek and Rickey Gates decided to make a Bob Graham Round attempt, starting their epic run at 3.10am from the Moot Hall. However, the pair did not find it easy. Scott said: 'We cut it real close in the end, with only 16 minutes to spare, but we did it! Quite possibly one of the most difficult courses I've done in my life, but so beautiful.'[1]

Very little is known about Bob Graham's own preparation for the round, but by common consent the main training he did was to walk and run regularly on the fells, often during the night and covering considerable distances. He certainly knew his way around the fells and was a good navigator.

Phil Davidson commented that 'Bob was particularly good at downhills. I thought I could travel a bit, but I couldn't do anything like his speed downhill. When it came to graft uphill I could stick with him. The hardest part was the second [leg]: 12 hours of continuous walking. You had to really persuade yourself to go on, at least in my case. You had that feeling 'why

---

1 *Cumberland and Westmorland Herald*, 25 April 2014

the dickens am I doing this'. Who is benefitting and what is the use? After that there was a sense of achievement.'[1]

Eric Walmsley remembered that although Bob Graham never took part in rock climbing, he was quite comfortable on scrambles like Broad Stand. But he couldn't recall Bob ever competing in the guides races. When Graham did go walking it was for all-day efforts, not short strolls. This was despite having been turned down for service in the First World War because he had flat feet. Nonetheless, he moved fast over the Lakes terrain:

> He took a lot of keeping up with as he always moved at a trot or a jog. He never ate much while out on the fells and never carried any protective clothing, just a jacket which he'd tie around his waist if the weather was warm. On his feet, he wore plimsolls or sandals, much to the disapproval of one friend who suggested he should wear boots. Bob took his advice for one walk only with the result that he slipped and fell down a gully. That was the last time he wore boots.

It is unclear whether it was the same incident noted above, but one accident on the fells that Graham suffered actually made the newspapers. If he did only wear boots once, then it's highly likely that it is the same incident, since he comments on wearing boots. The incident was reported in the *Yorkshire Post and Leeds Intelligencer* in March 1937, under the headline 'SLID 300-FEET ON GREAT GABLE. Champion Fell Walker Saves Himself':

> Mr Bob Graham, of Keswick, the champion fell walker, escaped serious injury when he slid 300 feet down the East side of the Great Gable on icy snow. He climbed the Gable with Mr. F. Ratcliffe, of Keswick, bank clerk, and Mr. P. Stanger, a Newcastle dentist who plays for Keswick Rugby

---

1   On the soundtrack of a programme called '*It's Bob's Round*', made for Border TV in 1995, directed by Jannicke Wallace.

Union club. They went up the breast of the Gable and were descending the rock-strewn, precipitous East side towards Windy Gap when Mr. Graham, who was leading, felt himself slipping. 'I dug my heels in and fell over on to my face,' he said. 'The weight of my boots swung me round, and I went sliding feet first for about 300 feet, nearly to Windy Gap. I clawed at everything to keep myself from gathering speed and going over the side of the Gable or down into Windy Gap, and I tore my finger ends. I was unable to stop myself. I was wearing a lumberman's thick coat, and that saved my body. All I got were severe bruises and abrasions on my arms and legs. Mr. Ratcliffe started to slide, too, but he managed to keep upright. Some climbers with ropes and ice axes helped me down to Styhead Pass, and I was able to walk and run to Seathwaite, where we had left a car.'

A report on the same incident in the *Lancashire Evening Post* mentioned that he was from Balmoral Castle, Keswick,[1] and that he 'found it difficult and dangerous going at times owing to the snow having thawed and then frozen. They were descending by the east side, where they found the boulders filled up with frozen snow ... he was assisted to Styhead Pass by some climbers from Burnley.'

Eventually, various events commemorated either Bob Graham or his round. Most notably, in 1971 the Bob Graham 24 Hour Club was instigated. Further details of the Club are given in Chapter 15. Later, the December 1982 issue of *The Fellrunner* reported on a Bob Graham Jubilee Relay that was held to commemorate 50 years since Bob Graham's inaugural round, involving 35 members of the Bob Graham 24 Hour Club (i.e. round completers).

Present at the start of the run at the Moot Hall, Keswick, were Eva Graham, niece of Bob, the Mayor of Keswick, Mr S Crawford, and Phil Davidson who had accompanied Bob

---

1   Presumably meaning Balmoral House, his guest house at the time

for part of his record run. At 7.30pm on the warm, humid evening of Friday 4 June Phil Davidson, who celebrated his 80th birthday a few days earlier, placed a baton made up of the tip of a Herdwick ram's horn on a leather thong, round the neck of Alan Heaton, the Club's first member, who led a small group of runners up Skiddaw on the first section of the relay. The form of the baton was chosen specially in recognition of Bob Graham's founding of a local rambling club known as 'The Herdwicks'.

Those first runners reached Threlkeld at dusk, and another team took the baton to Dunmail. Into the dawn and further teams took it over the Scafells to Wasdale, then to Honister, and so over the final leg back to Keswick.

At 3pm on Saturday 5 June, nineteen and a half hours after the start, Jean Dawes, the first lady member of the club, led the final group, whose ranks were swollen by the inclusion of many earlier runners, to the Moot Hall to be warmly greeted by a large, enthusiastic crowd. A few hours later, on a piece of land beside the Watendlath Road, formerly owned by Bob Graham, a memorial cairn built by Fred Rogerson was unveiled by Eva Graham. The long day was concluded at Barrow House Youth Hostel with refreshments and a film show presented by the club chairman Fred Rogerson, showing highlights of many successful attempts on the Bob Graham Round spanning a period of 20 years.

The memorial cairn is a pleasing and unobtrusive memorial to the man and the event, sitting as it does on the attractive minor road that skirts the back of the grounds of Barrow House, on the way to the excellent tea room at Watendlath. The cairn bears a plaque with the inscription: *In memory of Robert Graham 1889–1966 of Keswick who on 13–14 June 1932 traversed 42 Lakeland peaks within 24 hours. A record which stood for 28 years.*

There was more to Bob Graham than first meets the eye. He was a member of Keswick Rugby Club (though he did not play the game), and a keen tennis player. He also had a keen interest in music. There was a piece entitled 'Lakeland's Champion Walker on the Air' in the *Lancashire Evening Post* of 5 Dec 1935 which showed another side of 'Lakeland's Champion Walker':

> Not many ramblers who listened-in to the Mountain Singers [of Keswick] on the North Regional a fortnight yesterday realised when they heard Bob Graham, the compere, that they were listening to the finest walker in the Lake District. One could hardly call Bob a rambler, as no ordinary rambler could keep up with him. Only one man has been found so far, an Arctic Explorer, who can keep up with Bob when he is out on one of his long walks. . . . He has frequently been one of the search parties that have had to be organised when people have been lost on the fells. Owing to the nature of his work most of his rambling has to be done during the winter, and even on the coldest days he dresses as most ramblers would in the middle of summer. He travels light and often wears rubber plimsolls which he prefers to heavy boots. His strength of endurance is amazing.

The Mountain Singers of Keswick were on the 'Harry Hopeful' tour of Lakeland that August, and they included workmen from all types of trade in the district – quarrymen, engineers and farmers. They were organised in 1922, and the choir that Bob Graham compered had performed for radio in a studio in Newcastle, their repertoire including 'authentic versions of John Peel, adapted from an old Scottish rant'.

Chapter 3

The Round

The Bob Graham Round is 62 miles in length, takes in the 42 peaks listed here, and has 27,000 feet of ascent. It is tradition-ally considered to be made up of five sections, or legs. These are defined by the four road crossings, where support vehicles may provide food, drink, kit etc., and are nowadays the normal changeover points for pacers to start and finish their stints. Going clockwise, the normal support points are at: Threlkeld, Dunmail Raise, Wasdale Head and Honister Hause.

The 42 peaks that comprise the round are certainly not the highest 42 in the Lake District,[1] but linked together they do form a fairly natural route that joins up several watersheds, by means of the intervening crossing points. You can be sure that if you get good visibility you will see some of the finest scenery in the Lakes as you traverse the round.

The peaks and support points (in order for a clockwise round)

No.	Name of peak	Height (feet)
1	Skiddaw	3053
2	Great Calva	2265
3	Blencathra	2847
Threlkeld		
4	Clough Head	2381
5	Great Dodd	2807

---

1 The lowest two, Steel Fell and Calf Crag, are 145th and 154th highest respectively, if ranked by the Wainwrights list.

6	Watson's Dodd	2584
7	Stybarrow Dodd	2770
8	Raise	2889
9	White Side	2317
10	Helvellyn Lower Man	3033
11	Helvellyn	3118
12	Nethermost Pike	2920
13	Dollywagon Pike	2810
14	Fairfield	2863
15	Seat Sandal	2415
Dunmail Raise		
16	Steel Fell	1811
17	Calf Crag	1762
18	Sergeant Man	2414
19	High Raise	2500
20	Thunacar Knott	2351
21	Harrison Stickle	2403
22	Pike o'Stickle	2323
23	Rossett Pike	2106
24	Bowfell	2960
25	Esk Pike	2903
26	Great End	2984
27	Ill Crag	3040
28	Broad Crag	3054
29	Scafell Pike	3210
30	Scafell	3162
Wasdale Head		
31	Yewbarrow	2058
32	Red Pike	2707

33	Steeple	2687
34	Pillar	2927
35	Kirk Fell	2630
36	Great Gable	2949
37	Green Gable	2603
38	Brandreth	2344
39	Grey Knotts	2287
Honister Pass		
40	Dale Head	2473
41	Hindscarth	2385
42	Robinson	2417

Section 1: Keswick to Threlkeld[1]

A short amount of road to the small car park on Latrigg then a steep pull up onto Skiddaw itself. A steep descent to the track leading to Skiddaw House, straight over this and up Great Calva, then a beeline for Blencathra. Finally a descent of the steep Hall's Fell to Threlkeld. Once on the fells the going is at first a slate/shale path then boggy or heathery with a rocky final descent. Distance: 12.5 miles, Ascent: c.5150ft.

Section 2: Threlkeld to Dunmail Raise

A slightly involved section in the valley to gain the slopes of Clough Head, once the summit of this is reached then it is high level ridge running along mainly grassy paths to Helvellyn. At Dollywagon Pike a steep descent is made to Grisedale Tarn then the two outliers of Fairfield and Seat Sandal are taken before descending to the road at the summit of Dunmail Raise. The going is mainly grassy with some easy stony paths around Helvellyn and Fairfield. Distance: 13.2 miles, Ascent: c.5900ft.

---

1 Descriptions from: http://bobwightman.co.uk/run/bob_graham.php – which also has information in more detail, including water sources.

Section 3: Dunmail Raise to Wasdale Head

This is the longest section and also the roughest underfoot. A steep climb from the road to Steel Fell leads to an undulating section in and around rocky hummocks to the Langdale Pikes. A moorland section then leads round the head of Langdale to Rossett Pike. A cunning scramble leads to Bowfell which marks the start of the roughest section of the round. Speed is difficult to maintain over this terrain as it is mainly composed of large boulders. Eventually Scafell Pike is reached. The quickest way to Scafell is via Broad Stand which is a rock climb, though admittedly easy, where a rope may be required. It is then a long descent on grass to the car park at Wasdale. Distance: 15.2 miles, Ascent: c.6500ft.

Section 4: Wasdale Head to Honister Pass

This is another tough section especially since it follows the long central section. It begins with another steep climb direct from the car park at Wasdale to the summit of Yewbarrow. Generally easy running ground then leads around the head of Mosedale over Pillar to Black Sail Pass. Kirk Fell and Great Gable (which along with Green Gable is the last rough section) are then traversed before easier ground leads to Honister Pass. Distance: 10 miles, Ascent: c.6300ft.

Section 5: Honister Pass to Keswick

This is the shortest fell section with only three summits to cross before the final road section is reached. Follow the fence up to Dale Head, there then follows a high level ridge over Hindscarth and Robinson before a long ridge is descended to the road. Generally grassy underfoot. Distance: 10.6 miles, Ascent: c.2500ft

The 'rules' for a Bob Graham Round are flexible. You can go either clockwise or anti-clockwise, provided you start and finish at the Keswick Moot Hall. In the early days, by far the more popular was anti-clockwise. However, as we have seen, Graham himself went clockwise, on the advice of mountaineer and pioneer photographer George Abraham.[1] The anti-clockwise route gives the flattish section to Newlands in the early part, and finishes with the long descent off Skiddaw. You could also argue that it is easier to ascend Hall's Fell ridge on Blencathra than it is to descend it. There is a considerable range of start times in use these days, although a clockwise route starting in the latter part of one day to do the northern fells in some sort of light, before taking the Dodds-Helvellyn range ('relatively' easy navigation) in darkness, and finishing before dusk the next day is a popular option. How long you are expecting to take does, of course, come in to play here. But, we will see as we explore various rounds that there is still some variation as regards the timing and tactics used.

The normal start point for a Bob Graham Round is the Moot Hall in Keswick. Usually there is a photo opportunity on the steps at the NW end of the building, often with a celebration drink on those same steps after successfully completing the round. A moot hall is a meeting or assembly building, tradition-ally to decide local issues. It was called Keswick Town Hall in Graham's day.

The present Moot Hall building, dated 1813, was erected at a cost of nearly £1,200 by trustees of the Royal Greenwich Hospital. They took over the sequestered estate of the Radcliffes after the 1715 Jacobite rebellion. Records show that in the 1820s the lower floor was used as a market for meat, butter, eggs and poultry. Upstairs, the Moot Hall continued its tradi-tional function as a court house. Here the Lords of the Manor, the governors of Greenwich Hospital, considered claims and arguments over land and tenure. The open-air market held in the shadow of the Moot Hall continues a tradition that goes back to the charter of 1276.

The Moot Hall is an iconic building, with major significance

---

1 It is one of Abraham's pictures that forms the centrepiece of the Bob Graham Club certificate.

for the subject of this book. It is not particularly impressive architecturally, but sits in a prime position within the town. It has been roundly criticised by commentators such as William Hutchinson, who in his monumental *History of Cumberland (1793–1797)* condemned the Moot Hall as 'of the most uncouth architecture'. George Bott, in his book *Keswick. The Story of a Lake District Town,* comments that the Moot Hall has had several functions, including being the home of the Keswick Literary Society. The hall currently contains the town's Tourist Information Centre, catering for the needs of the streams of tourists who come to the town of Keswick.

The current values given for the Round are given at the head of this chapter. Over time, details of the distance covered have varied. In *Long Days in Lakeland* Ronald Turnbull reckons that if:

> measured with string or a little wheel it is 60–62 miles.[1] However, factors can be added 'for wiggles', or 'distance up the slope' or 'to make it more exciting'. The generally quoted figure for the Bob Graham is 72 miles. I've used the distance as measured, of 62 miles. The climb of 27,000ft is found by counting contour lines.

At the time of Bob Graham's original completion of the round the achievement was reported in some sources as being 140 miles and 30,000 feet. The Bob Graham 24 Hour Club website[2] currently states:

> The use of mapping software and GPS devices has led to a re-evaluation of the distance of the Round. Mapping software gives figures as low as 61–63 miles. GPS systems (which have been carried and operated throughout several successful

---

1   This was written in 1998, which was before hand-held GPS devices were as readily available as they are now. These will give a reasonably accurate figure of how far completers actually travelled

2   http://www.bobgrahamclub.org.uk/

attempts) give a figure of between 65–66 miles. The tradi-
tional ascent figure seems to be more accurate, though some
calculations have produced a figure of 26,000 feet. The
distance continues to stimulate debate depending on how it is
measured, but a figure of something between 60 and 66 miles
is more accurate than the traditional 72.

Chapter 4

First challengers

It is generally considered that Graham's 'record' stood for 28 years. Westaway, in *Men who can last*, when writing about the Bob Graham Round, records:

> . . . the mountaineer, explorer and Sedbergh School alumnus F. Spencer Chapman attempting it in 1932. Spencer Chapman noted that 'Dr. Wakefield was a Sedberghian, and had been paced over part of his route by Bobby Woodhouse, a Sedbergh master.' He also indicated that Wakefield and Woodhouse were keen for the prize to go to an Old Sedberghian. Chapman lodged with Wakefield and was coached by him. He set off on 17 May, 1932 but was defeated by navigational problems in the mist. He was also certainly hampered by a knee injury sustained on the 1930–1931 Greenland Expedition.

In the latest edition of *42 Peaks*, Paddy Buckley stated that:

> F. Spencer Chapman had begun to run over the fells when he was at Sedbergh School, claiming that he could average six miles an hour. In 1933, between his two Greenland expeditions, he made an attempt on the record, wanting to recapture it for Sedbergh. He set off from Keswick at midnight on 17/18 May going anti-clockwise, supported by pacers. He took breakfast at Wasdale Head. On Bowfell he was met by Bob Graham with hot cocoa, and on Helvellyn by Dr

Wakefield with hot coffee. It was raining hard by the time he got to Great Calva, he was an hour down on schedule, and his supporter had given up and gone home. The final climb up Skiddaw was "almost a nightmare" and he reached Keswick at 1am having taken 25 hours.[1]

The first date is prior to Graham's successful round, and the latter is clearly after it. This implies that Chapman failed once (before Graham) and then completed it (after Graham), but in a time over 24 hours. Pacing, and helping later aspirants, is not just a recent feature of rounds. In providing evidence of this, Bob Wightman notes that 'Graham himself also paced on both prior and later attempts at the record by Freddy Spencer Chapman'.[2] Spencer Chapman was certainly an interesting character. He believed in pushing himself to extremes, once while at school encouraging his fellow pupils to hit him over the head with a cricket bat 'to see how hard he could take it.'[3]

In the 1950s there was renewed interest in Graham's achievement. There were several more attempts, with both Ted Dance (a laboratory assistant with ICI at the time) and Des Oliver coming near to success but being thwarted by bad weather. There was also a joint attempt on the record by a team of four on 13 May 1960, two of them, Maurice Collett and Paul Stewart, getting round an almost similar course to Graham's but taking more than 27 hours to do it. Three of them made another attempt the following year, but had to give up before completing the full round.

The real impetus came from Harry Griffin. Fred Rogerson

---

1   An intriguing report in the Sedberghian Magazine (about Hugh Symonds' BG round in 1995) says that 'Mr F. Spencer Chapman completed the round but unfortunately his time in 1937 was over the 24 hour limit' – a date four years later than that noted in 42 Peaks.
2   In an FRA Forum post, 14 Nov 2010
3   Guardian, 21 Oct 2009

wrote an article in the *Alpine Journal* in 1976, entitled 'In quest of the ultimate', in which he noted that,

> About 1960 Dr Barbara Moore was receiving a fair amount of newspaper coverage by walking from Land's End to John O'Groats. Mr A. H. Griffin, author and journalist, wrote an article in an evening paper stating that anybody could do this sort of thing provided they had the time. Far better, he suggested, if people wanted to prove their stamina to have a go at Bob Graham's record – a test of endurance perhaps unequalled in this century.

In *42 Peaks* it is reported that 'Maurice Collett, a 37-year-old teacher from Kendal, and Paul Stewart, a 27-year-old builder from Windermere, planned an attempt on the record for 13 May 1960. It was a very gallant try; they experienced rough weather but battled on to complete the round of 42 peaks in 27 hrs and 20 minutes'.

Two fell runners from Lancashire also read Griffin's article. An attempt was made by Ken and **Alan Heaton** on 25 June 1960. Alan was 32 years old at the time, and worked as a clerk. As it turned out to be such a significant event, a full report of the round is included here. My report leans heavily on Gerry Charnley's account, which was published in Fred Rogerson's excellent loose-leaf 'booklet' – *History and Records of Notable Fell Walks, 1864–1972, Within the Lake District.*[1]

Alan Heaton was interested in a range of sports besides fell running. He was a very proficient orienteer and keen mountaineer, frequently climbing in the Alps. Among his notable endurance running achievements were winning the Fellsman Hike ten times. When asked what his favourite fell races were, he identified The Three Peaks, The Mountain Trial and

---

1 There is a copy in the excellent local history section in Cumbria County Council's Kendal Library, and two more in Carlisle Library.

Pendleton. In *Studmarks on the Summits* Bill Smith recalls that Alan Heaton 'was loath to stop for refreshment, preferring to eat while on the move, a practice not entirely looked upon with favour by his companions'.

For his round in 1960 Alan Heaton set off from Keswick Market Place at 10am in the company of Stan Bradshaw (a food processing manager), his brother Ken Heaton (a planning engineer), and Alistair Patten. They were all friends and members of Clayton-le-Moors Harriers. The weather forecast was for a very hot day, with temperatures expected to rise to the upper 80s Fahrenheit (30°C). They were seen off by Harry Griffin, who wrote for the *Lancashire Evening Post*, and is also notable for several accounts of BGR exploits in his excellent books, which include *In Mountain Lakeland*. Also there was clubmate Gerry Charnley, who was nominally their only support person, and who intended to meet them at the crossing points with food, drink and changes of clothes.

They used the same route as Graham, but differed from him in going anti-clockwise. Wearing lightweight road running shoes, shorts and vests they set off on the road to Newlands Valley, initially climbing the 800 feet or so to Newlands Hause.[1] It was so warm that Ken removed his vest to wring out the sweat accumulated during that first hour (covering seven miles according to the report). Then an incident occurred as they drank from a small stream as they started up Robinson. Ken took off his glasses, another member of the team stumbled, and the glasses were stood upon. They went on over Hindscarth and Dale Head and down to Honister Hause to meet Gerry Charnley. The Heatons arrived at 12.12pm, followed three minutes later by Bradshaw and Patten. Their 'schedule' was for a 23 hours

---

1 In an interview with Bill Smith in the June 1990 *Fellrunner* Stan Bradshaw admits they went via Newlands Hause because 'it was then erroneously thought that Graham himself had descended from Robinson to Newlands Hause' and they were replicating that, albeit in the other direction.

30 minutes round, and they were just ahead of their predicted 12.30pm arrival time.

Stan Bradshaw was already suffering cramps. He had suffered from a carbuncle on his face for a week, during which time he had managed very little sleep. Ken was feeling the disadvantage of limited vision without his glasses, but agreed to carry on. They quenched their thirsts and who should arrive but Harry Griffin, along with Bob Graham himself, who by then was a fit-looking 71 years old. Charnley notes: 'Graham put forward a theory of his own (not generally accepted) that the exceptionally hot weather was ideal for such an event. He made one or two personal observations on sections of the route and wished the runners the very best of luck'. At 12.30 the runners set off for Grey Knotts.

They went over the Gable peaks and down to Black Sail Pass. On Brandreth Ken Heaton became dizzy and decided to abandon. Patten had only been a pacer, and he stayed with Ken and they returned together via the pass to Mosedale and Wasdale. As Stan had to stop to massage out his cramp, Alan was now alone. He went by the top of the pass at 2.25pm, 35 minutes ahead of schedule. On the way down to Mosedale Ken Heaton and Patten met an ITV cameraman who was hoping to film some of the event, having seen the schedule in a newspaper report. He was told that Alan Heaton was well ahead and that he had missed him.

Gerry Charnley drove round to Wasdale Head, to park by the old school there. Amazingly, considering it was a Saturday, he found an optician in Cockermouth, who repaired Ken's glasses. Alan Heaton ran in to Wasdale Head alone at 4.15pm, looking a little the worse for wear due to the heat and the lack of water on that section, which is over some of the biggest peaks. All he wanted was fluids and some cream for his sun-blistered arms and shoulders. After 45 minutes rest he was remarkably well recovered. He set off again at 5pm, still 30 minutes ahead of schedule, now heading alone for the Scafells. He achieved the main summit in 66 minutes.

Meanwhile George Brass, the former Three Peaks race record holder, had arrived on his motorbike from Clitheroe. Stan Bradshaw had taken a fall coming down Yewbarrow and dislocated his thumb. He took almost an hour's rest, including leg massage, thumb bandaging and liquid intake, then finally also set off alone over the Scafell range, about 90 minutes behind Alan Heaton. Heaton descended Broad Stand, and Bradshaw chose Lord's Rake. By Stake Pass Heaton was 80 minutes ahead of schedule, and obviously going well.

The support crew, now consisting of Gerry Charnley, Ken Heaton and Alistair Patten, drove across to Dunmail as the light faded. Alan Heaton came off Steel Fell at 10.53pm, appearing surprisingly fresh. He hardly sat down, but refuelled with masses of sweet tea, tinned fruit, and tinned rice. He also changed shoes as his cross-country shoes were falling apart, and took on a tracksuit top as the temperature was at last dropping. Ken Heaton was to pace Alan for the rest of the round. Kendal's Maurice Collett arrived just after they had left at 11.35pm, to be told they were now an hour up on schedule. Collett noted that on his 27 hours 20 minutes round five weeks earlier Paul Stewart had accompanied him as they took nine hours to do the Dunmail-Keswick section, admittedly in the other direction and at the start of their effort. Heaton had 10 hours to beat Graham's time.

A couple of hours later Stan Bradshaw appeared, having traversed the Langdale Pikes in the dark without a torch. At one point he had managed to turn down to Codale Tarn and had to climb back up for Calf Crag. Realising that he was stretching the support too far if he was to expect them to wait for him at the Threlkeld support point, he decided to abandon and try another day. Having passed some folk camped on Helvellyn in order to see the day break, sunrise eventually came for the

Heatons as they were on Watson Dodd at around 3am. They arrived at the Threlkeld support point at 4.10am, and took a 25-minute break there. Alistair Patten joined the Heatons for the last stretch, and at 5.27am their outlines could be seen atop Blencathra – not a bad ascent time.

Gerry Charnley's report notes:

Running well within himself and with the knowledge that the record was his, barring accident, Alan made the pace fast across the moorland of Long Brow direct for the detached peak of Great Calva. At 6.24am with the sun climbing high in the eastern sky the three runners surmounted Great Calva and gazed across the vast depression towards the 3054-foot summit of Skiddaw, the last peak, at 7.30am and from there on it was downhill all the way to the Market Place.

Being a Sunday the main street in Keswick was much quieter than the day before when they had left. Alan Heaton leapt away from the other two and sprinted off to finish at 8.18am. Still looking remarkably fresh, his time of 22 hours 18 minutes took 1 hour 21 minutes off Bob Graham's time from 28 years earlier.[1] He celebrated with a cup of tea.

Harry Griffin records (in *42 Peaks*) that when Bob Graham heard the news of the record finally being broken he 'could not have been more delighted. "About time, too" he said, for he was a modest man, not caring for the limelight'.

A fortnight later **Stan Bradshaw** was invited to join an attempt on the round being made by a Kendal AC team, which

---

1   Alan Heaton attempted to be the oldest man (at the time) to complete the BGR when in 1995 he tried a repeat crossing 35 years (to the day) on from his first, at the age of 67. It was done in a heatwave, which previously hadn't been a problem for him. But this time lack of water on the Langdale section made him dizzy and lightheaded, forcing him to retire at Dunmail.

included Collett and Stewart from the earlier attempt. Bradshaw completed it to become the second person to emulate Graham's feat. The weekend in between he completed a hard training run from Dunmail, doing a half-Bob Graham-plus of 48 miles. A pretty fit guy for his age of 48. At this time he regularly trained over the Three Peaks course, or did 26 miles on the Howgills, 38 miles over the fells from Keld, or a solo 56 mile Five Peaks run in Ribblesdale, as well as regularly going into the Lakeland fells. He told Bill Smith the story of the round briefly in an interview in *The Fellrunner* in 1990:

> We left Keswick at midnight to go clockwise. Heavy rain on the Dodds and Frank Carradus and Paul Stewart retired before Dunmail. [Maurice] Collett got down to Dunmail okay and the weather brightened. Ted Dance was our support and we went very well to Mickledore, but up Broad Stand, Collett, who has a paralysed arm, had to retire. It was hard luck on Maurice and we were very sorry to have to leave him to make his way to Wasdale. I can remember having to warm my own soup here but was in good spirits. Can't remember who supported me from Wasdale to Honister. I went in the Youth Hostel at Honister and was treated well, being given soup. Two of Collett's friends accompanied me from Honister to Robinson. I was in good form and ran all the way in to Keswick to finish in 23 hours and 25 minutes.[1]

Reporting on this attempt in the July 1982 *Fellrunner*, Fred Rogerson commented that Ted Dance accompanied Stan Bradshaw from Dunmail back to Keswick, traversing 27 of the 42 summits, and said of Dance:

> His ability to ascend steep ground, hands on hips, with

---

1 In 1977, at the age of 65, Stan Bradshaw made two further complete traverses of the Round, failing to get inside 24 hours on the first occasion due to sickness. In that year he logged 4,500 training miles altogether.

apparent ease, despite being loaded with food (solid and liquid) and spare clothing, etc., for the contender and himself, was to me one of several memorable features of the attempt.

The next person to complete a round was **Ken Heaton**, but he went further, managing to include 51 peaks and still be five minutes faster than brother Alan had been for 42 peaks. On 24 June 1961 Ken Heaton set off in a clockwise direction, but started from the Old Dungeon Ghyll Hotel in Langdale instead of from Keswick. The round was reported in *42 Peaks*:

Conditions were very different from the previous year. Between Keswick and Threlkeld thick mist caused problems and more than once the party went astray. They had strong, cold winds during the night section on the Dodds and Helvellyn. Despite this Ken was always up with the schedule and he finished in 22 hours 13 minutes, to set a new record of 51 peaks. Ken had left out one of the original 42, Rossett Pike, and Scoat Fell was claimed as an extra, although undoubtedly it had been done by Graham, and either omitted from his tally, or put in as Steeple.

Fred Rogerson claimed it was 'the start of a new era of epic achievements', and speculated that Ken would attempt to add extra peaks at a later date. When asked, Ken Heaton apparently replied instantly:

I have accomplished what I set out to do and do not intend to make any further attempts on the Lake District 24-Hour Fell Record. I will give assistance to anyone making an attempt, undoubtedly my brother Alan will have a go and in all probability improve upon my record.[1]

Ken did not have another go, but did help his brother to take the record onwards and upwards.

---

1 *Notable Walks . . .*

In his time **Eric Beard** set some amazing endurance records, including those for the Welsh 3000s and the Cuillin Ridge on Skye. In 1963 he set about the Lake District 24 hour record, at the age of 31. His reputation drew in pacers of the calibre of Alan and Ken Heaton, Stan Bradshaw, Des Oliver and Joss Naylor. Beard chose to travel light, wearing his Leeds AC vest and shorts, and kletterschuhe (more often used for rock climbing) rather than running shoes.

The attempt was on 6 July, going clockwise, with Beard fit and raring to go. They reached Threlkeld in just 2 hours 21 minutes, and Dunmail in a further four hours, taking in Great Rigg as an extra peak. Early on Beard had developed a blister, which he had declined to have dressed. When Margaret Rogerson finally got to treat it, at Wasdale, there was about four inches of skin on the ball of his foot hanging off. He just got his head down and carried on. The weather was fine and at Aiken Knott he was clearly going to break the record. In *42 Peaks* the report continues:

> Instead of turning right for Scar Crags and Causey Pike, two of the tops covered by Alan Heaton, he turned left to include Sail, Crag Hill and Grisedale Pike, a much more worthy variation, before trotting back to Keswick at 5.35pm on a fine afternoon with 25 minutes in hand, to complete a round of 56 summits,[1] involving about 88 miles of travel with 34,000 feet of ascent.

It was inevitable that **Joss Naylor** would appear in the Bob Graham Round story. Like Eric Beard before him, and Ken Heaton too, he didn't bother with the 42 peak version.[2] Instead Naylor included 61 peaks in his own first 'extended' round,

---

1 This was two more peaks than Alan Heaton had managed in his extended round the year before.

2 Ken Heaton's 51 peak round in 1961 was pretty remarkable, his 22:13 being technically the fastest BGR so far.

which he extended even further later. On 26 June 1971 Naylor set out to top Alan Heaton's total of 60 peaks within 24 hours, which had been set six years earlier. He started from Wasdale Head, just a mile down the road from where he lived. He had delayed his start for an hour because of low cloud, rain and high winds, but then set off with Danny Hughes for company. Over Pillar and the Gables to Honister took them three hours, already ahead of his planned schedule. Alan Heaton joined them for the Buttermere fells which were traversed in just 50 minutes, a remarkable effort. Heaton, fresh from a three-day Pennine Way run, continued with Joss over the Grasmoor and Coledale fells.

They arrived in Keswick 34 minutes ahead of schedule and with two extra peaks in hand. Over the Skiddaw/Blencathra section Joss had Pete Walkington, Mike Nicholson and Ted Dance as pacers. By Threlkeld they were 71 minutes up, and stopped for soup and hot sweet tea. Ken Heaton and Alan Walker took over support duties for the night run over the Dodds and Helvellyn. By now they were facing strong cross winds and heavy rain. Just after midnight they reached Dollywagon Pike, where Stan Bradshaw and Frank Milner provide hot tea. Joss reached Dunmail at 1.30am and after a 30-minute break continued over the Langdales to reach the Old Dungeon Ghyll just after 5am.

Alan Walker and Pete Walkington carried on with Joss, and they met Bradshaw and Milner at Thunacar Knott for more cups of tea. A navigational error on Sergeant Man lost them a little time. Joss was tiring by the last section, but had an hour in hand. Walker and Dance went with him from there, with Alan Heaton joining them at Esk Hause. Pete Walkington was at Broad Stand, which was a trifle greasy, so they used a safety rope.

Naylor had intended to include Lingmell as well, but missed it out due to the wet rocks and stiffening legs starting to slow him down. Having put in two additional summits, Base Brown and Causey Pike earlier, his total was 61 peaks. Including his total rest time of 2 hours 14 minutes, he was round in 23 hours 37 minutes. Joss is quoted as saying shortly afterwards: 'I've been planning to do this for four years and I wanted to do it when I was 35. I never felt weak, never had one touch of cramp but my legs were stiffening up at the end'.[1] Given that he was SO dominant in the long fell races when he was at his peak, and could outrun anyone over 20 miles or so, I do wonder how fast Joss might have done a standard Bob Graham 42 Peak Round if he had set himself to do it.

Naylor did, of course, go on to add another peak to the total in 1972, and then to complete an extended round of 72 summits in 23 hours 11 minutes on 23 June 1975, at the age of 39.[2] This extended round total was taken to 76 by Mark McDermott in 1988, and then to 77 by Mark Hartell in 1997.

The following table gives the statistics for the early completions of the round.

New completers per year *(brackets = peaks if more than the standard 42)*:

1960	2	Alan Heaton, Stan Bradshaw
1961	1	Ken Heaton (51)
1963	1	Eric Beard (56)
1971	4	Joss Naylor (61), Pete Walkington (43), Don Talbot, Michael Meath
1972	2	Ken Brooks, Jim Loxham
1973	5	Harry Blenkinsop, Eric Roberts, Dennis Weir, Boyd Millen, Bill Smith
1974	13	
1975	14	
1976	13	

---

1 *Lakeland sheep farmer sets up new fells record*, A H Griffin, in *Notable Walks . . .*

2 Chris Brasher was so impressed by this feat that he and Eric Roberts started a fund to help Joss go to Colorado later that year and take part in the Pikes Peak Marathon. There was no real international aspect to the sport at the time.

After the four completions in the early 1960s there was a gap of eight years before the next successes. 1971 to 1973 showed just four, two and five completions respectively, and then the numbers started increasing significantly. The following graph shows the data[1] for each year since 1971.

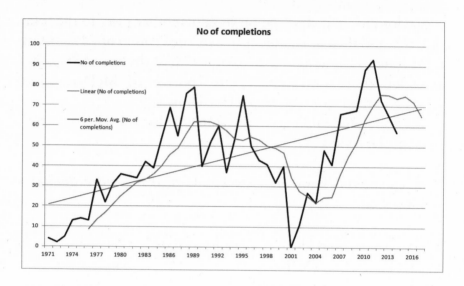

The thicker solid line shows the annual numbers of completers. The thin straight line is the overall trend-line and the grey line a 6-year moving average. Unsurprisingly, the figures increase gradually during the 70s and 80s. In the 90s they fluctuated year on year but were trending downwards, until the anomaly of 2001 was reached. This was the year of the foot and mouth outbreak, when the fells were out of bounds for the whole of the spring and summer, when normally attempts would be made. It took a while for numbers to return to previous levels, possibly because people weren't able to get onto the fells to do the appropriate reconnoitring as part of their building for an attempt. The numbers appear to have peaked at the high point of 93 completions for 2011.

---

1   Calculated from data listed at: http://www.bobgrahamclub.org.uk/index. php?page=members

It was a while before a successful round by a woman athlete was recorded. On Saturday 31 July 1976 **Jean Dawes** set out at three minutes past midnight to attempt a clockwise round. Dawes had stated in advance that she intended to complete the round irrespective of the time it took, although a sub-24 hour schedule was prepared.

Dawes started at the same time as Stan Winstanley, who was also attempting a round. He remarked that she burned him off going up Great Calva. Quite possibly this had some impact on their respective outcomes. Dawes, accompanied by Brian Tatham, reached Threlkeld in under four hours. Dunmail was reached at 8am, with Stan Bradshaw pacing that section. On to Wasdale with Alan Barber joining them, with Bradshaw hoping to find a pair of binoculars he had lost on an earlier walk. Dawes was going well and took just over six hours on this leg. They went on to Honister with Alan Barber navigating. Boyd Millen had been at Esk Hause with refreshments, and did the same at Beck Head, before moving on to support from Brandreth. Meanwhile, Dawes was having a bad patch going up Great Gable.

They left Honister Hause at 9pm, the support being husband Pete, Peter Beesley and Stan Bradshaw. After going over Robinson, Dawes started almost dropping off to sleep through cumulative tiredness. Supporters down in Newlands watched their lights coming towards them increasingly slowly. The time was now slipping away. But, fighting sleep, Dawes was deter-mined to finish, which she did in 24 hours 50 minutes.

There was an explosion of interest in 1977, with 33 new completers registered. Jean Dawes came back to the Bob Graham Round that year, setting out on a clockwise round at 8am on 25 June. An impressive list of pacers was lined up, with Chris Bland agreeing to start things off along with Pete Dawes. They had rain and mist on Skiddaw, but husband Pete's navigation was up to the mark. They descended Hall's Ridge to a welcome cup of tea at Threlkeld.

Boyd Millen and Steve Tosh led off up Clough Head into more mist, gathering more runners as they went. Jean Dawes commented that she had the chance to 'catch up with all the news from Joan [Lancaster] and Anne-Marie [Grindley]. Boyd says "save your breath for running" or words to that effect'. There were drinks at Grisedale Tarn, before misty ascents of Fairfield and Seat Sandal.

They reached Dunmail at 3.19pm for tea and stew, Jean feeling she shouldn't get too comfortable at support points. The support party still seemed to be growing, and the weather was now dry but windy. More food was consumed at Stake Pass. They met Eric Roberts on Rossett waiting for Harry Walker and Bob Whitfield, who were going the other way on a round with Pete Walkington as pacer. It was cold on Bowfell, and Dawes took on salt tablets and worked through one of the pacers' supply of butterscotch. Dawes had huge self-doubts halfway round, thinking of packing up at Wasdale, but didn't want to let her supporters down. She recalled 'Broad Stand, wet in places – *slape* you might say. Chris and I up first. Chris counting heads as they appear over the rock edge. Rough descent of Scafell and the rest of the team catches up. Chris leads us down a beautiful scree run. We sit and remove stones from our shoes. Then down to Brackenclose Lane for our supper'.[1]

At 9.58pm they were off up Yewbarrow. Dawes was now feeling tired and lost the pacers temporarily in the dark, and then dropped and broke her torch on Kirk Fell. A short sit down to mend the torch and she nearly fell asleep before moving on. They met Pete Dawes coming up from Beck Head, and took some tea with a drop of brandy before hitting Gable.

Soup and tea were taken at Honister at 4.05am and Dawes set off with Bill Smith leading the way over the last three peaks. Eventually they came over the rock steps of Robinson and down to the river path, with just the road home to do. There was

---

1 From her report in *Notable Walks* . . .

not much running, but an attempted sprint up the main street to finish in 23 hours 27 minutes, which included a total rest time of 1 hour 23 minutes. The first ladies sub-24 Bob Graham Round was in the bag. She was the 69th BGR completer.

Chapter 5

Male record setters

At the same time as Heaton, Beard and Naylor were increasing the number of peaks climbed in 24 hours, faster times for a standard round were also being set. First to do so was **Pete Walkington**, who was number 6 on the BGR Club list. On 10 July 1971 he completed his own round, having previously often helped others as a pacer. He had a running time of 18:54, with 1:49 rest, making a total of 20:43. He was paced in part by Joss Naylor, who had arrived home only a few hours earlier, after running up and down Ben Nevis, Scafell and Snowdon in record time.[1]

The next record was set by **Boyd Millen**, who knocked five minutes off Walkington's time with his round in 1973. In a profile of Millen in the June 1997 *Fellrunner*, **Bill Smith** mentions this achievement, but with no more than a comment that the time was not beaten until 1976. Even more remarkably, in his own book (*Stud marks on the Summits*) Smith only tangentially gives himself credit for being the new joint holder of the record:

> On 17/18 August, Bill Smith teamed up with Boyd Millen (Kendal) for a joint attempt in perfect conditions which resulted in Pete Walkington's record being reduced by 5 minutes to 20 hours 38 minutes – Walkington himself urging them on to this achievement.

1 See *It's a hill, get over it* for the story of Joss Naylor's International Three Peaks challenge, accomplished in an astonishing 11 hours and 54 minutes, starting and finishing at sea level.

In a long article in the Spring 1976 *Fellrunner* magazine, Smith wrote further about some of his extended runs, including this (much edited down, the whole article taking up 17 pages of the magazine) account of his and Boyd's record round:

At 9.32am Pete [Walkington] set off from Keswick to accompany us over Robinson, Hindscarth and Dale Head to Honister, where Eric [Roberts] would take over. Pete would then drive Eric's car round to Wasdale Head to prepare refreshments for us, and would afterwards be ready to join us at Dunmail for the night section. We were well up on schedule by the time we reached Honister and here we had tea, cake and jam butties. Conditions were ideal.

Eric shouldered the rucksack containing our spare kit and food and led off up Grey Knotts. His route finding was flawless: not once did he hesitate, nor refer to map or compass. Broad Stand was the only area with which Eric was not intimately acquainted. In fact, his sole experience of this moderate rock climb had been on his own 42 peaks circuit, when Alan Heaton had led him down it. Nevertheless, he showed Boyd and me the way down with expert ease.

At Wasdale Head Pete had everything laid out in preparation, with hot tea and soup ready for us as soon as we trotted in. Following Eric's advice we towelled ourselves down and donned fresh clothing in order to retain our body heat. Then we sat in the car and ate and drank all the good things Pete offered us. We took almost the full half-hour's rest scheduled for us before setting off at a walk up Lingmell Gill, Brown Tongue, and so on to Scafell summit. At Angle Tarn we made our first stop of the day, apart from Honister and Wasdale, and rested for ten minutes, while refreshing ourselves with jam butties and orange juice. The pace Eric had set for us was ideal, we were running easy and relaxed. At Dunmail refreshments were provided by Pete, Mavis [Kenyon] and Eric's wife Gladys. Here we changed clothing once more. Pete led off up Seat Sandal, and we also had an additional pacer in Mike Pearson.

It was fully dark when we reached the summit of Fairfield. On the way up Dollywagon Pike the moon rose from behind the clouds, rendering our torches unnecessary. Just below the summit of Raise we rested for about 10 minutes and had biscuits and orange juice. We were careful not to get too enthusiastic and stuck to Eric's rule about not running uphill. On Clough Head we signalled with our torches to let Mavis and Eric, stationed at Threlkeld, know we were on our way.

We rested and feasted for the full half hour again here, and Pete Trainor replaced Mike as our second pacer. Off we went up Hall's Fell, or 'Kneewrecker Ridge' as fell runners refer to it when descending. It is a fine, narrow, rocky spine. Blencathra's summit was quite clear when we reached it, but mist descended as we dropped down to cross the River Caldew. We were feeling great now, and Pete Trainor, the Singing Fell Runner, serenaded us over this section, scattering the sheep in terror.

The mist cleared from Great Calva as we approached. While we were thankful for this, we heartily cursed its knee-deep heathered flanks, both on the ascent and descent. At the summit of Skiddaw we met three walkers who seemed a bit disconcerted to find us there (it was 5.23am). We also threw in Skiddaw Little Man as Peak 43 for good measure, then set off at a fast pace along the grassy ridge and down the fellside. Sunlight flooded brilliantly across the fells. Boyd, who had been running and chatting with Pete Walkington, holder of the 43 Peaks record (20 hours 43 minutes, 1971), drew level with me and said: "We've got 12 minutes to get down and beat the record!". We raced down to Keswick faster (it seemed) than Dave Cannon does in the Skiddaw Race. Eric was waiting at Moot Hall, overjoyed at our time of 20 hours 38 minutes. The two Peters staged a mock sprint, then we all shook hands. Pete Walkington then solemnly suggested we all do a lap of honour.

Boyd admitted that when he'd told me we had 12 minutes to get in we'd actually had 17, but he'd said 12 to make sure I moved myself. Pete Walkington's gesture in helping us to beat his own record was typical of the spirit of true sportsmanship which exists in amateur Fell Racing.

In 1977 Boyd Millen completed a double BGR. A clockwise run in 21 hrs 30 mins was followed 30 mins later by an anti-clockwise traverse in 30 hrs 30 mins. In 1980 Roger Baumeister topped this with a double BGR in 46 hrs 34 mins 30 secs, although he did it Keswick to Yewbarrow clockwise, then reversed the route to Keswick and on to Yewbarrow again, before turning round again and finishing clockwise back to Keswick. Joss Naylor, Selwyn Wright and Martin Stone were among his pacers.

Millen and Smith's time survived many more attempts, until in 1976 one-time Fell Runners Association (FRA) Chair **John North** produced a new fastest time with an anti-clockwise round that started at 10am on 19 June. As well as being the FRA Chair for three years in the late 1970s, he was also a keen mountaineer and cyclo-cross competitor, being one of the select band of fell runners who have also won the Three Peaks Cyclo-cross race.

On his Bob Graham Round he was untroubled on the leg to Honister, having Dennis Beresford for support, who also carried on to Wasdale. The weather was good to Wasdale, but on Green Gable the sole came off one of North's shoes. A temporary repair with spare laces was performed. They found a good line off Yewbarrow and then had a short break with their support crew, which included Fred and Margaret Rogerson. Donning a tracksuit as he was cold, North went on into the mist, which his pacer Alan Heaton navigated through very efficiently. An enthusiastic ascent of Scafell gained John 20 minutes on his planned schedule.

In his report on the round[1] North noted that:

From here Alan set the pace. On the Scafells my watch strap broke so I had no idea of the time. Whenever I asked Alan

---

1 In *Notable Walks . . .*

how we were going all I was told was 'You're doing OK, keep it going'. This was the best part of the run for me as I had done enough to feel I was getting somewhere and still running well.

The mist cleared as they came off Steel Fell down to Dunmail, with a chance to refuel before the night section. They had a flask of tea at the top of Stake Pass provided by Alan Heaton and one of his other supporters. It is intriguing now to see how the early rounds included refreshment breaks 'on the hill' as well as at the road crossings (and on rare occasions *instead* of). That is much less prevalent nowadays.

With the weather improving Heaton carried on to Threlkeld with them. Beresford paced the last section, which they attacked after a short break. They climbed Hall's Fell ridge with the first light of dawn breaking the sky. Blencathra was in mist and the wind was still troublesome, but the rain had now stopped. On the way to Great Calva they encountered the River Caldew in flood, and North promptly fell in. Over Great Calva and Skiddaw, North was shivering after his almost total immersion. Atop Skiddaw they were surprised to meet Jim Loxham, who had a very welcome flask of hot tea for them. Going up the road to the Moot Hall, North tried to sprint, but after nearly 20 hours had nothing left to offer.

His total running time was 18 hours 34 minutes. With the 1 hour 34 minutes cumulative resting time he had completed his round in 19 hours 48 minutes. He had pushed that particular endurance boundary just a bit further. North's attitude to fell running, and to the Bob Graham Round, is summed up by his comment that 'it means a lot to me. Really fell running is all about self-satisfaction – you against the watch'.

Meanwhile, **Billy Bland** had burst on to the scene.

It was a beautiful moonlit night when, back in August 1976, Billy Bland and his pacers, including Mike Pearson and Mike Walford, left the Moot Hall at midnight on what was claimed to be a 23-hour schedule. The following account is Billy's own, edited down from the one published in Fred Rogerson's *History and Records of Notable Fell Walks, 1864–1972, Within the Lake District.*

After having three or four hours sleep in the afternoon, the seven of us set off for a nice, steady, uneventful section, arriving at Threlkeld on schedule, hoping that daylight wouldn't come – the conditions for running being ideal.

We reached Clough Head together, apart from Neil who was now beginning to lag behind. Howard insisted that Calf How Pike was one of the tops included so, being a little ahead of schedule the two of us added this. Having a job to hold Howard back as we were all tending to split up slightly but we managed to stay together until we met Fred Rogerson at Grisedale Tarn with a welcome flask of tea, then on to Fairfield and Seat Sandal. Neil was now a long way behind and we were starting to leave Chris. We arrived at Dunmail 30 minutes ahead of schedule.

After breakfasting on tinned fruit in a 25-minute rest, four of us set off up Steel Fell with Mike Nicholson and Mike Walford as pacers, leaving Chris who said he was going to hang on for Neil (eventually he set off on his own). We stayed together until High White Stones then we began to leave Howard and Mike Walford, the three of us pressing on with Mike Nicholson. We arrived at Rossett Pike at 10am, where Joss Naylor had kindly left an orange drink.

It was beginning to get very hot now but we were still going well. We reached Bowfell at 10.28am. I was going rather better than David and Anthony so Mike decided that we should press on by ourselves. At 11.29 we arrived at Scafell Pike and decided that Broad Stand would be a much better way to get up as everything was dry and should cause no problems. We made a fast descent to arrive at Wasdale Head at 12.15 for a 26-minute stay and more tinned fruit.

As we set off up Yewbarrow I turned round and saw David and Anthony arriving at Wasdale Head. After having a struggle to climb Yewbarrow we arrived at the top at 13.21 and went on to Red Pike and Steeple, both of us both suffering from the intense heat. Then on to Pillar, now going well again but getting very thirsty as there was little water because of the dry time we had been having. On reaching Black Sail Mike decided to go for water leaving me to do Kirk Fell and meet him at Beck Head. I reached Kirk Fell at 15.11, had a chat with a climber, being glad to see him to prove I'd been there. I dropped into Beck Head feeling shattered and cramming Mars bars in, one after the other, together with all the water Mike had brought. After five minutes rest I set off up Gable, Mike deciding to go for more water. After struggling up Gable I arrived at 15.45, the water/Mars bars getting through my system and I began to go well again. I met Mike on Green Gable and we then did Brandreth and Grey Knotts where we again met up with that man, Fred Rogerson with his cine camera, then down on to Honister Pass arriving at 16.20.

After thanking Mike for the excellent job he'd done and now feeling really good I set off up Dale Head with Mike Walford after five minutes rest. We arrived at Dale Head at 16.49, Hindscarth 17.03, Robinson 17.24, then down on to the Newlands road – the hardest part of the course for me, Mike having to really urge me on. We arrived at Keswick at 18.50, downed two bottles of cider – and I said 'never again'.

Billy Bland concluded that he was already beginning to have second thoughts on the 'never again' quote, and that he was delighted that David and Anthony made it in together, with Howard finishing on his own but still within 24 hours. Chris didn't make it though, probably due to the fact that the team had split up.

As part of my research I interviewed Billy Bland about his later BGR record. I wanted to get as close as possible to the truth about that fantastic effort. In talking, however, we also discussed the 1976 round. Billy offered some interesting reflections on the event, admittedly with hindsight nearly 40 years on. As he remembered it, the team was Billy, Anthony Bland (his cousin), David Bland (brother), Chris Bland (cousin) and Howard Pattison (who Billy went to school with – and by coincidence went past Billy's house earlier in the day I interviewed him doing the 10 in 10, which finished just down the road in Rosthwaite).

The 1976 round was instigated by my cousin Chris Bland. I became the 52nd to do the round. I can't remember what time we started, but we were all supposed to go round together. Just to do it. We went over Skiddaw range together, and then up on to the Dodds. Chris was first to start struggling because he was always going to be the weakest of us. Anyway Howard started going 'come on Chris' and that sort of thing. A little bit of ... [*a pause, and then the thought was not articulated*] – but you know that when you are trying your best you are trying your best. Somebody was nipping away and wanting you to go faster. Let's face it we were only a few hours into the job anyway. So it started to split up. Once we split up – which wasn't instigated by me, although plenty think it would be, but it wasn't. Then we started to splinter, and because we had plenty of pacers everyone had someone to go with. Or maybe Anthony and David went together for a long time, and they may have finished together, I can't remember. Anyway even before Dunmail, can't remember if Anthony and David were still with me or Howard was with us, I sort of pressed on from there in my own way and ended up doing much of the round on my own. I was on my own before Scafell or thereabouts, and ended up with 18:50, was it. I think it was a new record [*it was*]. I was just left with the memory that it was useless, I could knock spots off it. After '76 I became a lot better runner. I wasn't even winning races then.

Billy Bland did become a lot better runner. *Up and Down* magazine noted (in its Jul/Aug 1991 issue) that 'on 15th June at the Royal Dockray 17-miler Billy Bland scored his 100th career victory. The 43-year-old veteran's winning streak dates back to 1967 when, as a 19-year-old guides racer, he won his first race, at Patterdale.' Billy repeated this the following year but then had to wait another ten years before winning a race again, this time his local Borrowdale race. He was not exactly setting the sport alight in his early years. That round, noted above, was when he was just finding his way, figuratively speaking. He returns to the story with an even more startling round, though.

Mike Nicholson was a pacer on Billy Bland's 18:50 record round reported above, but was not considered someone who had his eye on a fast round himself. In 1977, following a good run in the Borrowdale race, Nicholson was relaxing (with a drink) at the post-race dance and barbecue when he suddenly announced he would be making an attempt on the BGR the very next weekend. Over the next few days a schedule was worked out for a joint attempt with Mike Walford. Nicholson had gone well pacing Billy Bland so a fast time was planned with a 5am start. They were going clockwise and aiming for an ambitious 17 hours 30 minutes.

It was warm but overcast as they left, and all went well to Blencathra. Because of low cloud they couldn't locate the summit, but still arrived down at Threlkeld in 2 hours 45 minutes. They had a short break then encountered cloud on the Dodds, where a navigation error meant they lost time taking in a view of the Greenside mines and the summit of Stybarrow Dodd twice. On Helvellyn they had a welcome drink from the first person they had met on the fells all day.

Jim Strickland, who was on his way to Black Sail to meet them, met them on Fairfield, accompanying them to Dunmail. After a 15 minute break for food, Mike Nicholson left with Billy and Stuart Bland at 11.40, with Mike Walford leaving soon after with Jim Strickland. They caught up with Nicholson on Rossett Pike and Jim left for Black Sail. Janet Sutcliffe was on Scafell Pike with liquid refreshment and accompanied them to Wasdale via Broad Stand and Scafell, arriving at 16.26. Mike Walford was eager to take food whereas Mike Nicholson was having problems with what his stomach would take, but did manage some tinned fruit.

Mike Nicholson left Wasdale Head after a 28-minute stop, with Billy and Stuart – with the Blands enjoying the bilberries they found ascending Yewbarrow. Honister Hause was reached in 3 hours 19 minutes. Mike Walford now had Chris Bland and Janet Sutcliffe for company and reached Honister Hause in 3 hours 48 minutes. Mike Nicholson had a foot bath and a little fruit before leaving with Boyd Millen at 20.30. The last three summits and run in from Newlands took 2 hours 15 minutes. This meant a total time of 17:45 (of which 1 hour 3 minutes was rest time). They arrived in time to visit the nearest pub.

Mike Walford was making his third attempt and completed 45 minutes later (in 18:50, with only 52 minutes rest time). He apparently drank a can of beer without effort, and had enjoyed a bottle of reviving Mackeson at each of the feeding stations on the way.

In the five years from Mike Nicholson's round in summer 1977 to the summer of 1982 a further 140 runners completed the Round. In summary, in the 50 years from Bob Graham's 1932 round to 1982 there had been well over 200 successful rounds, which had brought the best time down on seven occasions from 23 hours 39 minutes to 17 hours 45 minutes, as the table shows.

Bob Graham	23:39	1932
Alan Heaton	22:18	1960
Ken Heaton	21:13	1961
Pete Walkington	20:43	1971
Boyd Millen/Bill Smith	20:38	1973
John North	19:48	1976
Billy Bland	18:50	1976
Mike Nicholson	17:45	1977

Chapter 6

Billy Bland

As has been noted, **Billy Bland** felt that his own 18:50 round was not a true reflection of what he was capable of. In discussing this he commented to me that his effort,

> Kinda sowed the seeds for one of these days I will have another go at that because my name is on there as record. Mike Nicholson came along and did 17:45. You hear people say that Mike Nicholson beat Billy Bland's record. Well yes he did, but it wasn't a record I was at all proud of, because I knew I was capable of better anyway. I was taking part in races and I was getting better. That was the best part of my running career if you like, the good part as you are getting better. Once you get to the top of summat, you are just there to be shot at. Toeing the line as the underdog is not as nice as toeing the line as favourite. It just isn't.

On June 19 1982 Billy Bland set out determined to put his mark down, which he did by blowing the existing record into oblivion. Setting off at 5am in a clockwise direction he finished in a stunning 13 hours 53 minutes. It was such an outstanding achievement that it is talked about in tones of wonder and astonishment even now. However, it received some strangely muted commentary in the years afterwards, partly because Bland chose not to indulge in self-aggrandisement, or even really talk or write about it much. Even Bill Smith's authoritative tome *Stud marks on the summits* (published in 1985), in its

27 pages given over to the Bob Graham Round, allows just one paragraph on Bland's record round, a paragraph which lists the pacers and the times taken for each leg. He concludes with a quote from Fred Rogerson, who said afterwards that 'he had never seen anyone look so fresh and undistressed at the end of a 42 Peaks circuit'. Even more remarkable is the fact that *42 Peaks: The story of the Bob Graham Round*, in its 46-page 2012 edition, merely notes that 'the Bob Graham Round is not competitive in the sense of having winners and losers, but there have been many outstanding performances which are worthy of note. The fastest time for a round at the first attempt is 14 hours 56 minutes by Stuart Bland of Borrowdale, and the fastest overall time is held by Billy Bland, also from Borrowdale, who recorded 13 hours 54[1] minutes in 1982'.[2]

Billy Bland provided some great copy to the reporter who wrote up his feat in a fairly long piece in *The Times* (Wed Jun 30, 1982). In summing up his achievement he said (tongue firmly lodged in his cheek, I suspect):

> In fact there are them as won't believe I've done it. I was lucky with conditions, with the people pacing me, who made sure I didn't run a yard more that I needed to, and I was in really good form ... Training takes up 10 or 12 hours a week, covering 100 miles or so across local hills ... I do have bad patches but I know when they are coming because my eyelids start to flutter. I just bang in another Mars bar and wait for it to hit the system. It's like putting coal on a fire.

Fellrunner magazine had an account of Billy's round in its July 1983 issue, written by Tony Cresswell, who was one of his

---

1 Different sources give it as either 53 or 54 minutes. It is more often recorded as 13 hours 53 minutes.
2 The Bob Graham Club gives an 'Achievement of the Year Award' (by a Club member) each year. Billy didn't win it in 1982, although admittedly it was often given for other 'extended' endurance event achievements. Mark Hartell *was* awarded it in 1999/2000 for his 14 hours 54 minutes round.

pacers for some of the round. His pacers were of absolutely the highest calibre, including Kenny Stuart, Joss Naylor, Jon Broxap and Pete Barron. The article was entitled 'Bob Grahams – the Bland way' and detailed both Billy's record round and also his brother Stuart's shortly afterwards that same year. It had two photos from Stuart's round within the article, and the cover of the magazine had two more, but none from Billy's. The part of the report that refers to Billy's round is reproduced here, largely as it appeared in the magazine.

Largely unreported until now, the antics of Billy then Stuart Bland's epic rather swift BG's would make riveting reading. That is of course if any one person could have stayed in long enough to report on them. Ideally, Billy and Stuart should write a report themselves but the likelihood of them singing their own praises is as likely as me running the next 12-odd hour BG! Anyway, as I was involved to a small degree in both I will do my best to paint a picture of these amazing lightning tours.

The weekend nearest to the longest day of 1982 was the stage for Billy's effort. Having run (and won) the Ennerdale the previous weekend as a depreciation run our Willie had most of Keswick AC and more dotted round the region in readiness. I was labelled for the Dunmail-Wasdale leg (might have slowed by then?). Billy had started at the crack of dawn going clockwise like Mr Graham had and as Mike Nicholson had when he set the existing record of 17:45 in 1977. I wasn't able to make Dunmail in time for Billy's schedule due to work so set off up Langdale and hot foot for Rossett Pass. I had still missed him – information kindly supplied from some of John Gibbison's pacers, also doing a Round. The day was still and mild but low cloud obscured the tops all day. Should I go to Ore Gap and miss him there? I opted for Esk Hause and alas I had still missed out but the gap was now down to apparently 5–10 minutes. Keep going son, you've got all day and thanks to the abundance of walkers (doing the Four 3000s) I gained progress reports of the elusive 'Have you seen three fell runners, mate?' until Jon Broxap faintly made out one such enquiry in the mists in the Ill Crag region. At last, contact!

There was Stuart also going in support and, going great guns, Billy. He graciously declined my offers of one flask of tea, ditto coffee, squash, milk, butties, cakes, having humped them all the way. I could have made a fortune flogging the stuff on Scafell Pike but if we stopped I must have blinked. Broad Stand was the riot it commonly is. Stuart was shoved up to pull up Billy then Jon who went on for the Scafell summit. I was last and nearly had me and Stuart down Mickledore Chimney; 'By lad, yer 'eavier than our Jon', he said. Our time off Scafell was ridiculous as I remember and a small group was assembled at Wasdale Head. He only stopped a very short while but I recall him with a butty and bottle of Mackeson as I stood croaking behind Joss's car. Only Joss continued with Billy on up Yewbarrow leaving me trying to flog those drinks and things to Joss's kids. Having failed there as well I set off for Sty Head after Jon and Stuart bound for Borrowdale and I returned to Langdale via Rossett once more. Over my shoulder I understand Billy had a few minutes halt on Yewbarrow but Joss saw to that [with a Naylor shake]. Barring that momentary flutter he speeded up if anything and from Newlands into Keswick it was a job for any including the fresh to live with him. So at 6.54pm, just 13 hours 54 minutes after setting out, Billy shaved a clear 3 hours 51 minutes off the record. The record was likely to go all right. He told us pacers that 16 hours was the target, it was the amount under that target that stopped the world turning. It turned out to be an ultra depreciation run for the Wasdale a few weeks later – which Billy also won, with a record time.

Tony Cresswell concluded the article with these thoughts:

In trying to gather information for this article I was told not to waste my time, 'I'm telling you, someone will go out soon and do 12 hours . . .' Well, while there are maybe one or two about I thought I had better write this article and let the brave come forward.

I have to apologise for the depth of detail supplied which can only revolve around my own tiny contributions. There were loads of folk involved who performed their own marathon efforts but rather than make this a great factual account they are left out of here . . . a few split times to close should make some of us squirm. I was only too glad to be along and very proud to be part of a bit of history.

Keswick to Threlkeld	2:13	3 minutes rest
to Dunmail	2:41	3 minutes
to Wasdale	3:43	2 minutes
to Honister	3:09	13 minutes
to Keswick	1:47	
	13:54	21 minutes

What would Billy Bland himself reveal about all this?

On a weekend when my wife was doing an open water swimming event in Derwentwater I had arranged to chat with Billy Bland about his record BGR time. I zipped up Borrowdale, past Bob Graham's old haunt near Ashness Bridge, and pulled in to his house, to be met by a still fit-looking Billy. We settled in with a bit of banter about ageing, before I started teasing out the story of his record round. Billy explained much of the background to his record, the build-up and the earlier 18-hour-plus effort. He seemed to have been reluctant to say too much previously, as he is naturally tough but modest by nature. Indeed, he implied that he had been misrepresented by others in their reports and comments about how things panned out, and why. I somehow feel it was a chance to tell the story from his own perspective that he had waited some while to take, but was now pleased to. Billy kindly dug out some original photos from the round and generously allowed me to take them with me to scan and return to him, after identifying the pacers and supporters in them. My one regret was not thinking on my feet at the time. Billy referred to some handwritten notes when talking about the times for each leg. These were the leg times written on cards, which he has kept. I should have realised the historical significance and asked to copy or photograph them for this publication. It was also quite weird being in Billy's sitting room and seeing figures flash (or more often stumble) by the window in an endurance event that finished just down the road in Rosthwaite.

What follows is a transcript of the interview I conducted with Billy Bland. It gives his take on the unfolding story of his build-up to his record round, the round itself, and some connected post-round comments from him. It is told in his own words, usually transcribed 'as said', sometimes re-ordered; so it includes some colloquialisms. [*'Prompts' from me are in italics*].

The Build-up

Would you say you had a different, more single-minded approach to your second BGR? Absolutely. This is a bit of story that I don't think has been written actually. Me brother Stuart had started running. He was a one-man-band farmer up the road there. I can't remember what age he was, but his first race was Borrowdale and he came third. He was terribly good at downhill. He was mekking inroads on the downhill. He still finished third on merit without a doubt. He was a good downhiller, as I was meself. Anyway, he thought he would do a Bob Graham, and he would have a go at doing it real serious, not to go round in 24 hours.

Because of Joss holding the 24 hour peaks record I never ever wanted to tek it off him. I did have a go once but didn't finish. I was talked into it, but me heart wasn't into it from day one, because I didn't want to take it off t'old lad.[1] That is silly thinking, actually, and I should have. *How many peaks was it at by then?* It was at 72 peaks I think. Me brother was going to have a go at BG. With the mentality that I didn't want to tek it off Joss, I knew that if me brother went and set a Bob Graham record I wouldn't have wanted to tek it off him. He was going in August I think so I needed to be getting this, as I'd have not wanted to tek it off him. And that is how I then went between winning at Ennerdale and Wasdale. [*We had a discussion of timescales. My prepared information showed his BGR being 1 week after Ennerdale and 3 weeks before Wasdale, Billy thought there was an extra week in there.*]

You had a good knowledge of the fells. Did you specifically recce any legs for your round? No, no. Because I had been on them all. I didn't set out to do any particular thing apart from do it my way. Do it like I felt. The reason I was doing it was because me brother was going to do it. *There is a myth that you said you set out to do 16 hours.* Well, no. I knew I was gonna brek it. I had done 18 hrs 50 without trying, basically. I had become a lot better runner after that, so I did know I would brek it. I had no idea what time I was gonna do. All I was gonna do, which was a great way to do it, was just run as I felt. Did what I wanted to do, don't get dictated to by anybody. I was the boss on the day. I didn't need any pacers to show the way cos I knew the way. *So, doing your own navigation?* Oh aye.

Did you change your training for the BG? No, it was stuck

---

1 In an interview with Andy Hyslop in *Climber and Rambler* Magazine in March 1983, Joss had this to say: Well, given the right day I think Billy could go well – adding a few onto the 72 peaks record. He knows where his weaknesses are, he's got to have plenty of food, and I hope he does it. *You wouldn't feel any remorse if he took the record from you?* Not at all, because he'll have to work hard to do it and on the day he'll suffer. I paced him from Wasdale when he did the Bob Graham Round in 13 hours and he was going well that day.

in between an Ennerdale and Wasdale, which meant more to me than any Bob Graham Round. I said to meself I will ga around there, of the three it would be third on my priorities. People are now talking as though that was the best thing I ever did. I pull folk up every time, and say well no. Wasdale and Borrowdale records to me are better achievements than the Bob Graham. The Bob Graham I did was just what I wanted to do on that day. Whereas in a race you are dictated to, or can be, by the opposition. *You did a 20+ mile race at Duddon in the build-up to the 1982 round.* Beaten by someone there, I can't remember who. *Was it a blip in that season?* You don't get everything right. I remember setting off in one Duddon and by Harter I was kicking stones. Basically, I was buggered before I set off.

The Round

When going that fast, what is the point of pacers? Carrying water? Of course they are. Set off in pair of shorts or what-ever is suitable for the day. In races I see lads on a fairly warm day in a bit of rain and they set off in a cagoule. I just used to smile to messel. What have you got between your ears? That cagoule is gonna pull all the juice out of you in no time. Just put it round your waist and put it on if you need it, otherwise keep it off. Sweat is gonna come pouring out of you.

Did you plan it on that day, to get the pacers available? Or was it that you waited for a good day and did it then? Living here, if it had turned out a bad day then it is off. That is how we are fortunate up here, we can play it that way. So, yes I went as I felt. *People time sections and predict times and get a pacer who can do that time now.* Load of crap. Get yourself fit and put one leg past the other and do it as you feel. Forget the times someone else has done. *Did you think you could do it in a period of daylight?* Yes. Absolutely. Out of Keswick at 5am. I have still got a card with the times on.

[Finds the record of leg times] Must have been 5am. Kenny [Stuart] was on that leg – the little bugger could run, but his navigation wasn't up to much. We departed Threlkeld 7.16am. *[Reads times]* 53 minutes to top of Skiddaw, 1:20 Calva, 1:59 Blencathra, 2:13 Threlkeld, and back out in 3 minutes. *You had pacers on each section?* Only Kenny on the first leg. On the Dodds certainly Peter Barron and I think Ian Charlton. After Dunmail it was Stuart that would be one. Tony Cresswell on some of that, but not it all. Jon Broxap was among it, on some of that section too. Joss came out of Wasdale and did his famous Naylor shake out of there. Martin Stone was standing at Wasdale, not sure whether he actually went out on all of that section. He certainly was on Kirk Fell with us and came into Honister with us. On the last leg Chris Bland, Jon Broxap, Peter Barron, Stuart and I think ole Joss carried on, and I think me brother David. I don't want to miss anyone out.

What about this blip you had on Yewbarrow? It is a struggle up Yewbarrow. I consciously said to myself, I had just eaten something and that is the wrong place to force it. Blood goes to your stomach to process food. *What was your feed strategy?* Me wife's malt loaf, and date and walnut cake. There is a thing called barmbrack [*yeasted bread with added sultanas and raisins*]. Nice moist stuff. The odd sandwich mebbe, just whatever you fancy, but you do get sick of eating. It has got to go in, hasn't it. If you don't put the food in you run out of petrol, which I duly did.

Someone timed your rests at each road point, and they were 3 minutes, then 3, 3 and 13. What happened? I know exactly how it happened. We were climbing up towards the top of Kirk Fell and I heard Martin say 'what a fantastic climb, we are going really well' and I heard him and Joss talking, and they were saying 'he's gonna get under 14 hours'. I heard them say it and I wasn't bothered. As far as I was concerned I was doing what I wanted. I was doing what I thought was [*pause*] quite well. [*laughs*] With them talking about that I think mebbe they meant to, mebbe they didn't, but they just started nudging us a bit faster. You are working to fine lines anyway. Living on the edge as I call it, of being almost just a fraction out of fuel, not bloated and not over-eating. But close to running out of petrol. An awful lot of people are sick, although I never was.

So, why the long stop? I think to call it an injection of pace would be ridiculous. But obviously just a little bit of raising of effort took its toll. Over Gable it is a pig of a climb, then across to Green Gable, Brandreth and Grey Knotts. I was coming off Grey Knotts and I could see Honister. There is a fence line that comes off the top and down, although they don't do it know, they stay over more where the Borrowdale race line comes down. I would know that. Why I chose to come down the fence line I don't know, I was doing it my way. Coming down the fence line I was just going dizzy, and pish – was out of petrol, just as quick as that. Within two minutes my legs felt wobbly and I went dizzy. I just sat down. It has been reported that I got given something to eat there, but I don't think I did. I just sat a couple of minutes – like I say within 300 yards of the feed station. Got up and went down there and that is where I had the 13 minutes. I maintain that nothing was done to upset the thing really. But I think that slight raising of pace and talking about being under 14 hours, if they had just left us and said nowt. I would have come in to Honister 2 minutes later at worst and would have gone out 2 minutes sooner.

Did you have any navigation problems on the day? Certainly – it was at back o'Skiddaw. Can't remember whether I was compassing it. Probably did from Calva, I hit the sheepfold probably on a bearing. I certainly knew when I set out the navigation was down to me. Most of t'others it was clear on. I had a hell of a knowledge of this lot round here [*Borrowdale*]. As it is my training ground. With Wasdale and Ennerdale races I kinda knew near every stone and every little sheep trod I had to find. *How did you get between the*

Scafells? No rope as I remember. There was quite often a short bit of rope with a pin left there. Can't remember, I think Stuart kinda bunked us up. I used to go training over there on a summer night running like. It is only because you are mebbe fatigued that it is better to be pushed up and someone holding it. I could get up and down it myself if I went now. *What shoes did you wear? Walshes?* Aye, Walshes. I wish I had kept them, as the pair that I did BG record in. But it is neither here nor there.[1]

Post-round thoughts

Other people have said it will throw the whole season out if they trained for the Bob Graham. Haha. Soft buggers. When you are fit, you are fit. If I went to bed and wasn't recovered, if you don't recover in maximum 3 days you are not fit. That is how I have seen my training. If you all of a sudden went and did Ennerdale off very little you would be knackered for a week. Bear in mind I used to go training on the fells nearly every night. My body was adapted for taking that sort of load.

You would do Borrowdale Saturday, Latrigg the next day. So you had good recovery. That is what the body was used to. It adapts to a load. Now if I had a trainer, and this is where I think a lot of people and a lot of sports fall down. They will not let an individual be an individual. They try to tek it out of you. Take footballers. [*The World Cup was a few days off*] You get someone who would now be classed as a maverick. All he is doing is expressing hisself on the pitch. I'll hardly watch athletics on telly because they interview them and they are all just the same. Not individuals, they have been

---

1 A recent exhibition at Keswick Museum on *Fell Running on Skiddaw and Latrigg* included the pair of Walshes that Kenny Stuart wore to set the course record for the Skiddaw race in 1984. His 62:18 is still the record for the race.

produced if you like, that is the kind of thing I am getting at. I was an individual, I wouldn't let anybody influence me. I did it my way or didn't do it at all. Be I right or be I wrong. Yes, you make mistakes, but if you have a head on your shoulders you will learn off them.

Stuart Bland

Actually Stuart tried a month later and he held my times until Scafell Pike, and he lost it after that, I saw it cos I was with him. He had his wobbly patch coming off down off Scafell. *Did you do a Naylor shake on him?* Because Joss had done it to me, and I don't know whether it is so much the shake as someone showing concern over you. Because you do, when you are buggered you withdraw into yourself. I never considered messel buggered, but I think Joss was quite anxious about me. Someone must have told him about it, he couldn't have known. So we did a shake on Stuart, but more or less he wanted a pep talk really. He did the same as I did at Honister, he ran out of petrol coming down off Scafell. He was just an hour and 3 minutes slower than me and then Mark Hartell beat that by 1 minute.

Further thoughts

How fit are you now? I did the Fred Whitton[1] until two years ago, coming in first 50 places at my last one. Toed the line two months before me 64th birthday. I might have done a triathlon like the Wasdale one, but I am no swimmer. Don't like it, never front crawled. Don't do any running now. Knees are alright, ankles are the problem. Used to be 5ft 10.5 and

1 The Fred Whitton Challenge consists of a 112-mile cycle sportive around the Lake District, starting at Grasmere and taking in climbs of Kirkstone, Honister, Newlands, Whinlatter, Hardknott & Wrynose passes.

went for MOT and am now 5ft 9 [*laughs*]. No spring in them ankles any more. If I had to run to Seatoller, a few hundred yards, then my ankles would ache. To be quite honest I am not bothered. Took fell running as far as I could take it. Me biking I get nearly the same kick as I used to get out of running. Gotta be realistic. What is the point of toeing the line and limping all way round. I can ride a bike and get no pain at all. *I see Gavin Bland making a sort of comeback.* Gavin could have knocked spots off anything I ever did. More talented than me, but that is only part of it.

Is someone going to beat your time soon? I said it to Ricky Lightfoot, because there is some talk of him doing it. I am saying never mind what times others have done. Just set out for a day on the fells and do what works for you. If it comes out alright, it comes out alright. Don't get hyped up about hitting times. So, I think there was possibly another 10 minutes there. It was like putting a nozzle in the car. I got that food down me and was away as if nothing happened. It just was a fuel thing. *Do you think you got the optimum performance you could get?* I hadn't the pressure of beating anyone's times. I wasn't under any pressure at all. I think it was quite fortunate. Anyone who does it is going to be under that pressure.

You never really thought you could take the 24 hour peaks total upwards? No, nothing to do with that. Didn't think it was right to tek it off the man. Which is bad thinking really. Realise that now. It wasn't right thinking. We are both from the same background, families had known one another for years and I just didn't have the appetite to want to do it. Just like this feller now that has broken Joss's Wainwrights. He had sussed out, and I sussed out years ago, that old Joss always went bang into everything till he had reduced himself to nought and stayed on because of his dogged determination. Steve [*Birkinshaw*] would be armed with that sort of talk. I have talked a lot to people about what Joss used to do. I have great admiration for his hardness, but he never learned how to pace himself. Even now, I had a word with Steve on Dale Head the other day and he was down to two sticks, and he had been walking for 3 days. Although it was a more measured approach, he isn't as good an athlete as Joss. By going with less sleep and refining the route that Joss took, and now he has got it.

Why did you only win the British Fell Championship once (in 1980)? Because I wasn't good enough! *Were you not good enough on the short races that were included?* I was good on long 'uns. If someone had said 'Right Billy you can pick races this year' I could have won a few probably. You know some short and rough ones and that. I never saw meself as the bees knees at all. Cos I always knew someone with more ability who wasn't winning as many races as they should. My application was my strongpoint. I liked what I was doing, and my attitude was some nights I came home and didn't fancy training then I would think well if you don't someone who is main opposition will be. So I was out and away, so it was application that got me there. I certainly wasn't the most talented. I had a talent for running downhill, and my only other talent was for training hard.

Tell me about your walking round. It was instigated by a talk with Ken Ledward. I said three mile an hour and you've got it. That is how it started. I said to Gavin [*who was then 18 yrs old*] do you fancy coming? We had some pacers, but no schedule, just setting out to walk as fast as we could, never ran one step. We were far too early in Wasdale, and pacers weren't there. We had to walk between Wasdale up on to Scafell and across on to the Pike on our own. Then whoever had come had scuttled up to join us. Actually even though we had sat down by the wall on Scoat Fell and had an orange or summat to kill some time – a minute or too there maybe.

Can you imagine someone taking your BGR time? Of course I can. *But no-one has?* And I think I know why. You see what happens now with this Wainwright round [*Steve Birkinshaw*]. You get an aura, and people put you on a pedestal that you shouldn't be on. Naylor has been on a pedestal for ages. People didn't think it was possible as it was Naylor. Then because I was dominant in long fell racing and did this thing. Then McDermott and Hartell had taken the 24 hour total on and both tried for my time. I kinda knew they wouldn't get my record. That puts it even more on a pedestal. Even though they weren't regular fell race winners, but they were long distance specialists. I never saw myself as anything special. That is where they fall down, they don't train hard enough. I don't think I am hard mentally, but you certainly get a confidence out of what you can do, knowing your ability and harnessing that in the proper manner.

Could Ricky Lightfoot do it? He may be doing the mileage. He is doing mountain running, which is fine, as I don't think it is about focus. My focus wasn't on the BGR. I just stuck it in because me brother was gonna have a go. Which coach would have told you that was a good idea, stuck between two long races? None. *What about Kilian Jornet?* [*pauses*] Would he want to come here? If someone said to me when I was at me best, do you want to go to Spain to have a go at this and that. Spain means nowt to me, this is what means something to me, where I live. Jornet would need the right people with him to show him the best way. If he is capable, then fine. I couldn't care less if someone took my record. What I know is that is about as good as I was, within a few minutes. That is the satisfaction.

Joss never tried a fast time? Was he capable? I don't think Joss could have done that time. I have better times over the years in long races. *He had a lot of health issues?* He likes the publicity, which is not my scene. We are different in that way. But no, I am confident that anything Joss did I think I could do. Just in my own mind, and I think he would know it as well. Mark McDermott and Mark Hartell, I knew they wouldn't break my record. I had a pretty good day, and didn't do much wrong. I am not trying to sound bigheaded, just being realistic. *What do you think of people soloing or doing it in winter?* Clutching at straws or trying to make a name for themselves. Because a winter Bob Graham would not appeal to me one little bit. That is just me. Even Ricky – word got out that he was going to try to set a winter time. He could do that hopping on one leg.[1] I said to him what is wrong with summer – get stuck in to that. Everyone to their own. I like competition, but I couldn't care less if I got beat. If I have done my best and get beat, then they were better than you. I was brought up on defeat. You don't win first time out.

Ending

Thanks for your openness. There is an awful lot that gets printed that isn't right. When I was in my footballing days, in my 20s, I said 'what is old bugger like Joss doing winning races'. That was the mentality then, somebody that was 40 had to have a pipe and slippers and a pot belly. There is one thing about me, if I said it, I will stand by it.

I left Billy Bland's house with plenty to ponder, some of which I will return to later in this narrative.

Billy Bland obviously worked hard to achieve his amazing fitness, as is evidenced by this view from Joss Naylor (quoted in *Feet in the Clouds*). 'There was no bugger trained harder than Billy. He put the miles in, and he put them in hard. He was so self-centred, so self-destructive – he put himself through a hell of a regime. But I'll tell you what: he had a lot of bloody guts and determination in his training'. Bland also had a terrific 'feel' for the mountains, yet had a strange take on navigation. On this aspect of his ability Askwith quotes him as saying, 'I've never been lost in training. I had a good memory, and I could read ground, especially in the Lake District. For long races I would write bearings on the back of my hand, but if I ever got the map out, it meant I was lost. Generally I'd find my way off memory'.

---

1 Ricky Lightfoot did have a try, but it didn't go quite as Billy suggested (see Winter chapter)

One of the thoughts talking to Billy Bland prompted in me was of comparing the record breaking rounds over the years. Looking back over the record progression described in this chapter I had a feeling that there would be some interesting detail within the various times. Reading the pages of Fred Rogerson's *Notable Walks* ... I noted that the individual rounds reported in that volume had their individual rest times recorded, together with finish times. The amounts of cumulative rest time seemed to be coming down dramatically over the years. I hypothesised that these time gains would be a major contributor to reduced completion times. For instance, Alan Heaton's 1960 22:18 round included a total of 2 hours 10 minutes rest, whilst Billy Bland in his 1982 record only took 21 minutes rest. The following table shows the rest times[1] for all the new record setters, where known. It shows a rather different picture.[2]

Year	Name	Time for round (hrs-mins)	Rest time in minutes	Actual running time (hrs-mins)
1932	Bob Graham	23:39	75	22:24
1960	Alan Heaton	22:18	130	20:08
1971	Pete Walkington	20:43	109	18:56
1973	Boyd Millen/Bill Smith	20:38	n/a	n/a
1976	John North	19:48	94	18:14
1976	Billy Bland	18:50	64	17:46
1977	Mike Nicholson	17:45	63	16:42
1982	Billy Bland	13:53	21	13:32

---

1   Rest in this context is taken to be the amount of time at the support points, ie feeding/drinking and not moving.

2   Ken Heaton's 21:13 in 1961 is not included in this analysis as he did 51 peaks, whereas all the others did 42.

It is assumed that Bob Graham's times show him having a relatively small amount of 'rest' as he was predominantly walking, being 'on the go' for nearly 22½ hours. After that, each record breaker took progressively less rest than the last (data for Millen/Smith not being available). However, the calculated running times also become shorter in each and every case too. From this it is possible to extrapolate the contribution of reduced rest times and increased pace to each new record, as shown in the next table.

Name	Record reduced by (mins)	Rest reduced by (mins)	Run reduced by (mins)	Contribution of reduced running time (% of record reduction)
Pete Walkington	95	21	74	78
John North	55	15	40	73
Billy Bland	58	30	28	48
Mike Nicholson	65	1	64	98
Billy Bland	232	42	190	82

Billy Bland's first record is a slight anomaly, in that it is the only time where reduced rest contributes more than reduced running time. All the others have figures of 73% or more for what might be termed the 'running pace effect'. Mike Nicholson's effort of being on his feet for over an hour less than the previous record holder seems pretty remarkable, until that is the figure of over three hours less run time for Billy Bland is considered.

Chapter 7

Female record setters

In 1978, one year after Jean Dawes became the first female BGR completer, a second woman runner joined her. This was **Anne-Marie Grindley**, who became the 98th member of the Bob Graham Club, going round with husband Will. Her time cut over 2 hours 20 minutes from Dawes' time. In the period before her successful round Grindley did several months of training at 50/60 miles per week, and once topped 100 miles. This was mostly off-road as she disliked road running.

Anne-Marie Grindley's anti-clockwise round on 17/18 June 1978 came in at 21 hours 5 minutes, including a total rest time of 1 hour 36 minutes. It was noted in Fred Rogerson's '*Notable Walks . . .*' in the following way, in a report written by Grindley herself (and edited down by me for this publication):

Not only have I never been so pampered – never have I been so bossed. As we ran up the first gentle inclines along the road from Keswick John Haworth shouted "You'll regret it later". I appreciated John's concern even if I did appear to disregard it. He (and my husband, Will) were convinced that I would 'blow up' later on, but we women fell runners are made of sterner stuff.

The sunny weather was infectious and the whole proceeding had an air of light heartedness. We had a marvellous tea party at the top of Rossett Gill, devouring food like a plague of locusts. Alastair [*Patten*] caught a frog going up Dollywagon and wondered if it was doing the BGR.[1]

The fates were smiling kindly on me that weekend with curious crises smoothed out by my helpers without worry to me – although Will had a bad fall on Kirk Fell. He was able to continue after a short rest at Black Sail Pass. At Wasdale we were so far ahead of schedule that we left before the arrival of one of our support team for the next section. It was the most enjoyable day on the fells that I have ever had, due to our wonderful companions.

When we discussed it, Anne-Marie felt that the extract quoted above might read as though she didn't take the Bob Graham Round very seriously. This was far from the case, and she added the following thoughts on her memory of the days when she and her husband were involved with the Bob Graham Round:

Above all the generosity of people – who drive hundreds of miles from their homes to the Lake District. They then drive around for whole weekends, just to assist the contenders. Whatever the weather, runners turned out, often with partners and children in tow. Their reward – just a good day out on the fells (even if it was wet, windy, foggy with route finding problems), good companionship, food and drink supplied by the contender. This even occurred when the contender may not be thought to have much chance of success. Wonderful camaraderie! Friendships forged then continue to this day.

---

1   There is of course the Frog Graham Round. The website (http://www.froggrahamround.co.uk/) explains: The Frog Graham Round is a running and swimming challenge that was created by Peter Hayes from inspirations from the classic Bob Graham Round but with an added twist. Along with covering just over 40 miles and ascending and descending 15,750 feet, the competitor must swim across Bassenthwaite Lake, Crummock Water, Buttermere and Derwent Water before finishing where it all started in Keswick.

It took another year for a third female runner to complete a round. In 1979 **Ros Coats** became the 129th Club member, and she brought the fastest time down further to 20 hours 31 minutes. Coats was the inaugural Ladies Fell Running Champion that year, further emphasising her abilities, which had been honed in her earlier mountaineering and orienteering experiences. Coats' start time happened to coincide with a Dark Peak Fell Runners multi-BGR attempt, and Will and Anne-Marie Grindley attempting a 58-peak round; so it was extra busy around the Moot Hall that particular Saturday. When reminded of this extended round, Anne-Marie Grindley commented:

> When I completed 58 peaks there was some comment about my counting of peaks, but we had been in touch with Fred Rogerson and established that I could include peaks with two 50 foot contours around them. That led to counting two peaks on Kirk Fell and other extra peaks. Of course, the main addition to distance was the Causey Pike to Whiteless Pike ridge, giving six extra peaks. Most of the others were ones which various men had included in their 42+ rounds. As the first female to do more than 42, I felt it was my choice of route. My record stood for about 15 years, before Anne Stentiford beat it.

Wendy Dodds made an unsuccessful attempt to complete the Bob Graham Round in 1978, her failure due mainly to insufficient preparation. She had been inspired by the sub-24 hour traverse the previous year by Jean Dawes of Kendal AC. Dawes had completed the Round in 1976 but exceeded the allotted 24 hours by 50 minutes and her example, in returning to have another go, led Wendy Dodds to mount her own second attempt in 1979, when her 23 hours 30 minutes circuit resulted in her becoming the Club's fourth lady member.

It should be remembered that at this time female distance runners were struggling for recognition in the fell running community. Both Dawes and Grindley were described as 'housewifes' in a report in *The Fellrunner*, and they had been among the women agitating for equality in race opportunities. This period is covered in *It's a hill, get over it*, where I noted:

> 1977 had seen shorter ladies races set up in parallel with some of the long classic Lakes races like Wasdale, Borrowdale and Ennerdale. Langdale also had a short ladies race, up Pike O'Blisco, although this soon changed to have all entrants traversing the full course. Earlier, on 2 April 1977, the Pendle Fell race had held the first official ladies race.

Strangely, in relation to someone who has had such an impact on the sport, there is very little reported on the various BGRs that **Helene Diamantides** has completed, often in fast times or in an innovative fashion. She was the first female runner to do a solo/unsupported round in 1988, unknowingly setting a new record of 20 hours 17 minutes, subsequently setting another record when she brought the time down to 19 hours 11 minutes in 1989. The following is Helene's own account of her 19:11 record (and final of her 'Big Three in a month'). It is from Adrian Belton's archive collection:

> In the fell running tradition the decision to 'go for it' was made a mere 14 hours before the start. As gale force winds and showers were forecast it seemed ideal to make the attempt. Adrian (brainless) Belton had decided that 18 days rest between records was excessive and he was also keen to complete his hat-trick. Hence a truce was drawn up and a mutual support party organised.
>
> The grot and clag on Skiddaw lifted for Calva as we left Martin (schizo) Stone who was supporting another attempt. Dawn broke descending to Threlkeld where we had a wonderful breakfast of Ambrosia creamed rice and tea. We spent the Helvellyn section chasing Tim Maitland on his solo round, when I wasn't busy competing with him for the most pees per round.

The cloud lifted, and with it our spirits. The work-to-schedule ruling by the pacers' union necessitated a mid-shift handover to Paul [Stone] from Bowfell to Wasdale. I was bonking well up Red Pike, and Great Gable loomed out of the mist again, and again, so we had to double back to the summit.

At Honister a reception committee of 'I'd rather do the Buttermere' types waited like vultures at a painful death. Their encouragement propelled us up the final lumps and on to Robinson. The sun on the heather in Buttermere and the glowing evening light on the hills almost made it worthwhile.

A quick change of shoes at the road, pick up more loo roll, and grit the teeth for the grind back to Keswick. The finale: dodging chip eating grockles, and ice cream wielding children, on the last 100m to the Moot Hall. A highly appropriate finishing tape of loo roll summed up my thoughts on the 3 completed Big Rounds.

I wanted to rectify the situation with regard to the reporting of Helene's achievements, so sought to get the stories directly from her, and made contact to ask her for an interview.

Helene Whitaker (née Diamantides) was the first of two people I interviewed while researching this book who I had already spoken to in writing my first book. She was again very receptive to my questioning, answering freely and openly. We relaxed into talking about her various BGR experiences, both as completer and pacer for others. We covered her earlier round, her planning and execution of the first solo and unsupported round by a female athlete, before finishing on her fastest time round of 1989. She had got out her photo albums from that era and kindly allowed me to borrow some BGR photos to scan for possible inclusion in this book.

Helene explained that she initially found everyone around her seemed to be doing the Bob Graham Round. It was seen as a long day out on the hills. Her club was Dark Peak, which supported contenders well, and the members supported each other. There were also fewer races then, and she remembered doing her first Edale race.

I asked her if someone in particular had influenced her. 'No, I didn't realise that women hadn't been allowed to do long stuff,' she replied. 'I just turned up and ran round the long course. I do remember that most women did the short course.' Going on to her BGR, Helene pointed out that it wasn't done as a Dark Peak round. 'I was at college with Alison Wright in Durham, and we were running together,' Helene explained. 'She had done it, and may have been the youngest woman.'

Helene had done a reasonable amount of preparation for the round. 'I hadn't been on all the tops. I knew where the sections went, and probably couldn't have navigated my way round it all at the time,' she noted. 'I could get myself round things, and was safe, and could have got off things – with my climbing background. I wouldn't have known best lines for instance. I basically got taken around.'

On that round she went up Broad Stand, as she was a climber. 'I think I stood on Martin Stone's shoulders, and then hoiked him up,' she laughed. 'I think we left someone behind there. On every round I lost pacers.' The weather wasn't great on the round, and the photographs show them in thermals. Talking about Broad Stand got us into a discussion about whether or not people's attitude to Broad Stand has changed, with us being more and more safety conscious. But Helene disagreed. 'I think it is more that it has got worse. I think it is much more slimy and has just got very worn.'

On the round Helene's supporters were people she knew from climbing. She explained that it was nominally 'her round'. She had been advised not to set off with two or three other people setting off on their round. 'I believe that very strongly,' she said. 'If there is more than one person setting off now I say I am that person's pacer and make it quite clear. I am going with my person.' The main reason is that she has seen so many go wrong with their pacing. She pointed out the advantage of going solo. 'I could stop and eat when I wanted to, and where I wanted to. It wasn't at road crossing points, interestingly. It was where there were streams or whatever. I remember sitting on a hillside above Ennerdale having a food stop, and then later trotting through Dale Head and stopping at Hindscarth as that was a better spot. The natural stopping points were when I was hungry, and I am sure that helped me have a fast round. I was eating when I wanted to and needed to, rather when was convenient for the crew.' She agreed with a comment that Billy Bland had made to me: that holding your own 'agenda' is really important. It also seemed to be a good example of someone contradicting my earlier point about contenders not having breaks 'on the hill' on more recent rounds.

We next moved on to talking about her ideas on going it alone. I started by asking if she took anyone's advice. 'I didn't really talk to Martin Stone at the time, who had already gone solo,' she replied. 'I remember talking to Fred Rogerson, as I was concerned how I would get it validated. I said I would leave cards at the road crossings so that at least if I didn't turn up someone would know which section I was lost on.' Fred just laughed at her and said 'why would you cheat?'. Having established that, she said there was then only one person who she told when she was going, Andy Sheath, 'so that if I didn't ring at the end they could send out the rescue.' It was planned and delivered as a solo/unsupported attempt. She had done a lot of practice navigation on her own, and was now confident. 'On the day, really early on, going up Skiddaw because it was dark I took a bearing on a sheep,' she laughed. 'Fortunately it didn't move before I got to it. That was a bit of a wake-up call.'

Helene's aim was to get round in under 24 hours, as no women had done that solo/unsupported. Her plan was based on the schedule she had used before (in 1987). Having said that, she tried to see how much she could take off each section. 'I genuinely remember feeling OK, thinking this is rather nice,' she said. 'I was really nervous setting off in the dark. I thought if I ran as fast as I think I can I will finish before it gets dark again, and not have to navigate in the dark when tired. The worst patch was going up Red Pike, it is such a long pull. As I got to the top it was the Ennerdale race and it was a hot, hot day, which doesn't cause me too many problems.' Here she had a conversation with one of the race marshals. 'He (and I don't know who it was to this day) spotted me and said 'are you doing what I think you are doing?' 'Er, possibly'. 'You are nearly home', he said. She stopped soon and had something to eat, rather than near Red Pike. 'I felt fine running home and running in. I honestly felt better then than on any my other rounds. I had no idea what the ladies time was,' she claimed.

I asked if, looking back, she would choose to do anything differently with regard to that solo round. 'It is funny, because everything now is geared to times,' was her response. 'That wasn't my plan. I just wanted to get round the Bob Graham. I never set my sights to do a fast one, ever. I don't think you can set off to do a fast time like that – maybe some people can. I am sometimes not very confident, and my intention has always been to get round as comfortably as I can. I always feel that you are just a gnat's crotchet away from disaster, especially the longer you do. The bigger, the longer, the harder it is, the closer you tread the line between having a good run and success, and a dire time and failing. It is only ever a twisted ankle, or a blister, or a chaffing, away from failure.'

Having said that, I wondered if there was any point in the solo round when she thought 'this isn't going to go'. She didn't recall that being an issue. 'It is incredibly easy to appear arrogant when you are young. I suppose it was arrogance, because I honestly thought I could do it. It crossed my mind that I might not get round in 24 hours. But I knew I could by then, so I just wanted to see if I could get round on my own. It wasn't for anyone else, or for a time, it was just for me. I think people make too much of these things sometimes.' She felt it is easy to look back and think it was simple at the time. She didn't worry about nutrition, just ate what was on the supermarket shelves. She didn't worry about hydration, just drank water out of streams. There was obviously a need to navigate, as there was no GPS then.

I was interested in the kit that she would have carried. She decided to carry a heavy cagoule and waterproof, and a bivi bag, plus a first aid kit. 'I thought if I do prang myself, there was no mobile phone then, I am going to be out at least 12–14 hours before someone found me. So I had full kit and a Gore-Tex bivi bag. I could stuff it with heather for insulation if I needed to, lying on the hillside with a broken leg or whatever.' The heather idea reminded me of the foot treatment that someone had suggested to Steve Birkinshaw on his Wainwright's week. This was sheep's wool between the toes to 'protect' soft spots. He rejected the idea, apparently.

With her seeming desire to increase the level of challenge I asked Helene if she ever thought of doing a winter round. She had, and chuckled at the thought of it, as she told me the story of that effort.

I set off two years ago [Jan 2013] to do a solo/unsupported winter BGR. I had done all the legs in summer, and been round all the legs I was likely to have to do in darkness actually in darkness. I stayed at Steve Birkinshaw's and Yiannis Tridimas came to see me off, and was going to check me through road crossings. I had a GPS to verify it and in case I got lost. I also had an ice axe and crampons, and the kit weighed about 10 kg, which I got down to about 6 kg. I set off up Skiddaw on a beautiful warm night. Because it was so warm the mist was so thick I kept wandering off the path going up Skiddaw, which wasn't a great start. I was well within time at the top, but went slightly wrong coming off, and I remember thinking this is such a great night for a night run, but wouldn't it be good if I *wasn't* doing the Bob Graham. I carried on up Blencathra, and a shooting star went past which was glorious, and then I went back into the clag. All the time on that first leg I was well up on the schedule but kept thinking I am dreading the next section along the Dodds because that will be dark and snowy. Then the next section in the daylight will be icy but that is OK. Then it will be dark again and that will be grim. I am thinking I am not looking forward to this. All I can think is how miserable the rest of this run is going to be. If I was only out for a little run I would be really enjoying this. I thought, I could go home – so I did. I had a really nice run out. I actually bumped into someone else, who should probably remain nameless, and who was also doing a solo BGR that night. He was making all sorts of navigational errors, so I kept catching him up. We ran off Blencathra together, and I went home. So, it was an attempt, but it made me think actually it is really grim out there in the dark for hours on your own. I put a lot of effort in making sure my equipment was right. I invested in decent head torches and had decent spare batteries, and kept them warm. I was ready to go and I thought it was just miserable. I thought it was a long way to go being miserable. It would be nice to do it, it would be nice to do with friends, but that has already been done.

In 1989 Helene did the three big rounds, so I asked her to talk about her 19:11 BGR record that was part of the trio. It was the fastest time until Anne Stentiford did hers, which was 45 minutes quicker. 'I was knackered after the other two rounds,' said Helene. 'After the Scottish and Welsh rounds I felt it would be really nice to finish it off and do the BGR under 24 hours too. I was tired and sore. I really struggled from Red Screes onwards. I do remember flogging along the road and thinking 'thank goodness this is nearly over, I never want to run ever again'. It was a really nice idea to finish all three rounds, I wasn't going for a time. I was on a high as everything was going well. I was running it with Adrian Belton, who was also running well. We had a lot of friends out helping, who had helped both of us do our three that summer. It was like a party.'

I asked her if she was at her physical peak that year, or whether the Dragon's Back represented the peak. 'It is different for different things, isn't it?' she replied. 'I would get myself fit for World Cups and things taking say 40 minutes, but that is just completely different from a 100km road race, or a round even. I don't think you can compare really.' In my discussions with different people it has become clear that some wouldn't be able to do a decent fell race after a round, but Helene picked up after the first and did two more rounds. She claimed that she just didn't worry too much, just expecting everything to hurt. 'I think people may analyse things too much these days, but this may push on performances,' was how she looked at it. She has always put in the homework she feels is needed for an event. She worked on the basis that if she could get round the Charlie Ramsay Round she was probably fit enough for the others. Each one is progressively about an hour less than the last, according to perceived wisdom. 'I didn't set off to do the three that year from the start,' she said. 'The Charlie Ramsay is the hardest, by a long shot. Each hill is a good big hill. The technical difficulty both in navigation and terrain is significantly tougher. It is a hard round for pacers and runners alike. If you have got a pacer who can support you on the Ramsay they can probably do it themselves. The Bob Graham isn't quite like that. You can pop up and do a couple of tops and pop home again and be done, and be none the worse for wear. The Welsh round is pretty rough. You find yourself dropping to some little spot height which is defining the round and it is a bit frustrating.'

I do feel that Helene doesn't get enough recognition for the fell running records she has set. She told me an interesting story from when she set the Borrowdale record, for example. 'I really badly gashed my foot coming off Scafell. I had cut through my shoe and into my arch on a pointed rock. I was coming along to the finish, hobbling long and Scoffer said "come on Helene you can beat the record". I just tapped my watch and said "oh no". Scoffer turned round and said to Martin Stone "I think Helene needs a new watch". I had no idea what the record was, and wasn't going for it. I wish I had known. I think sometimes setting that sort of target for yourself and you don't achieve it you feel you had a bad run. I don't work well that way.'

Plate 1. Phil Davidson, Bob Graham and Martin Rylands at Dunmail Raise,
13 June 1932

Plate 2. Lizzie Graham (sister), Gordon Graham (nephew) and Bob Graham

Plate 3. Bob Graham, with friends Ruth and Alfred Taylor in 1959

Plate 4. Balmoral House, Lake Road, Keswick – Bob Graham's guesthouse in the late 1930s

Plate 5. Barrow House, which Bob Graham ran as a hotel in the 1940s and 1950s

Plate 6. Derwentwater Independent Hostel (formerly Barrow House) as it is now

Plate 7. Ken Heaton, Alan Heaton and Stan Bradshaw

Plate 8. Joss Naylor on his 60 @ 60 round, 1997

Plate 9. Billy Bland and his support on the run-in through Newlands Valley, 1982 (?, David Bland, Martin Stone, Stuart Bland, Billy, Pate Barron)

Plate 10. Billy Bland, flanked by Pete Barron and Stuart Bland, at the Moot Hall after his 13-53 record round, 1982

Plate 11. Billy Bland and support, (incl Fred Rogerson, Jon Broxap and Joss Naylor) after his record round, 1982

Plate 12. Billy Bland at the Langdale race, 1990

Plate 13. Helene Diamantides/Whitaker at Dunmail on her 1987 round

Plate 14. Helene Diamantides/Whitaker at the end of her solo round in 1988

Plate 15. Anne Stentiford/Johnson celebrates on the last peak of her 62 peak extended round, 1994

Plate 16. Nicky Spinks, with Joe Mann and Tim Whittaker on Scafell Pike, 2012

Plate 17. Nicky Spinks contemplates yet more rice pudding on her record BGR, 2012

Plate 18. Nicky Spinks on Steel Feel during her 18-06 record round in 2015

Plate 19. Mark Hartell finishes fast, with Steve Birkinshaw behind, at the end of his BGR, 1999

Plate 20. Mark Palmer, and Dave Nuttall on Watson Dodd, on his BGR, 2011

Plate 21. Mark McDermott at the Wasdale support point on his 76 peak 24 hour record round, 1988

Plate 22. – Mark McDermott's support at Grisedale Pike, the last summit on his 76 peaks record, 1988. (Tim Laney, Mark McDermott, Martin Stone, Andrew Addis, John Brockbank, and Steve Wood)

Plate 23. Colin Donnelly

Plate 24. Steve Birkinshaw at Wasdale on his BGR, 2005

Plate 25. Jonny Muir being told he has to eat, at the Wasdale support point on his BGR, 2012

Plate 26. Martin Stone shows where his safety card will be at Honister for the solo/unsupported round, 1987

Plate 27. Jim Mann at Honister, supporting Patrick Bonnett, 2012

Plate 28. Jim Mann pacing Patrick Bonnett's BGR, 2012

Plate 29. Fred Rogerson, Eva Graham and Phil Davidson

Plate 30. Duncan Archer and Adrian Belton at Dunmail, supporting Patrick
Bonnett's BGR, 2012

Plate 31. The Bob Graham memorial, near Ashness Bridge, Borrowdale

Plate 32. Bob Graham's gravestone, Stonethwaite churchyard

As with other interviewees, discussion turned to speculating on whether anyone might beat Nicky or Billy's BGR record times. Helene felt that, for the women's round, if you extrapolate from Billy's time the women's time should be under 17 hours. 'I think the most logical person who is capable of that is Angela Mudge,' she said. 'I would be really interested to see what Jasmin Paris could do. There are a lot of very good young women coming into fell running now, which is lovely because there has been a bit of a dip. I think it will take someone with a mountain background and it tends to be women who have that sheer strength and mountain ability. I would like to see the women's record under 17 hours. I thought Nicky Spinks would be able to do that – she was jolly close. I wonder if she felt she could have gone under 17 hours.'

She feels that, among the men, Ricky Lightfoot is capable of it. 'The problem is you would have to be of the calibre of Ricky and Jasmine as far as sheer speed goes, but then have the ability to sustain the speed over a large distance. That ability isn't always there,' she thought. 'You have got a rare fish who can do that, I think.' She then said she was amused when Wendy Dodds got back to her after her Welsh round last year to say she had used her timings. 'She said "you started off very slow, didn't you". Perhaps I do, but I have never thought so. I just don't slow down as much as some others. That is what I used to find. Any schedule I was on I used to struggle to keep up in the early stages, but after 12 hours or so I was knocking times off. I would think I will see if I can knock six minutes off this one rather than five. I suspect it is probably my ability not to slow down rather than my sheer speed.'

We talked briefly about Kilian Jornet. 'He is amazing, but he is going to have a very short life, some of the things he does! But it will be a happy life. He is an astounding athlete. But who would pace him [*if he tried a BGR*]? I think he would have to vet people's ability.' She remembered meeting Mark McDermott on the Langdale Pikes with a Mars bar and something else, and being unable to keep up with him as he descended, even though he had been running for about 14 hours. She was pretty fit at the time, and had just come up from Langdale. 'Seeing the speed that people need to go at I think Kilian's problem would be who could keep up with him. I have seen the footage of his outstanding stuff and it is often on rough rocky stuff – he is clearly a very able athlete, but he likes the big mountains.'

Towards the end of the chat we discussed whether Helene had ever thought of doing an extended round to take that record. Apparently people have often suggested it, but it didn't really fire her imagination. 'To do something like that you have *really* got to want to,' was her view. She was also pretty clear on why many more do the BGR than the other rounds. 'Access is the biggie,' she said. 'It is easy to get people in, and out, and is close to population centres. The Welsh round is harder in terms of terrain underfoot. You are not going to get someone getting round who is not a fell runner. Just simply because of the ankle twisting ground. Same goes for the Scottish round, which is a mountaineers round. Unless you have a head for heights and are happy scrambling along airy ridges with tired legs, and you can sort yourself out in big mountains, and are prepared to take at least two hours longer than a Bob Graham, then you are not going to get round. There is also the weather. The further north you go the bigger the hills the more iffy the weather and the smaller the window of opportunity.'

My final thought was about the Cuillin Ridge, as I don't remember seeing any female running attempts. 'I thought of that, the Cuillin and the Red Cuillin as a round. I was interested in that at one point. I went along the Cuillin Ridge with Rex Stickland and Adrian Belton and it took us 14 hours to do just that. It is hats off to anyone who can run it quickly.'

The next female athlete to beat the best time was **Anne Stentiford**. Four weeks after setting the record for the Paddy Buckley Round, Stentiford decided to test her fitness by tackling the ladies' BGR record. She set out in dodgy weather in a clockwise direction early on the morning of Saturday 21

September 1991. As she was going round, Stentiford wondered whether she had fully recovered from the Paddy Buckley. She also found eating difficult, a situation not helped by the food supply being with a supporter who got lost. She also lost some five to six minutes on Sergeant Man as the weather deteriorated. Martin Stone covered the new record she achieved in his column in *The Fellrunner*:

After five hours of darkness she was still inside her 19-hour schedule. Fred Rogerson was at Dunmail Raise and his encouragement spurred her on when after seven hours of cold and mist she was considering retiring. The weather deteriorated and by the Scafells was gusting to gale force. She arrived at Wasdale with a few minutes in hand.

The Pillar and Gable section became a fight for survival as the wind hit storm force, lifting the team off their feet and throwing them to the ground. At times it pinned them down and it was necessary to scramble behind boulders, choosing routes sheltered from its blast.

Climbing Gable, the sky went black and a terrific storm of horizontal hail raged for 15 minutes. Quite unbelievably, Anne still kept to her 19-hour schedule and was given an emotional welcome at Honister. Fred was there to greet her and said that in all his years of association with the BG club he had never known anyone cope with worse conditions, let alone be setting records. Darkness came after the final descent off Robinson and Anne completed the last few miles of road to Keswick in torrential rain.

Her time of 18 hours 49 minutes reduced Helene Diamantes' two-year-old record by 21 minutes. It was one of the most sensational rounds ever and a performance that took great courage and determination.

The following day it all caught up with Anne, as she had to go to hospital and was diagnosed with a stress fracture of the foot, which, looking back, was believed to have happened somehow on Bowfell. With a pot on, this put an end to the idea of doing a Ramsay Round as well. I caught up with Anne (Johnson now) just as she was about to move house.

The very next day after speaking to Helene Whitaker I was to interview her friend and rival Anne Johnson (nee Stentiford), at her home near Halifax. Leaving from my son's house in Leeds I headed for their farmhouse, which turned out to be up a fairly steep minor road off the Calder Valley. I was welcomed by Anne and her husband, to be told that they were moving house very soon, and packing had commenced. Over coffee we talked of her background and early running and climbing experiences. It was fascinating to talk to this unassuming athlete who achieved breakthrough endurance performances, and is now turning to triathlon after keyhole surgery on both knees, probably due to 35 years of running.

We started by talking about Anne's running background. She has been a runner since she was about 14. 'I did track running, cross country and road running,' she said. 'I did my first marathon at 16 (in 3 hrs 28 mins), similar to Helene Diamantides.' At 17 years old she was already road running, with the Macclesfield club, meeting a few people who did the Karrimor Mountain Marathons, including Colin Ardron and Pete Nolan. 'They took me to a couple of very local fell races. Shuttlingsloe fell race was probably my first.' Anne lived in London for a while, but, when she came back to Macclesfield, she got in with a group who were also doing long things. Her first husband, Geoff Pettengell, had done the BGR and said he thought she would be good at it.

She was fairly new to fell running in 1989, and was in Macclesfield Harriers then. 'I thought I would quite like to do the BGR. I did most of the sections with Geoff, John Amies, Phil Cheek and Colin Ardron.' Her first attempt on an actual round was a failure. 'I think I got as far as Wasdale,' she recalled. 'It had rained for about 17 hours, absolutely torrential, so I had to call it a day.' She went off then to the Pyrenees for three weeks, and did most of the High Level Route with Geoff Pettengell and John Amies. She got very fit doing that, as it was like altitude training. 'A week after we got back I thought I would have another go, with a very small group of pacers, about three or four. They worked harder than me, and I got round in 20 hrs 35 mins as I remember.' This was in 1989, at the age of 24. She didn't do Broad Stand on that first round. 'No, on the very first one it was Lord's Rake. The people on that round didn't want to do the Stand.'

Although quite young and green, she did a fair amount of recceing. 'I went up there quite a lot. Those I was running with often went up at weekends. There was always someone in the club wanting to do a section of the round.' I was interested in knowing who was 'mentoring' her, and whether the two Marks [*McDermott and Hartell*] were a significant early influence. 'At that point I didn't know them,' she replied. 'The main influences at the start were John Amies, Phil Cheek (who was quite an inspiration), and my husband Geoff. It was only later on that I met Mark Hartell, which was after my rounds, but I met Mark McDermott fairly early on.'

That time of 20:35 was a great start, but did she feel it was good, bad or indifferent? 'I didn't really have much concept of BGR times. I was just running on a 24 hour schedule,' was her response. 'But Phil Cheek, who had done loads of pacing for others, was getting really excited as we were knocking off chunks of time. We were really flying and he was thinking "what is the record"? I was really pleased and was fine at the end.'

In 1991 Stentiford went back to finish the High Level Route, spending another two weeks in the Pyrenees. Leaving there, she did the Swiss KIMM with Helene Diamantides. Anne was talking to Helene about possibly doing the Paddy Buckley Round, as she had done a good amount of it already. 'She said "you will be fine, I will pace you and you could have a go at the record" [*held by Helene at the time*]. I said "don't be silly",' she recalls. A week or so afterwards she decided to have a go. She had been round all of it over the summer, and had a 24 hour schedule. However, Martin Stone knew she was running well, and he had secretly set a record schedule. 'So we set off on the 24 hour schedule, and two-thirds of the way along the first leg he said "we are on record schedule", and we switched to the record schedule. He kept his eye on both, but we stayed on record.' Martin Stone did leg one, but the problem on that Paddy Buckley Round was that because of the planned 24 hour schedule the pacers weren't there as they were so far ahead. 'Martin ended up doing quite a lot with me, and then often people would end up doing a section later, and it was a bit chaotic,' she chuckled.

I characterised the situation as Martin Stone being more confident than her in her ability. 'Yeah. I just didn't feel confident,' she agreed. 'I hadn't done huge amounts of ascents and massive mileage each week. I did go out for the weekend and do a day in the Lakes or something and then another long steady day, and maybe one or two runs in the week, but not the mileages others did. I never thought I could run quickly for a long time. I just ran how I felt.' On the Paddy Buckley she felt really comfortable and enjoyed it. At the end of it Martin Stone said why didn't she do the BGR, and go for the record even. 'That was a completely different kettle of fish. So I set off a month later with the record in mind and that was much more stressful. The schedule was so much harder, starting off with the record in mind. I remember starting up Skiddaw and thinking this is hard, I can't possibly maintain this.'

Her start for the BGR was at 1.40am, banking on a quick round to make it in as little darkness as possible. The weather was awful and then got worse. It came in over leg two, then deteriorated, torrential rain and gale force wind. 'Later on going up Kirk Fell we were crawling on all fours,' Anne recalled. 'Fred Rogerson was waiting down in Honister, he had never been in weather like that before. He was sitting in his car being rocked around by the wind and assumed we had abandoned.

He couldn't believe it when we came down and were ahead of schedule. As the weather got worse I seemed to get stronger, physically and mentally – I was very together.' She claimed the weather doesn't bother her when she is doing something, she just has to focus.

The pacers were just Martin Stone on leg 1, Paul Driver on leg 2 with Andy Thornton, Phil Cheek on 3 with Andy again. On leg 4 it was Martin again, with Mike Lawrence and Paul Driver. The last leg was Martin, Phil and Mike. The pacers were navigating and carrying, and motivating. 'I knew them all really well and had run all the sections with them,' said Anne. 'Andy Thornton didn't know the route very well and had just come back to England from living in New Zealand for five years. He was very keen to get back on the hills, and was a great motivator. There was a nominated navigator for each leg: Martin on 1, Paul on 2, Phil on 3, Paul on 4, and Martin on 5. I hardly had any rest, maybe a couple of minutes at each section.' On the round she ate a lot of rice pudding and tinned fruit. 'I also seemed to eat a lot of satsumas for some reason. I found I could eat a lot early on, and then from Wasdale I couldn't get much down.'

Despite the deteriorating weather they didn't have any real navigation issues in the clag. 'No, I think it was spot on,' Anne remembered. 'We did Broad Stand with the aid of a rope set up by Stuart Gascoyne from Macclesfield Harriers. It was OK, as I was so focussed. At that time I had been doing a fair amount of climbing, so was fine. I wondered whether if the weather was better I could have done it any quicker. It must have slowed us down, but I might have been able to go quicker, but not a lot.' She has never gone back to try though.

To Anne the extended round of 62 peaks was a natural next step. 'Yes, but in between I met Mark Hartell, when he joined Macc. He was really enthusiastic and he was keen to do the men's 24 hour one. He suggested I should have a go at the ladies' record.' She went on a lot of recces with him, and planned which peaks to add. She was working in the south as a computer programmer at the time, and remembers spending time in the evenings poring over maps and pencilling in which peaks to add, and checking they were valid. Then she spent some time recceing those extra peaks to see how long they would take her. On the day itself she recalls, 'I had built in four, but I bottled out on doing Fleetwith Pike because I was feeling horrendous, with stomach problems. I thought if I did it I might be outside 24 hours. Then I did start to recover and was going well again, and picked up Grasmoor and knew I could do that in 17 minutes. It is a nice run out and quite grassy. I regretted at the end that I didn't do Fleetwith Pike because probably I could have got it. I changed shoes at Newlands for the run in, both on the extended and record rounds.'

Surely at some point Stentiford had wanted to do a solo or a winter BG round, I mused? 'I wouldn't be able to now,' she sighed. 'My knees are bad. I don't think I am going to get back to the point where I can do very long distance again. The consultant thinks they are pretty worn out. One is worse than the other. I know what I can do now.' She is getting into triathlon. Not being able to swim a couple of years ago, that was her first target. She has done some sprint triathlons, and would like to work up to the Olympic distance.

Anne didn't really think that these endurance efforts affected her other commitments. 'I wasn't really into doing the champs races, although I have since,' she noted. 'I just did local races, coming 5th lady or whatever. I just enjoyed races. Often at weekends I would be in the Lakes or Wales doing sections of rounds. I wasn't really a serious fell racer at the time.'

Having said that, I was interested to know what she felt was her crowning achievement. 'I think when I got the ladies BG record it felt well-earned, as the weather was so awful,' she commented. 'My one regret was not being able to do the Ramsay Round. I was thinking of doing the Ramsay a month after. But at the end of the BG I could hardly walk. I had done something to my foot. I went to the hospital on the way back and they said it was really severe tendon problems. They said it would have been better if I had broken my foot, and they put a pot on it for a month. So I couldn't do the Ramsay after that, as the muscles would have wasted a bit. I was up for doing the big three with a month in between. Maybe I needed another week after the Paddy. It was quite late, September already.'

We then discussed anyone being capable of taking on Billy or Nicky's BGR times. 'I had the record for about 20 years, which I am amazed at as there were some extremely good fell runners.' After thinking briefly, she reflected, 'I always thought Menna Angarharad or Angela Mudge would go round, but they didn't. Now, Jasmin Paris is phenomenal – I am convinced that if she set her mind to it she could knock quite a chunk off it. Not sure about the men. Mark Hartell had a couple of attempts, but didn't quite do it. It would be fantastic if Ricky Lightfoot did it.'

Anne then commented that she always had the Ramsay Round on her radar. A few years ago she got very fit to do it, maybe even fitter than when she did the BGR, so she had every intention of breaking the Ramsay record. 'It was an absolute disaster, we didn't even get to the start. We set off at 3am and on the way there was a car that had gone off the road and was turned over in the ditch, and the driver was trapped and died while we were there. We were there for hours, we rang for the ambulance, the fire brigade came and we couldn't leave for three hours. By then the time and mood was gone.'

We talked briefly about her Macclesfield clubmates (Mark Hartell and Mark McDermott) and the comments made about them by some 'traditional fell runners' when they were doing extended rounds, and seen as outsiders. 'I think there was a little bit of "it should be kept in the Lake District". They both put in a lot of effort,' commented Anne. 'Not everyone can live in the hills. It was most unfair really, this stuff wasn't thrown at Steve Birkinshaw, who lives in the Lakes now.'

Finally we covered Anne's very varied career. 'My first job was as a forensic scientist, specialising in fire investigation, in London for the Met Police. But that didn't fit in with fell running. I used to hitch every weekend up the M1 to go

climbing or fell running with Clive Davies, a superb climber.'
She is not working fulltime now, though. 'Before children I was
doing computer programming for ten years. I then retrained in
reflexology and did that part-time. Now I help a friend out with
dog walking – which fits in with my lifestyle.'

Anne kindly gave me a copy of her schedule for the day of
her record-breaking round, which shows estimated and actual
times for each leg/peak in detail. Studying this shows that she
set herself strict support point times. They were two, three,
three and one respectively (for a clockwise round), and she kept
right on time. As far as the overall schedule is concerned, she
obviously knew herself and her potential pretty well by then.
Against her schedule she lost four minutes on leg one and five
on leg three. However, she gained nine minutes on leg two,
three on leg four and just one minute on the last leg, meaning
she was four minutes ahead overall.

Chapter 8

Nicky Spinks

The next person to move the ladies' record on was **Nicky Spinks**. In 2005 she had done a Bob Graham Round in 23 hrs 30 mins. In 2012 she came back to make another attempt. The following account of her record-breaking round is edited down from her own blog posting.

The day before the round was a busy day for me as we were haymaking on the farm. The weather looked promising but I knew more rain was forecast for Saturday. I have always advocated that the weather is one of the most important things to get right but what was influencing my decision this time was (1) It was my only weekend to go this year (2) good training for Dragon's Back Race which I was doing in September (3) the forecast was exactly the same as for the Wasdale race which actually turned out perfect for running. How would I have felt then if I hadn't even started? (4) I thought I could break the current record of 18 hours and 49 minutes in semi-decent conditions.

When we arrived I got my tent up and cooked more food then sat around eating with my supporters. I got into my tent around 10.30pm and did a bit of reading before actually falling asleep (a first for me as I never usually sleep before a big challenge). I heard rain overnight but could see stars through the clouds when I got up at 3am. The wind didn't seem bad and I couldn't decide what to wear. The support on the first leg was Neil Talbot and Simon Cox. Simon was sleeping at the Skiddaw car park as he was worried about the pace (having completed his Paddy Buckley only two weeks ago) and would set off early up Skiddaw.

A lot of people had turned out to see me off and Yiannis even appeared at the Moot Hall reassuring me he would be on Blencathra. We set off at 4am at a steady pace. Neil said it was quite fast so I slowed down. The clag came in at 500m but it was light so at least we could turn the head torches off. I started eating, hoping to stave off the sickness I felt on my 24-hour round. By the top of Skiddaw the wind was very unpleasant, blowing us across and making talking unrealistic. We ran over the top and descended to the fence where we saw the stakes but not the path. We went on and soon hit the path lower down. The valley was soggy – also a reminder that the Lakes had had a lot of rain. I was trying to assess the conditions to see if I should make adjustments to my pace. We had made up time on the early splits, but lost a bit on Calva. I realised that the pace was fast and minutes were not easy to gain in the conditions so pushed on. I was constantly comparing myself to last year and couldn't decide whether that was good or bad. Mungrisdale Common felt energy sapping – I thought about Raise as it's similar and hoped I would feel better by then.

Meeting Yiannis on Blencathra was great, a quick loo stop and we were off. I really enjoyed the descent and even the clag lifted and I could see right across to Clough Head. 'At least it's not too hot', I thought. Neil had a couple of spectacular tumbles – quite worrying Yiannis but Neil, like a toddler, just rolled over and got back up!! *Schedule 3:27 Actual 3:09*

My support team were there at Threlkeld with tea and beans which I ate easily. Setting off with Digby Harris, he said Ian Winterburn would meet us on Clough Head. I was now thinking I was glad it wasn't too hot – this was where I started to overheat last year. I knew this leg would be fast as most of the splits were mine from 2011. Ian was his bouncy Tigger-like self so I thought it must be OK. I concentrated on more eating and left navigation to them. The clag had lifted and we could see across to Scafell. I kept looking round for more weather coming in but couldn't see any. Running down to Sticks Pass we could see someone laying out goodies. It was Neil and his tea was superb! Carrying on he said the pace was much quicker than Leg 1 but we were bang on most of the splits, so I just kept going. Dropping to Grisedale Tarn a very sharp shower came across before we had time to get our waterproofs on. Fairfield came and went quickly. I tried to eat something more as I had been eating well – beans and rice pudding were going down very well. I thought I could make up a bit more time on the schedule on the next leg. I hadn't gained any more time on Leg 2 but I didn't expect to. *Schedule 3:33 Actual 3:32*

I ate some pasta and changed to a long-sleeved top, as it was now obvious that it wasn't going to get hot. Setting off with Tim Whittaker and Joe Mann I enjoyed Steel Fell and made up a couple of minutes on schedule. Trotting to Calf Crag and then High Raise I was in good spirits. I could see clag on Bowfell but that is not unusual and didn't worry me. We got a couple of showers but they passed quickly. The tops came and went quickly although I noticed the ground was boggy, and knew that would be slowing us down. I added another top and my jacket across to Rossett Pike as I could tell the conditions were going to be worse on Bowfell. Yiannis waved from the top of Rossett Pike and then ran off to get the kettle on! The coffee he handed me at the col was definitely the best thing I consumed on the whole round. I shot up Bowfell making up more time until we hit the clag and rocks.

The rocks worried me as they were very slippery but we continued to Esk Pike where we met Willy Kitchen and Lewis Ashton doing the Cumbrian Traverse. It's lovely meeting people, exchanging a few words and knowing you will see them later to catch up properly. The wind had picked up and route finding became difficult and caused us to miss a grassy line or two across to Ill Crag. I only hoped to do the rest on schedule as up to now we had been gaining and were now 22 minutes up. I knew on Ill Crag and Broad Crag that I was going too slowly, as I had to hold onto the rocks while descending but tried to climb faster to compensate.

Yiannis asked us to pose on Scafell Pike for a photo. In Mickledore I saw some ropes to the right and thought what mad climbers in this weather and made for the crack. There weren't any ropes there though and then we heard shouts from above. It was Ian Fitz. Having never done Broad Stand before and having come down from the top he thought he was in the right place. 'Oh my God' I thought. 'There is no time to go round, I'm going to have to go up that!' At least with a harness and also a rope with knots in it I had a lot of safety – and I needed it. I couldn't find purchase with my shoes at all and a lot of the time poor Ian was just man-hauling me. I remember leaning back and thinking 'I hope he's got me'. He had.

Reaching the top I was shaky and took the harness off. I had a rest and drank some Lucozade while I waited for my nerves to calm as I knew there were still a lot of horrid slippery rocks above that I had to get over. I started off up glad that I had reccied this bit, when we had taken our time and been down and up to learn the way. Following the obvious worn bits I contoured back and forth across the rocks having to slither on my tummy sometimes as my shoes wouldn't grip anything. I heard a voice below and gave a sigh of relief. Tim had climbed up behind me and was soon catching me. We summited the plateau and ran off – in the wrong direction at first, before I gathered my wits and headed left to the stone cross then up Scafell. Glad that was all over, we headed down to Wasdale. Unbelievably we hadn't lost much time and were still 14 minutes up. *Schedule 4:55 Actual 4:56*

It was sunny in Wasdale and although I could see clag on the tops I was heartened by the fact we hadn't had much rain across Scafell and the wind was drying the rocks on the descent. I changed my socks (thanks for the foot massage

Olly) which felt nice and although it cost me a few minutes I knew getting the shrapnel out of my shoes was the better decision. Last year I had run round with a stone in my shoe for 20 hours and ended up with a very bruised sole. Setting off up Yewbarrow with Olly Stephenson, Dave Sykes and Tim Whittaker I knew I could make or lose time on this leg as the schedule was quite tight. I wanted to start pushing it a bit, but to do this I had to breathe faster and therefore couldn't eat. But upwards we went and I tried to eat a little. The split to Red Pike was silly – I tried to do 35 minutes. I got really stressed and was very angry with myself for not working a proper schedule out. I sulked and snapped at Olly and Dave who were by now badgering me to eat. We actually did 39 minutes which wasn't bad at all, but by now my stomach had started to say it wasn't going to work at this pace and I couldn't think what I could eat. I was getting bits down, gel blocks and a couple of biscuits but I knew that wasn't enough. We weren't making very good progress. I was distracted by my stomach. The rocks were slippery. It had started to rain again, sometimes very hard and the wind was constantly blowing us around. We were also missing some of the best lines and ending up in rocks. All the stuff that generally costs you minutes.

One forecast had showed the weather crapping out at 4pm and it was. I knew then it wasn't going to get any better. I had come too far though and was still on for breaking the record so there was no giving up now. Losing time constantly I had an absolute battle with myself. I had two options: to keep eating bits (but what, as I didn't want anything) and gels: or to get something solid down like a rice pudding then suffer the consequences for 30 minutes while my stomach tried to throw it all back up. I knew the second option would get better results and I wanted to feel strong for the last leg.

So taking the plunge I asked for a rice pudding after Pillar. It got it down OK. For the rest of the leg till after Great Gable

I felt awful. Dave Sykes sympathised with me, which helped. Poor Olly got more of my sharp tongue though. I promised myself 'never again'. We met Neil once again with tea but too milky for me and it was nearly 1-0 to my stomach. Onwards to meet Ian off Great Gable, but with no-one being confident in knowing the way to find the grass. We just headed for Ian's loud cheery voice. It must have been freezing waiting for us up there, so thanks. Climbing Green Gable I felt good and could think about food again. And then what did we get but an absolutely horrid hailstorm. The wind and hail came across at us sideways. Pulling my hood right over and using my hands to shield my face I just ran as hard as I could. It wasn't worth stopping to put bottoms on. I just wanted out. It stopped on the climb to Brandreth and we all got our breath back. I started to see what I could run up and just cruised right across Brandreth and Grey Knotts. Running down into Honister I thought "Right, I'm not stopping, I'm going to get back as much as I can". I asked for tomato soup and coffee and just walked right through. I so wanted to get under 18 hours but we had lost a lot of time. *Schedule 3:48 Actual 4:07*

I was joined by Keith Holmes and Helen Elmore. Tim Whittaker, Olly and Joe Mann all tagged along but kept a wide berth after I snapped once again at Olly, who was trying to persuade me to stop and drink my soup. I got it down gulp by gulp (apparently I missed my mouth quite a bit). With a few more gels I felt good and was going well. I knew I should be running bits of the hill but on the other hand didn't want to push my stomach. So with a truce we continued, with me running what I could until I was breathing hard then walking. The wind was constantly buffeting us about and every now and again it rained on us.

I was tired of this weather now and just wanted to descend to some calm. Nick Cable met us on Robinson and I followed him off as I had confidence in his lines. Reaching the grassy track I tried a few knee-ups to see how the legs were feeling

– surprisingly good. Running along the road even the chatty supporters started to concentrate, so I knew I was going OK. Keith and Helen ran alongside giving me gels, water and energy drink. It was an excellent feeling to know I was going to do it. The only trouble was – not on schedule. I asked for a Dark Peak vest which Keith burrowed in his rucksack for and then sprinted to catch me. Oh joy, the end is in sight. Lifting my arms and knees I sprinted (was I?) on the road through Keswick, over the roundabout and up to the Moot Hall at 10.12pm 18 hours and 12 minutes after leaving it that morning. *Schedule 2.13 Actual 2.17 hours*

I was very pleased to have finished in style and to have broken the record. My only disappointment is being over 18 hours, but in those conditions I couldn't expect more. It was a very hard day out in fantastic company. I did stay awake long enough to shower, eat half a pot noodle and join my supporters for a beer in the 'shower room' back at the camp-site before retiring to bed.

I wanted to talk to Nicky Spinks about this phenomenal feat, and managed to be in the right place one weekend to catch this busy farmer/athlete.

I was visiting my son and Nicky kindly agreed to meet to talk about her BGR record of 18:12. We met in a Thurlstone pub with some fine beers on tap, but I was on soft drinks, as I was about to drive back South. I was particularly grateful because the day beforehand Nicky had been out on the fells for 18 hours, winning the 10 Peaks Xtreme – outright. Considering she had slept in her van before travelling back from the event she was remarkably sprightly. We chatted about the 10Peaks and about mutual acquaintances, before getting to her background and her Bob Graham efforts. I came away with the impression of a steel-willed person with phenomenal endurance and drive. You only have to consider the fact that she has set the ladies records for all

*three classic rounds (BGR, Paddy Buckley and Charlie Ramsay),
and even more impressively is the only person (male OR female)
to complete all three rounds in times under 20 hours, to realise
what an athlete she is. Furthermore, she is a beef farmer and has
had serious medical problems to overcome. Without specifically
mentioning particular challenges, there was a glint in her eyes
when I asked her 'what next'. I have a pretty good idea from our
conversation as to what that might be.*

During a fascinating conversation Nicky explained the lead
up to her record and some of her other achievements.

Nicky's Ladies Lake District Record came before her fast
BGR. She had already done a slower standard round by then.
In 2005 she had done a twenty-three and a half hour BGR. By
then, she said, 'I had done all three rounds and also done the
Grand Raid Reunion [*a 100-mile race*]. I wanted to do more
rounds. A friend of mine, Simon Ripon, suggested the Ladies
Lake District Record. I didn't think I was that fast – but knew I
could just keep going. Then when I did it, someone else pointed
out to me that I was running as fast most of the time as an 18
hour BGR, but was going for 23 hours.' (By coincidence, the
very weekend I spoke to Nicky, Adam Perry had a go at the
current men's 24 hr total peaks record – and had timed out at
77 peaks.)

I suggested that these events attract a different type of athlete,
from different backgrounds, for example Heather Dawes. In
Nicky's case, she started with shorter events. 'I started with
Penistone Footpath Runners,' she commented. 'There is the
Marsden to Edale race in December, roughly 20 miles, and I
started off trying to do that. Then the Three Peaks race, and other
20-mile fell races.' She was farming at the time, and pointed out
that she tended not to do a great deal of training. 'Sometimes
when I look back I think I haven't done any training. Especially
when people say "what training did you do?". I do the long fell
races, and the ones in the Lake District are very hard.'

So, going into the BGR I asked what her expectation was, timewise. 'My schedule was seventeen and a half, and I was about 10 minutes up on that when the weather came in. We lost half an hour across Scafell (on leg 3). I tend to look at what other people do. Mark Palmer, he said I should be able to do sub-17.'

Nowadays contenders tend to have sophisticated schedules, with timed stages over the whole route. 'I tend to do a couple of splits, as I know the Bob Graham well,' commented Nicky. 'I have a lot of schedules at home, and a lot of spreadsheets. So I look at them and I look at what I did first time. I think, if I have to knock off 15 minutes that can seem ridiculous. So I will go out on a recce and time one split, rather than a whole leg. Then I think I can do it or can't.'

For the 18:12 round there was a change in preparation, going to the Lakes more often. 'I reccied leg one more than I had done in the past, and also leg five. I thought I am going to carry on if the record is on, but it is going to get dark on me, so I need to do leg five better than I did. You recce it on the basis that it is going to be dark, which is a lot different.' It was later in the year because of other [*serious health*] circumstances.

It was a 3am start, pre-dawn. Nicky classified the pacers as mostly carriers, more than anything. 'I was navigating myself mostly,' she noted. 'It's a joint thing. When we got on the top of the first peak [*Skiddaw*] it was claggy, so running off we had a discussion of where we thought we should go.' I wondered at the relationship with the pacers in these circumstances, and whether she had ever had to use her 'vote' on route choices. 'No, because it was Neil Talbot and he is a very good navigator. At Billy Bland's pace it must have been hard enough for pacers keeping up!' The forecast was the same as for the Wasdale race two weeks beforehand, reasonable low cloud but cool. Nicky thought she couldn't cancel because it was not actually foul weather, but it was going to be showery. 'It was claggy on leg one, then leg two it was a bit windy but not claggy, and we got one little shower. By Bowfell the weather came in – rain and a lot of clag. By leg four and five I had blocked it out, just concentrating on going.' She noted, 'when you see the pictures it looks absolutely foul, the supporters are all wrapped up.'

Nicky explained her feeding strategy, which tends to be one or two gels per leg and solid food like rice pudding where possible, plus some baked beans and pasta at the various stops. 'I need to be forced to eat sometimes, by supporters,' she explained. 'What went wrong across leg four was that one of the splits was too tight and I started running too hard. While I was doing that I wasn't eating, and my stomach rebelled and I felt really sick. Eventually I got a whole rice pudding down.' She tries to go for short stops, so two minutes maximum usually. 'As I am running in, I order what I want. Usually I am off before the pacers.'

As she was going across Mickledore she could see this rope hanging down on the right. She just thought that were some mad climbers out in the awful weather. She went to the gap and heard a shout, and it was Ian Fitzpatrick. 'He had climbed up from Wasdale and then down, but he had never done the rope before. I can imagine that climbing down there are some awful slabs higher up. He said it was horrendous and he dropped the rope where he thought it was. It is a good thing that I had opted for a harness as I am not that confident at climbing. He had dropped another rope with knots on, so I ended up man-hauling myself up. You can't get purchase with fell shoes on wet rock. I have seen Yiannis hop up there like it is just a step.'

Nicky felt that the low point in her BGR record round was sometime after Yewbarrow. It was the split between Yewbarrow and Red Pike that she remembers getting wrong. 'I don't like Red Pike any more,' she laughed. 'It was down to not eating. The weather was the weather. Even though I had lost half an hour, I was still on schedule, that is the splits were still going well even with the weather. There is a picture of me eating rice pudding and I am thinking "how many more spoons of this do I have to take on board". I can eat on the go sometimes. About half an hour after eating that, I picked up. I have gone more on to fruit salads in warm weather now.'

The question I imagine all record breakers ask at some point is "was that the optimum time for my fitness at the time?". When asked, Nicky thought that she knew she could beat it, and that her powers of recovery are good. 'The 10 Peaks Xtreme was almost a Bob Graham and I did 18:26 supporting myself,' she said. 'I did the Ramsay Round four weeks ago and the 10 Peaks Xtreme yesterday and my legs are fine. My feet are fairly swollen. Your legs just get used to it. I have been up to the Lakes supporting two Bob Grahams, and just ticked over in between. Maybe a lot of people miss out on the rest, and train every day. Today I had to walk carefully round the cows and be careful of the dogs as they race up and down.' She also feels that she is probably better about body management now. 'It all depends how your stomach is. I don't think I have a very good stomach. But on my first Ramsay and my Paddy my stomach was fine. I drink a lot of water and I think that is one of the reasons I go well when I am not eating. I know the Bob Graham well and I know where the streams are, and I'd always look at the map to see where the streams you cross are.' [*I recalled having suffered badly on my Cuillin Ridge traverse, when we ran short of water – there are very few streams reachable once on the ridge.*]

In a subsequent discussion Nicky admitted that she did learn an important lesson last year. 'Although I thought I was recovering well after the Ramsay my performance at the Ultra Tour Mont Blanc has now led me to believe that I was too tired after doing both the Ramsay and the Extreme 10 Peaks to do the UTMB justice', she said.

When we talked of someone beating her and Billy's times, Nicky thought that it requires a different sort of person. 'Kilian [*Jornet*] is very fast, but racing is different to rounds,' she said. 'I think because there is so much more in your hands in rounds. Lots of people are fast enough, but everything has got to go right.'

Her reasoning why the BGR is so much more popular than either the Ramsay or the Paddy is simply that the BGR is more 'doable'. For Scotland you have to travel for six hours to get there, and your support has to as well. I reminded her that she is the only one under 20 hours on all three big rounds. 'It is weird. Even when I did the schedule I didn't know that. I think Mark Hartell and Steve Birkinshaw both did unsupported Ramsays, so that is why their times are not comparable to their BGR equivalents.' I proposed that an unsupported or winter BGR might be a suitable next challenge. 'Not winter, but unsupported maybe,' Nicky concluded.

We ended by me asking what I thought might be a slightly delicate question: whether having cancer in 2006 was a motivator for her endurance feats in some way. 'I'm happy to talk about it,' she replied. 'If anyone is out there who has got cancer, it might not be the end of the world. I had done a BGR and had just done a Paddy, but failed to get round in time. Then I was told a month later, straight out of the blue. I did apply the same recovery approach after the operation as after a race. Eating well, drinking well, putting stuff in place, and just trying to improve every day. Thinking "I need to sit up for eating breakfast" – and then accepting a lie down afterwards. I like to see small improvements.'

Just after I had submitted the manuscript for this book to the publisher, Nicky Spinks set a new ladies record of 18 hours 6 minutes, on 5 April 2015. She was going for the cumulative best time for the three big rounds (Graham, Ramsay and Buckley), which would have required a time of 17 hours 21 minutes. Having been on schedule for 17 hours 30 minutes for a good part of her record round in 2012, she felt this was feasible. Knowing that she struggles physically and mentally with heat these days, she wanted cool weather. On her blog[1] she noted that, 'choosing Easter would also give a longer weather window with availability of supporters so that's the date I went for. The weeks before Easter were stressful with snow then weather fronts disrupting my plans and determination. But I stuck by

---

1   http://www.runbg.co.uk/Bob%20Graham%20Record%202015.htm

my forecasts and after changing the day from Friday to Sunday I maximised on the high pressure that came in. My start time of 4 am gave me 2 hours of dark at the start and then (if on schedule) an hour at the end.'

She had a fall coming off Blencathra via the 'parachute drop' and badly cut her hand. Battered, bandaged, but not bowed, she carried on and was on target to Dunmail, but time started slipping away after that. She had a bad patch mentally and also couldn't keep food down, but with massive determination managed to knock six minutes off her own record. Her report finished: 'Running up and touching it [the Moot Hall] I looked at my watch. 18.06 it said! I was so happy to have finished and achieved a new record. Just showed how tough the old one was really. I sat and ate chips dipped in gravy while enjoying the celebrations for a while . . . then went to sleep in my van!' She then speculated that, 'maybe I should go for a bad weather attempt next time; if there is one!'

Chapter 9

Some fast 'near records'

Although Billy Bland's BG record is considered unbeatable by mere mortals, that hasn't stopped others trying for it – and achieving impressive times, as well, no doubt, as wonderful days out on the fells in the process.

After coming third in the Borrowdale race in 1982 **Stuart Bland** was heard to say 'I know I can do 16 hours . . .'. Tony Cresswell takes up the story of Stuart's round, which took place on 14 August 1982:

> I got up to see Stuart off from Keswick. Kenny Stuart went along as he had done for Billy, but in August it was still dark. Pete Barron and Jon Charlton went on from Threlkeld, again as for Billy with Dave Stones. I couldn't make Dunmail again (jobs have uses!) and this time I dashed down Borrowdale and up Grains to Esk Hause, electing to wait on Esk Pike. This was a grand day and views were extensive and the approaching runners were spotted on Bowfell. Billy and David Bland with John Gibbison were with Stuart but the regularity of Stuart's drinks hinted towards a slowing. The pace was very swift and Billy confirmed that at the time Stuart was well up with his own times. Stuart was reluctant to eat and sensed a fading, and after a drier and easier Broad Stand the drop off Scafell was halted. Part way down Stuart lay down and Billy saw his chance to try the 'Naylor shake' – a delightful little remedy performed by the said bod on Billy when he wavered on Yewbarrow. It was as much as

I could do to obey instructions, but with Billy holding his arms and me his legs we picked him up and shook the living daylights out of him. Gripping a Mars bar between his teeth for anaesthetic, poor Stu was shaken like a rag doll between two guard dogs.

It worked though; his eyes were all over his head but on we all trooped to Wasdale! It was during this time that Stuart lost that bit of time that made the difference between his and Billy's rounds. Off went the pair of them up Yewbarrow with Billy giving, shall we say, words of encouragement. I had feared it might all end in a punch-up on Pillar but Joss turned up and set off in pursuit as umpire. In true Bland style, Stuart got better as time went on and blazed into Keswick to record 14:56. While slightly overshadowed by Billy's effort, it ought to be remembered that this was a 'first time' effort and in as much was a voyage into the unknown.

Cresswell noted the two sets of splits and rest times for Stuart and Billy Bland. Taking out the rest times – 21 mins for Billy, 17 mins for Stuart – the differences between their running times were:

Keswick – Threlkeld	Billy 15 mins faster
Threlkeld – Dunmail	Stuart 3 mins faster
Dunmail – Wasdale	Billy 11 mins faster
Wasdale – Honister	Billy 23 mins faster
Honister – Keswick	Billy 20 mins faster

Seventeen years passed before **Mark Hartell** made a determined attempt on the BGR record – on 25 July 1999. On his club's website he gave this short report:

Last Sunday I got round the Bob Graham as quick as I could. I did set off with a schedule based around Billy's 1982 time of 13 hrs 53 mins, although I don't think I really believed I could better this. So it proved, I was on my schedule up to

Dunmail but lost a little time over the Langdales and more on the Wasdale to Honister section.

Final time was 14 hrs 54 mins which is two minutes inside the second fastest time (as was) set by Stuart Bland – 14 hrs 56 mins. Anyone interested can have minutes of fun looking at the attachment which shows my splits compared to those of Billy and Stuart [*See table on the website*[1]].

One nice thing about the day which saw perfect weather and excellent support from a cast of many (15:20) was that both Billy and Gavin Bland turned out to see me suffer.

Once again we go to Martin Stone, who gave a little more detail in his column in the October 1999 issue of *The Fellrunner*:

It was the perfect day he deserved and a team of 14 pacers and supporters were present to see Mark's romp over the fells. He set off at 6am attempting a clockwise round. Because the pace required would be too fast for most pacers carrying a rucksack, a careful plan was devised allowing pacers to take turns to 'col hop' while others were 'on duty'. Mark had had no opportunity to recce best lines and the odd minute was lost here and there. Early on he suffered with an overheating foot which troubled him for the first half of the round. Nevertheless, his renowned iron determination showed through and he reached Dunmail in about five hours!

Despite his bold approach to the run, he secretly doubted his ability to break the record but was determined to just do the best he could on the day. He passed through the valley crossings like a whirlwind and stopped for only three minutes the whole day. By Honister it was clear that he wouldn't break the record and it required true grit and determination to run the road hills back to Keswick so that he could beat Stuart Bland's time.

1   http://www.macclesfield-harriers.co.uk/fell/bg/fastestBG.html

Mark Hartell was the first interview I had done via Skype. He is in the States and I had just missed his recent flying visit to the UK. Although I prefer face-to-face for interviews it all worked well, and allowed me to get a good idea of Mark and his philosophy towards his sport. There were a couple of follow-ups about times and pacer details, but it was great to get the thoughts of one of the fastest BGR completers, who also gave me a much better understanding of the challenge that is ultra-racing.

Not knowing Mark's background I asked him to run through that for me first.

In 2007 he met Lynn, who is from the San Francisco Bay area and they got married in 2009. Initially she came to live in the UK, which coincided with two very cold winters. Discussions took place, and in 2011 they moved to Santa Barbara. She is a physical therapist and he is a project manager. 'I was brought up in Warwickshire, but have lived variously in Warrington, Frodsham, Leek and Macclesfield,' Mark explained. 'I still have a house in the UK, so I don't feel I have left the UK.' He was 50 that week, and was over in the UK and running the Borrowdale fell race two days after his birthday. 'It went OK, I finished it,' was his description. 'It was a pretty wet day. The winning time was over three hours, I think for the first time since 1975. It was a fitting return to fell running for me in some ways, as for a while earlier I had the nickname of 'Rain Boy'. Steve Birkinshaw was about five minutes ahead of me at the end. He came past me coming off Great Gable.'

Mark recalled that he didn't do any athletics at school, but got into climbing as a student. He got frustrated with that when he started work. 'Climbers aren't that good at finding stuff to be doing when the weather is not good. So I got into orienteering; even when it was foul you got a good workout.' In his orienteering club (Deeside) there were some fell runners. He started doing stuff with them, and supported five of them who were doing a Bob Graham Round. Only one got round. 'I thought I have trained with these people, I could do that,' he said. 'So I resolved to do it, which I did the following year – in 19 hrs 50 mins. I smoked at the time (about 20 rollups a day), and had three on the way round. I don't say that to upset people but to show how ridiculously amateur and naive my approach was in the early days.'

A couple of years later he became aware of the reputation that Macclesfield Harriers had for long- distance running. Mark was sitting on a rock on day two of the Saunders KLETS class (having a cigarette) when Alison Wright came past, and he said hello. 'She must have thought I was a joker but we got talking,' he recalls. 'That is how I got to know Mark McDermott, who was married to Alison at the time. Through knowing Mark and running with him every Monday, and almost keeping up with him, I moved the Lake District record in my mind from something mythological only achieved by proper runners to something that if I trained I could have a go at myself. That was five or six years earlier because it took me three attempts.'

'Through Mark I also got to know the likes of Martin Stone, Adrian Belton, Anne Johnson (née Stentiford) and Andrew Addis. Between them they held just about all the records for the big rounds then. I started doing stuff and realised they were focussed but not superheroes. So that is what made me decide that it wasn't completely laughable to go for the Lake District 24 hour record.'

Having achieved the ultimate 24 hour peaks record, surely a fast BGR would be next? 'No, that was never really a long-term objective. Firstly, I had been inspired at the Bob Graham Club dinner and was motivated by the honorary presidency that comes with the 24 hour record. Second, I felt that the fast BG was more for the true fell runners. I have run all the classic long fell races but I was never going to win them. In fact one of the things I did between the first and the third attempt at the 24 hour record was to learn to be a better descender. By that I mean being able to descend at the pace you need for a 24 hour record without trashing myself. My strengths were endurance, organisation and willpower. They got me a 24 hour record but I was never as fast a descender or as natural a fell runner as Billy Bland.'

'So, a fast BG was not in my plans. What happened is that I got severe food poisoning 24 hours before the Western States 100-mile race in California. That was my main event for the year so I had all this fitness and was not even able to start. I pulled the attempt together with about 10 days notice. I created a schedule but whereas for the 24 hour record I had run every split three, four or five times I did no specific training on the route in the build-up to the fast BG because there was no build-up. Even on the day I was desperately trying to remember which peaks I had to do as the standard BG because I knew the lines for all the extras on the 77 peaks and my worry was I would go haring off to peaks that are not even part of the BG.'

I put it to him that he must have set out thinking he could do a good time, whether or not he thought he could do the fastest time. 'Yes, I was always going to push for the best time I could but for the reasons I have described above there was no real confidence of any specific time. Once I fell off the pace completely over leg four (Wasdale to Honister) I lost a bit of focus but then going up Dale Head it started coming back and the brain started calculating what I could salvage – that is why I was pushing so hard at the end just to shave a minute or two off the second best time of Stuart Bland.'

Talking about a typical year, Mark commented, 'my year tended to be training hard from early December, through the winter building up the mileage. Then I would do the longer early season events like the Haworth Hobble, Calderdale Hike, High Peak Marathon. Training and intensity peaked in May with the Fellsman and the Scottish Island Peaks Race, and then in June I would throw myself into a round. By July and August it was often like the end of my season, as I was kind of burnt out.'

It occurred to me to ask what Mark thought was his best fell race performances. 'My best performances have not been in fell races but I was well pleased with a close third in Duddon one year and I had a couple of strong finishes in the old Buttermere 20-miler. I also surprised myself by winning the Cannock Trig points race one year – not really fells mind.'

He felt that Martin Stone had always been the barometer. A couple of times he had said that having done 10 hrs 20 mins on the Fellsman bodes well for a Lake District 24 hour record that summer. 'Let's face it, no-one understands better than Martin the type of form you need for record-breaking rounds. Although I never saw myself as a main contender in the pure fell races, I did feel some pressure there because there was this view that you had to be a 'proper' fell runner to be believable in terms of the bigger rounds.'

Mark felt the need to explain further. 'I was aware that one or two people had suggested that Mark McDermott could not have broken the record of 'Iron Joss'. It is a completely ridiculous thing to say and he was accompanied every step of the way as I was but the trouble is that people say these things in a roundabout way and it lingers. I didn't want that so I felt some pressure to establish credibility. There are some people that can only understand what they know so they figure you have to have won the race in their backyard to count. Never mind winning the longest ever Karrimor Mountain Marathon or the determination to get up Everest without oxygen,[1] they think that if you don't fulfil their preconceptions then something must be wrong. So, while I often ran races deliberately tired for training benefit I did occasionally try to do OK at the Lakeland classics.'

Mark then moved to 100-milers. 'I had done my BG. I had done my Paddy. John Amies from Macclesfield had come back from the States and told me about the Hardrock in Colorado. Back in the day if you were from another country you only had to say you knew what you were doing and you were in. Now

---

1   Mark McDermott is one of only four Britons who have climbed to the summit of Everest without supplemental oxygen – in 2001. The others are Stephen Venables (in 1988), Alison Hargreaves (1995) and Victor Saunders (2006) – data from http://www.8000ers.com

you have to have two or three other Hundreds in a decent time. Getting some mates together and going over for a couple of weeks to race there was what we did for several years.'

'Hardrock was fantastic – I ran it in 1996 and 1997 and then in 1999 we were a group doing the Western States which is when the food poisoning thing happened.' This was at the end of June. Hartell had got back from the States, moped around, and then wondered what to do with the fitness he had. He then gave his support crew less than two weeks notice of an attempt date. It was to be a 6am clockwise start, in the expectation of completing in daylight. The weather was good, certainly better than his 24 hour round. He took forward a hard lesson he had learnt on his second attempt at the 24 hour record. 'I was on the very first section and I hadn't been entirely clear about who was responsible for navigation,' was how he put it. 'Basically there was a mix-up. I thought I knew where I was and just ran off into the mist. That 24 hour round foundered when I couldn't find Coombe Height. After that I was very careful to be specific with pacers as to what their duties were. I then always said I am entirely responsible for the line. I would have one person who was responsible for times, one person who was responsible for food and drink. And they would all be given details of their responsibilities.'

Mark said that his feed strategy on all his UK attempts was based on the wisdom of Martin Stone. So, it was rice pudding and tinned peaches, bits of cheese pizza with the crust cut off, that sort of thing at road crossings. 'I became a bit of a fan of doughnuts for several years. I think Anne Stentiford started that one,' he laughed. 'Then jelly babies on each summit. I always steered clear of the engineered foods I suppose. Staminade was an essential ingredient for long runs in those days.' Mark said that he had been pretty lucky with stomach issues, until recent years. All this was organised to maximise his movement time, and he had three minutes rest time in the whole round. He explained in detail how things worked:

You have to see a Martin Stone-operated feed station. There

is a metal beer tray with stuff on. The pacers, or donkeys as he calls them, are already loaded up with water bottles and that sort of stuff. Maybe there was a bag with my waterproofs in, which are passed from one section to the next. Someone would already be halfway up Steel Fell, as sometimes at that speed pacers can't keep up. A road crossing is basically a rolling crossing. Martin would walk alongside me with everything laid out on this beer tray and I would scavenge from it then grab a handful of stuff and set off up the hill. I never believed in changing shoes or shirt unless it was really necessary. In the States it is hilarious. People would change their shoes after a stream crossing. How is that going to go down in somewhere like Borrowdale, changing your shoes a dozen times in a race? I don't think I even changed shoes on the run-in through Portinscale.

He remembers that he didn't have to be forced to eat and drink in later stages. By then, though, he was aware of how time was slipping away. 'I think I was losing a bit of time, particular on the Wasdale to Honister section maybe 20 minutes or so just on that section alone,' he thought. 'I started walking up Dale Head, with Gavin Bland and someone else. After the first steep bit I started running again. Someone said "here we go, let's pick it up". I started to feel a bit better. At one point someone will have said "well, there is this other time [*Stuart Bland's*] that is 14 hrs 56 mins". I am pretty sure I was 'eyeballs out' on the road towards the end to get that. By the time I came over the bridge I was throwing clothes off and almost sprinting to get inside that time.'

He recalls that there weren't really any navigation issues. They never got lost, but he still didn't feel that it was perfect. 'Whereas on the 24 hour round two years earlier I was pretty much foot perfect. That came from recent recces and familiarity with the route. I sat down after the fast BGR and went through it to see what I could I have done better. I came to the conclusion that even if everything had gone perfectly I could have been at most 25 to 30 minutes quicker. That was my process of reconciling myself to the idea that I shouldn't go back a year or two later and have another go. I didn't get the best time I possibly could, but I established to myself that the best I could get at that time was somewhat short of Billy's. I had already got the second fastest time, so what was there to go for?'

Going into Wasdale, and on the next section, it had become apparent he wasn't going to get the fastest time. Mentally he feels he must have slightly lost focus. Heading up Dale Head he re-assessed his expectations and realised the second fastest time was possible. 'It is interesting how quickly we can make a major revision of milestones or targets. Then I was totally focussed on going for the second fastest time,' he said.

On his 24 hour round Broad Stand was really greasy and Bob Berzins bodily threw him up it. 'It was a tense moment when I wasn't sure he was up it and behind me and safe. I thought, this is just for my personal gratification, and I didn't want anyone being hurt. On the fast one I can't remember who I was with but it was dry and it was quick. On the 24 hour one you usually go up Broad Stand and down Lord's Rake to get to Lingmell. When it is dry Broad Stand is OK. With my climbing background I am pretty comfortable with it. If you go to the most exposed part it is relatively easy. People tend to get themselves stuck in the corner because it feels secure but it is harder there. The thing is that it is not technically hard, just intimidating, but if it is wet and greasy it is a bit 'sketchy',' he commented.

Mark had no particular memory of how well or badly he recovered after his fast BGR. But he did comment that after the 77 peaks record he felt as though he was invincible. 'A month or so later Mark McDermott and I were scheduled to run the Hardrock 100 in Colorado, and we finished joint first. In the intervening time I basically ran with whoever was running longest on any given day. If someone said I am having a rest day, someone said I was running 10 and Mark said I am running 25, I would be out with Mark. In the Hardrock around halfway I was spent. I had a hollow empty feeling in my legs, but we were leading at the time. I said "I am done, you should go on". It is a measure of how good friends we had become, especially as I had just taken his 24 hour record, that he said we would stick together. We had agreed that plan, unless anyone caught us. I threw myself on the floor more than once, and he would say "you can sit there for two minutes and then we are going on". When I got back I got a virus because my body was so trashed and I couldn't shake it. I went to the doctor and was told I had pleurisy and it took four more months to shake it. That is the only time I have done that. Two months later I was still coughing.' By the BGR he suggests he was wiser, and by then he had a daughter so that stopped him getting out too much.

We discussed anyone being up to challenging Billy Bland's time or his 24 hour record, but he said he feels a little bit out of the loop these days. 'I feel it will be someone coming from fell racing,' he suggested. He had however got involved in setting up the Run Further series, and through that he got to know Adam Perry a bit. 'I didn't realise until his recent attempt how focussed on the Lake District 24 hour attempt he was. I am sure he will get it next time, given the right conditions. The only other person who I know who had a go at the 24 hour record is Steve Birkinshaw. He has come at it from the longer end though. Morgan Donnelly has the endurance, stamina and speed – he ought to have a go.'

At this point I referred to some of the comments made about Mark McDermott's 24 hour round – like "Ah, but he just did it on a computer". Mark Hartell responded, 'what Mark brought to the 24 hour round was a degree of organisation. Yes, he did have a spreadsheet. He had run every section several times before the big day. He knew the splits to the minute, as did I.' Hartell expanded on this, saying that, 'I have said to people that Mark McDermott had to tackle the legend that was Iron Joss. It is pretty well recorded that Mark said "hands up who thinks I can do this", and pretty much nobody did. It was seen to be Joss' domain, and people felt that you had to be working on the fells and living in Cumbria to stand a chance. Mark McDermott proved that wrong but there are some funny attitudes out there. One thing I have seen on forums and blogs is the idea that: "People should just let the record stand". I think that is ridiculous. Look at the mile record – are we all going to be amazed by Roger Bannister's sub-4 minute mile and leave it at that? There is some selective memory out there too.'

We then discussed Billy Bland's 'just go out and do it' approach. 'I couldn't have gone out and just run to my feeling,' said Mark. 'I guess I haven't spoken to that many people about mine. On my third attempt the weather was not great. After the first couple of tops I was a couple of minutes down. I made a decision on that day that I was going to run to the schedule whatever it took because I knew that if you lose 15 minutes off that schedule it is going to be impossible to recover. I got a few minutes ahead by the time I got to Dunmail and held it over to Langdale – through Langdale I felt nauseous because I was running quicker than I could sustain but I had held the schedule together (just!). It is interesting hearing Billy talk so differently about running how you feel. It tells you right there that there is still a fundamental difference in perspective. There are different ways to approach these things.'

I floated the idea that Ricky Lightfoot might be a candidate. 'There is no doubt he is talented and has good local knowledge. He recently ran round the BG with Scott Jurek from the USA and I just assumed he was going to have a go at a fairly fast one. It was interesting that they took over 23 hours.'

Mark also thought that Kilian Jornet is capable, as he is a true mountain person. 'He has skills over technical terrain so he can move fast over difficult ground,' said Mark. 'He has a sponsor to please, so things he does do have to have a reputation. He came over to the States to do the John Muir Trail. What prevented that was that he thought he could get a helicopter up there to film sections, and was told by the park authorities that "you ain't taking any helicopters into that wilderness". My perception is that he had a list of races and he has done those.

Next come big mountain challenges. But I think he would be a very strong contender for the BGR record.'

Mark had a few thoughts on the three big rounds, and was pleased that more go for the Paddy Buckley and the Charlie Ramsay rounds now. 'I did my Paddy the year after the BGR. The Ramsay was after my second failed attempt at the 24 hour record. I had basically lost confidence in myself and thought I was dragging people up to the Lake District for what was ultimately a wasted weekend. So I did the Ramsay completely solo. I needed to believe in myself before I asked others to do so.'

Mark then commented on topics he has ruminated on with Billy Bland over the years. 'Billy and I have had good chats at BG Club dinners. He has said to me that his wasn't some kind of genetic natural ability. He firmly believes that he simply worked harder than anyone in training at the time. "If the weather was bad then I would run on the spot in the kitchen for three hours". I am sure that is an exaggeration, but the point being made is that he may have felt a degree of disappointment that other people around haven't had a better go at some of these things.'

Mark had also had a conversation with Billy about the so-called 'Bob Graham machine'. He commented, 'I have been a bit disappointed to see clubs putting out groups who are being paced but don't really know where they are. I always think you should do your apprenticeship as it were. So, for me training for the Paddy Buckley round I wasn't enamoured at first, but grew to love it. I ran sections in winter, spring, early morning and late evening, and you get to know somewhere and respect it. My BGR was unusual as it was a fairly short notice decision to have a go at a fast round, but I knew the fells pretty well.' I suggested there may be a parallel between multi-contender club BG rounds and guided Everest climbs. At this Mark said, 'my daughter and wife have both made me promise not to attempt Everest. But if I was to, I would not want to be guided all the way up and down.'

At present Mark Hartell is President of the Bob Graham Club. 'The role is just honorary but one I am hugely proud of. It was going to the BG dinner after my first round that fired my passion for more. Fred Rogerson reverently read out all the "notable "achievements of the year and I sensed in that room such potential that I thought the greatest thing in the world would be to earn the respect of these people. In practical terms it means turning up at the dinner and making a speech and presenting some certificates but when Adam or someone else takes over the role it will still be one of my best ever life moments – standing up in that room being confirmed as the 24 hour record holder,' he concluded.

The next significant attempt was recorded in Martin Stone's long distance column in the October 2003 *Fellrunner*:

Andrew Schofield (Scoff) recorded a fine time of 17 hrs 1 min, making his round the second fastest on joining the BG Club, and the fourth fastest ever [*at the time*]. On a near perfect day he was paced by a who's who of fell racing, mostly members of Borrowdale AC. He set off at a furious pace, reaching Threlkeld in 2 hrs 35 mins. As he was by now 22 minutes behind Billy Bland's 13 hrs 53 mins schedule, Scoff concluded wisely that he wasn't on for a record! However, he did move swiftly throughout the day completing the Helvellyn ridge in 2 hrs 53 mins and the Langdale/Scafell section in 4 hrs 26 mins. Scoff's wheels finally came off at Honister and it proved a bit of a survival exercise from there to the finish. However, this was a top performance and the fastest round for a few years. Only Stuart Bland has completed a first round faster (in 14 hrs 56 mins) and Mark Hartell has completed a second BG in 14 hrs 54 mins.

Chapter 10

Mark Palmer

In 2011 a new contender for fastest debut BGR appeared. On 12 June **Mark Palmer** (Mynydd Du), already in the veteran runner category, put his marker down. He had set a schedule for 18:30, which he seemed to promptly ignore as he set off at an astonishing pace. He finished in 14 hrs 59 mins, making him the fourth fastest all-time, just missing Stuart Bland's fastest debut time. Martin Stone noted in the Summer 2011 *Fellrunner* that 'pacers were amazed at the pace which showed no sign of slowing in the latter stages and Mark seemed very comfortable and relaxed throughout the round.'

Mark himself wrote an extended report on the day in the Autumn 2011 *Fellrunner*, an edited-down version of which is included here:

The dawn had already arrived as we departed from Moot Hall at 4am. The overnight rain clouds were gradually dispersing to reveal patches of blue sky, whilst the cool morning air was welcomed as we made our ascent of Skiddaw. I had planned an 18:30 schedule that would give my support teams and myself a comfortable day out on the fells, but secretly felt I might have a 17-hour round in me.

We were soon crossing the first summit of the day two minutes down on schedule – fast starts have never been my strength! The low cloud hanging around the tops was no hindrance to Steve Birkinshaw's navigational skills, and Great Calva was bagged ahead of schedule. I was glad to reach the trod leading to Blencathra. All that separated me from my porridge was Hall's Fell ridge and in the daylight it proved to be no problem.

A quick change of shirt and partners and we were heading up Clough Head. We made good progress over the Dodds and up to Helvellyn, and reaching the top at 8.40am we had the mountain to ourselves. A fast descent to the west side of Grisedale Tarn, and with 15 summits in the bag it was time for a PBJ buttie at Dunmail.

Leg three has always been a favourite of mine, I have supported attempts in both directions and reccied it on numerous occasions. Climbing up Steel Fell the clear visibility made navigation easy and sightseeing ideal. Although the pace and terrain allowed little time to enjoy the panoramic views, I felt strong on the climbs and comfortable on the descents. With Broad Stand scaled and Scafell peaked we headed down to the Wasdale valley, another favourite of mine.

I was now two hours up on my schedule. This was a big surprise for me but an even bigger one for my support team who had just arrived. Having supported countless runners before, this professional outfit soon had me fed, watered, cleaned and on my way. I had heard stories of it being a graveyard for many BG attempts, so was glad to get the climb of Yewbarrow out of the way. Reaching Red Pike at 3pm it suddenly registered that I was now 11 hours into my BG; I had three legs in the bag, a comfortable two-hour cushion and was still feeling relatively good. Perhaps a 16-hour round was within grasp? On Pillar more supporters who had arrived after my departure from Wasdale joined us, one having come up Dore Head and two via Wind Gap.

Pillar now a distant rock, we ascended Kirk Fell and now my legs were starting to notice the steep climbs. Mentally I boxed this feeling and tuned into the wit and wisdom of my support team. Running on enthusiastic encouragement from my support, we soon knocked off the remaining peaks of the penultimate leg and were heading for the slate mines.

The crew were ready and my transition into dry top and trail shoes was complete before I'd finished my soup. I had mixed feelings as we climbed out of the valley, relieved to be on the final leg but sad that my fantastic day in the fells was drawing to an end. The good weather that prevailed was also ending as dark clouds loomed in the west. With fresh banter Dale Head was behind us and we were running across to Hindscarth with only Robinson remaining. And so at 17.59 I touched my 42nd peak, big smile, and a big emotional gulp. Finding all the grassy lines off the summit we rapidly descended into the Newlands valley. The rain finally came, but did little to dampen the high spirits as we hit the tarmac, mission almost complete.

Crossing the River Derwent I asked if a sub-15 was possible. The informed reply was positive but came with conditions: "Yes, but you need to pick the pace up!"

Once again the fell running community network led me to Mark Palmer, with an intro coming via Steve Birkinshaw, who had paced him on his round. Living as he does in South Wales it was going to be most convenient to arrange to meet when I was at my in-laws, who live not too far away. Crickhowell was the meeting place. We met in cafe Number Eighteen. That is its name, but could easily be the 18th cafe interview I have done as it seems to be my venue of choice. Getting comfy downstairs with our coffees we were soon swapping stories and I was finding out about Mark's background. A picture emerged of a hugely talented runner (and triathlete) who seemed less 'driven' than some I have interviewed.

As I didn't know Mark Palmer I started by asking him about his working life. He explained that after school he started doing engineering, worked in a factory, and did a number of jobs. He has now been in the fire service for a number of years. At school he was into all sports. 'We had a sports centre attached to the school,' he said. 'We did soccer, rugby, hockey, badminton and a bit of gymnastics. When I left school I started playing rugby, but my weight was not suited to it. I just used to run all over the pitch. At 16–17 I started playing squash, and running to keep fit for it. Then at 18 I started running for a club, just the normal thing up to 10k. Then I started triathlon, and was doing that for three or four years.' He got interested in fell running, and was doing a lot of running off-road. Through doing triathlon he met Jack Maitland, and it was Maitland who started the ball rolling for him becoming interested in the fells. 'I was always aware of fell running,' he explained. 'My parents did a lot of outdoor sports: walking, caving, climbing, canoeing and stuff. Then I left home and started doing my own thing. I met Jack and he gave me his contact details and I joined the FRA and got the races from the magazine.'

He wasn't immediately into long challenges when he started. Initially it was just racing, often in South Wales and then in the Lakes. 'I had been there before and was aware of the beauty of the area,' he noted. 'My first race there was Buttermere Sailbeck and I thought I have got to do more of this. The more people you meet the better it all is. A mate of mine from the club had done the Bob Graham Round. From when he said it to when I did it was about four or five years.'

I wondered at this point whether Mark had done the South Wales Traverse. 'Embarrassingly, no – I still haven't. It is on my doorstep, I have done numerous sections of it, and hopefully in 2015 I will have a go.' He then went on to talk about why he likes the Lakes events and about one of his ambitions. 'The BGR is the one round to do. The same applies to the Lakeland long fell races. I would like to do the Paddy Buckley Round. It is quite close and is on my radar.'

He has done just the one BG round, but has also supported a few other people on it and done a good few sections. He spent years preparing for his 2011 round. I quoted what he had said in his report about the schedule and outcome associated with his own round: 'Schedule of 18:30, secretly thought 17 hours, and ended with 14:59', and questioned whether that was really how it was. 'Yes, that was the basis of it,' he said, dead-pan. 'I looked at the times of people I had raced with. I had a sort of schedule made out for the support team. I felt that I could do it faster than 24 hours. People like Paul Cornfort and Dave Makin, who I had spent a lot of time with, said to treat it like a day out with friends, but I was a bit more competitive than that. I was thinking that if I did well I could do a 17, which would be nice.' But was Mark aware of other's times? 'I knew of Billy Bland's time, which is incredible,' he replied. 'I was aware of Mark Hartell's time, and that he had done it very scientifically. That is not me. Even when I was training for it I wasn't taking much notice of the leg times. Usually I was recceing to find my way round, and get 6–7 hours training in my legs.'

Surely then, the difference between the schedule and actual times must have caused some problems on the day? Mark felt that it caused very few, really. 'I was able to get messages forward to tell the support. Dave Makin was in charge and he knew the craic. The first two were fine. I was 40 minutes up by the second. When I got to Wasdale, Dave and Janet Makin and couple of others were sitting around having a cup of tea. They weren't even aware I was coming. They quickly got it sorted and I didn't really lose any time.'

I asked where he had gathered his pacers from. 'I knew Steve Birkinshaw from races, and had met him a couple of times. Paul and the others were from running and racing in the Lakes.' He had reccied it all a fair bit, the only section he wasn't too sure of was the first leg. 'I had Steve Birkinshaw on that as I knew he knew that leg pretty well. Skiddaw was not a problem, Steve had a good line off Great Calva and he navigated us brilliantly, including Hall's Fell.' I presumed that they had started at 4am so as to not run in the dark. 'I don't particularly like running in the dark. Some do, it doesn't do it for me. The whole point for me is seeing all the scenery and stuff. I had a head torch in the rucksack, just in case. Navigation was spot on all the way.

It was a clear day so you couldn't go too wrong. Paul Cornfort had a good route off Dale Head that I wasn't aware of. I was going straight down the race route, but he found a nice grassy descent. Once you are down there you are on the road.' He admitted that it was one of those days when everything just goes right.

We started talking about further details of the day and I just had to know whether he really had peanut butter and jam sandwiches as his staple food on the round? 'Yeah, at the support points, as well as soup,' he laughed. 'On the hills it was the standard bars and gels, although I got sick of those towards the end. PBJ sarnies – they are ideal for me, I love that. I do struggle sometimes to get food down.'

His report had just blandly stated that Broad Stand was scaled. I asked Mark to expand on that a little. 'I had arranged for someone to be up there with a rope, although I was confident that I could get up it on my own. I had done it a few times on my own. We were fortunate that we got there and it was June so there were a few doing the round that day. There was someone with a rope there anyway. I had done a bit of climbing as well so I was fine.'

All the way through the weather was good. It wasn't too hot, and they had hardly any wind. The first leg was pretty cool and they were in three-quarter bottoms, and after that Mark was in shorts all the way. It sounded like it was just one of the best days out on the fells. 'Yes, it is well up there,' Mark thinks. 'One of the best days I have had. When you look at people who have done winter rounds, or to Nicky Spinks for setting a record in dreadful conditions, I say hats off to people who do it in conditions like that. There is no way I would do it in winter, I struggle in cold weather. I would be warm enough running, but my extremities suffer. I wouldn't be able to open the wrappers on the energy bars!'

We discussed his policy for the road stops. 'I don't think I put a limit on road stop times. I just had some food and a change of clothes and got away, I wanted to crack on. I didn't want to sit down and rest too long. People did point out afterwards that *if* I had cut more time at the stops . . . but you can never tell.' Mindful that Mark had been faster than Billy Bland over last two legs, Steve Birkinshaw told him afterwards that he could have cut five minutes from every rest time and been a lot closer to him. Mark is not so sure [*Mark had a total rest time of 32 minutes, against Billy's 21 minutes*]. 'At the time the short rests may have helped. But at Wasdale, for instance, the last thing you want is to stop a while and be thinking about going up Yewbarrow. You might as well go straight through. But sometimes a short stop and a chat help.'

We diverted for a moment while I asked Mark about the Dragon's Back race in 2012, when he retired on day two (of the five-day race), when well up in the field. 'Coming off the Glyders I slipped and twisted my ankle,' he explained. 'I stopped at a stream and stuck it in the cold water for a few minutes. I struggled on, up over Snowdon and down the Watkin path to the end of the day. That night it swelled up. The next morning I knew it was wrong. Halfway through the second day I was running with Nicky Spinks and Tim Whittaker, and I was hobbling. I thought I would make it worse by carrying on, so I retired.' The obvious question is whether he wants to go back to it. [*laughs*] 'I have done a few multiple day races, for example the Goretex Transalpine on three occasions. I think I would like to go back and do it [*Dragon's Back*] but not 2015 as entries have closed. It is expensive though.'

I was thinking at this point that he must have the credentials for a solo or winter BGR. 'No to winter,' was the quick response. 'But I have often thought about a solo BGR, possibly. I might try a solo South Wales Traverse first, to see how that goes. That would be interesting.' [*At this point we had a brief discussion of Colin Donnelly's unreported solo BGR*]. 'I can see where he is coming from with that. Some things I do I think "yeah done that" and I just keep quiet about it. It was a little bit of a shock how my BGR got blown up.' I pointed out that it was fastest round for ages, but his response was that he had only done it the same as someone else, and that he was very fortunate that everything went his way. I do feel that his modesty here should take nothing away from what is a massive achievement, particularly for a debut round.

I then pressed on with the idea that he might be a candidate for increasing the extended 24 hour Lakes round. 'There are a lot of things out there you would like to do. I may get round to it,' was his laconic response, which he followed with this further parallel. 'Bob Graham is the Bob Graham, as are the other rounds. You can extend it but it is not the Bob Graham any more. You wouldn't extend Wasdale, or Ennerdale would you. Once you have done one of the rounds that is it really.'

We had a short discussion about how much Steve Birkinshaw took out of himself doing the Wainwrights, and how recovery should be managed. Mark said that he had spoken to Steve at the FRA Relays and he said it took a lot out of him. 'After my BGR Steve B's advice to me was to take a good couple of months off. For some reason I didn't. I had three weeks leave to do the BGR. I had a week off before, did it, and then had two weeks at my mate's. I couldn't sit around relaxing. I think the next day I went for a walk, the second day I went out on the bike, and on the third day I was running again. The following week I did the Great Lakes Race and felt OK on it. I felt mentally tired and seemed to get over it pretty well.'

I reiterated Billy Bland's views on recovery that he had revealed in my interview with him. 'I have met Billy, but he wouldn't know me probably,' Mark said. 'He did a [cycle] sportive after Borrowdale and I spoke to him. I know what he means. At the end of that week it was the Loughrigg race. I did that and I was feeling tired, but that is quite short and fast. Short races don't really appeal to me much actually.' When asked for his favourite of the Lakeland classics Mark had a definite choice, but went on to explain his 'taking part' philosophy of racing, and the fact that he doesn't record, or even remember sometimes, his performances. 'It has got to be the Wasdale. I am not ultra competitive. If I go out there and have a good race and finish high in the results that is good enough for me. My best performance is probably a top five in Wasdale. I know I have done a sub-4 hour time there.'

Mark competes for a reasonably small Welsh club (Mynydd Du) and I asked what its status is in the fell running world. 'Compared to some clubs in the North, we are small. We always try to get two teams in the FRA Relays. It is just a fell running club. I originally ran for Gloucester AC, and then ran for Forest of Dean for a while.' My next question, about the pecking order in the club, still didn't elicit a detailed response from him, and looking up some results I suspect he is something of a star in their firmament. 'I just enjoy running,' he laughs. 'I do a fair bit of training on my own now.'

We moved on to further ambitions and I asked whether the Ramsay Round is on his radar. 'It has been, but I know how long it took to recce the BGR. I always feel if you are going to do a round well you have to spend a good bit of time on those mountains. The Lake District was achievable, but going to Scotland is harder time-wise. I would like to do the Joss Naylor Challenge, now I am eligible. [*Mark is 51, at the time of writing*] My ambition is that I want to stay fit and enjoy myself. I enjoy ultras. I have done the Tour of Mont Blanc. The TMB is a lot in the dark and there is all that beauty around you. I don't see the point of running through darkness.'

On the subject of anyone beating Billy Bland's BGR time, Mark concluded that he is sure there are people out there. 'There is not a lot written about Billy's round – and some of that is myths, like that he did it on jam butties. I am sure Ricky Lightfoot is capable, for instance. It would be interesting to see Kilian Jornet over here to have a go at the BGR. He is absolutely incredible with what he does. He is the Usain Bolt of the ultra world.'

We were winding up and suddenly Mark started talking about his father. What his father had said and instilled in Mark may well be a clue to both his work ethic and attitude towards his sport. 'What my dad used to tell me as a kid I used to ignore.

But actually what he used to say to me made a lot of sense. He always used to drive into me that no matter how fit and fast you are, there is always someone fitter and faster. I have lived by that mantra. I guess that is why I have never got into times so much. I have always wanted to go out there and enjoy it, and come near the top. Don't get me wrong, there is a certain competitiveness there in me.'

He ended by talking about his feelings during his round. 'During the BGR I couldn't calculate how many hours I had done, kind of thing. It wasn't until near the end that I realised how well it was going. It was Paul Cornfort who said if you put in a fast 10k you can get under 15 hours. There I am working it out on my fingers, that is three hours less than I planned. I ran that last section in trail shoes, ones that I had on for a while. I felt I was dictating the pace myself. I felt comfortable with it. I hadn't had any really bad patches. Earlier, going up Gable, I was feeling tired and said so to Mark Roberts, and he replied 'you are allowed to by now'. So, I cracked on with it. I have supported rounds where people have struggled and have had to encourage them. But I didn't really seem to need that so much.'

Mark's final comments echo what all BGR completers must think, and generally say. 'I don't think doing the BGR would be possible without the support of the fell running community. After you have done it you appreciate it more. Not just on the day but in the lead up. The advice, the route choices, there are so many people that have helped you on the way.'

At some point we also had a discussion about tall stories. Mark left me with this anecdote, which nicely puts into perspective the sport and its participants. 'Scoffer tells a story about Joss saying that this and that happened in some race, and Billy Bland immediately chipping in with "you weren't even in that race", to bring him back to down to ground.'

In these last two chapters I have described some of the pretenders to King Billy's crown. Stuart Bland commented shortly after his own round: 'I'm telling you, someone will go out soon and do 12 hours . . .'.[1] But that has proved not to be the case. Over 32 years later no one has remotely approached that, and the only one to even beat Stuart's time has been Mark Hartell, and that by just two minutes.

There have been just three people under 15 hours since Billy Bland's 1982 effort, all within a range of times from 14:54 to 14:59 – all just over an hour slower, but within five minutes of each other. They were off his mark by the same amount but a look at the splits comparison show that they actually had three slightly different approaches, perhaps sub-consciously. Consider the numbers.[2]

Splits comparison (adding in the rest times to the leg they followed – bold = fastest)

	Billy Bland	Mark Hartell	Stuart Bland	Mark Palmer
Leg 1	**2:16**[3]	2:25	2:30	2:50
Leg 2	2:44	2:47	**2:40**	3:07
Leg 3	**3:45**	4:05	4:04	3:56
Leg 4	3:20	3:38	3:35	**3:17**
Leg 5	**1:46**	1:59	2:07	1:49
TOTAL	13:53	14:54	14:56	14:59

The time difference for Mark Hartell was made up of 9, 3, 20, 18, and 13 minute deficits respectively. He was slower than

---

1 Colin Valentine commented in 1995 that he thought Billy Bland's Bob Graham record of 13 hrs 53 mins to be such an enormous achievement that it will probably never be broken, and he [Colin] furthermore feels that it's never really had the appreciation it deserves. Colin partnered Billy on the Dunmail-Wasdale section of the Bob Graham Relay Challenge, over the Langdale Pikes and Scafell range, when Keswick AC set the record of 12 hours: 'The weather was atrocious, with torrential rain, high winds and low cloud, and I've never been so afraid as when going up Broad Stand in those conditions without a rope', he said.

2 The splits for Billy Bland, Mark Hartell and Stuart Bland are available on the Macclesfield club website (http://www.macclesfield-harriers.co.uk/fell/bg/fastestBG.html). Mark Palmer provided his splits.

3 Eric Beard did 2:21 for Keswick to Threlkeld on his 56 summit round in 1963.

Billy Bland on all legs, was 12 minutes behind Billy after leg 2, but over half his total time 'loss' was on the two long legs (2 and 3). Stuart Bland had time differences of 14, -4, 19, 15 and 20. He was actually the faster over leg 2 (Helvellyn), was only 10 minutes behind Billy after 2 legs, but gradually lost time over the remaining three legs. Mark Palmer had time differences of 34, 23, 11, -3, 3. He was the fastest of the four over leg 4 (Wasdale to Honister), was a massive 57 minutes behind Billy after 2 legs, but finished remarkably well, exactly matching Billy's time over the last two legs. Hartell had only one break, for 3 minutes at Dunmail, moving through all the other support points with no apparent rest. Billy had 21 mins rest, Stuart 17 and Mark 32.

A simplistic analysis is that Mark Hartell just did not have the speed required [*which he alludes to in his own interview*] – and that with just 3 minutes break he was moving all the while, but not fast enough. Stuart Bland had the second least rest time, started fast, but may have 'blown up' somewhat in the latter stages. As for Mark Palmer, you could argue that if he had started off at a faster pace, and worked through the support points with no timeouts, then he could have got significantly closer to 14 hours. All speculation, I know, but fascinating none the less.

Chapter 11

Winter rounds

Some people like to extend the challenge by doing the Bob Graham Round in winter conditions. What constitutes 'winter' is of course open to debate,[1] as it is with mountaineering ascents. The official Bob Graham 24 Hour Club website states that:

The Club perceives that there are two distinct types of winter Bob Graham Round which are:

- the 'Mid-winter' round which, taking its inspiration from the earliest attempts on a winter round by Pete Simpson and Martin Stone in the early 1980s, is attempted at any time from the weekend before the shortest day through to the first period of decent weather after the shortest day but to be completed no later than 10 January; and
- the 'Winter' round, which is a round not falling within the definition set out above, attempted during the period starting on 1 December and finishing on 1 March.

Even this distinction is artificial, because conditions on the shortest day could be quite benign, while full winter conditions could well be experienced at any time before or after within the wider definition of 'winter'. Ultimately, though, if records are to be kept, someone has to set parameters to keep them by. The Club is persuaded by the view of the early winter pioneers that the challenge represented by maximum

---

1   It is worth noting that the original concept was to use the shortest day of the year.

hours of darkness puts the 'Mid-winter' round into a category of its own.

The website then proceeds to list the records. **Pete Simpson** had done a round of 26 hours 22 minutes, with Martin Stone supporting most of the way before having to drop out, back in 1979. Stone explained in a *Fellrunner* article on the history of winter rounds (in Feb 1994): 'I was intending to have a go over New Year but after hearing of Pete's plans for the shortest weekend we agreed to combine forces. After a 4am start anti-clockwise we ran unpaced until Wasdale in classic snow conditions. I dropped out after an epic near Mickledore and Pete carried on in deepening snow, paced by Graham Webster and later by Martin Hudson.'

Selwyn Wright completed a solo mid-winter round in 1985 in 27 hours 38 minutes (which he wryly noted was about 10 minutes short of double Billy Bland's record), despite Joss Naylor suggesting at the Bob Graham Club Dinner that he was ill-advised to do it. Selwyn justified it by saying: 'I have always thought that a degree of danger has to be acceptable. The objective danger involved in a solo winter 42-peak round has been assessed on a par with an extreme rock climb. Not being an extreme rock climber, I wouldn't know. It's an interesting comparison, though, as we runners aren't really used to accepting danger in the same way climbers do. Simply because a run is objectively dangerous, does not mean that subjectively the runner may not feel able to tackle it.'

The first 'mid-winter' sub 24-hour round recorded was by **John Brockbank** and **Selwyn Wright** in December 1986, taking 23 hours 6 minutes. The first 'mid-winter' ladies round was **Nicky Lavery** with 22 hours 45 minutes in 2000, which was then technically the fastest mid-winter round. Lavery's round was reported in the *Westmorland Gazette* of 1 January 2000:

Nicky Lavery completed her second Bob Graham Round at the weekend. The 37-year-old mother-of-two, from

Kendal, completed [the round] in 22 hours and 45 minutes – 15 minutes ahead of schedule. Supported by a posse of 17 pacers over the five sections, Nicky enjoyed the benefit of near perfect weather conditions although it was boggy underfoot. She also took a buffeting from strong winds which she encountered on the Helvellyn range between 10pm and midnight on Saturday.

Her path on the night sections was clearly illuminated by a full moon and she hardly had to use her head torch. She set off from the Moot Hall, Keswick, in darkness at 6pm on Saturday and received a warm reception from family and friends as she returned shortly before 5pm on Sunday. 'I felt all right for the first 15 minutes after I had finished but after drinking some champagne and eating fish and chips, I felt quite ill,' said Nicky, who is a Grange-based health visitor for the South Cumbria Health Authority.

The high spot of the run for Nicky was watching the sun rise from Great End as she approached Scafell Pike on the stamina-sapping section from Dunmail Raise to Wasdale. 'It was absolutely fantastic,' she said, adding: 'I was feeling tired at that point but it gave me a real lift.' Nicky completed a summer Bob Graham Round ten years ago in 20 hours and 58 minutes.

'This time I did not put in as much training as I did last time,' said Nicky, who has been running for about 15 years. Her build up revolved around a three-hour run on a Sunday supplemented by six-milers on every other day of the week. Over Christmas she suffered from a chest infection and needed antibiotics to clear it. Road support was provided by her husband Mick Hoffe and Stephen Watson and she was joined on the last section by long- distance fell-running specialist Joss Naylor.

In 1981 **Steve Parr** produced what was the second fastest standard round time thus far, going round in 17 hours 58 minutes. It was also one of his ambitions to complete the first sub-24 hour Winter Bob Graham Round. Attempts in December 1985 and

January 1986 were thwarted by dreadful weather. During the 1985 attempt he was forced to retire when caught in a blizzard on Great Calva, with just Skiddaw to go. In December 1986 Parr completed the second sub-24 hour winter round. There was a short report by Parr himself in his mountaineering club's magazine.[1]

> I decided on a clockwise circuit for my third attempt and set off at 7pm on 22 December, 1986, with a schedule for 23 hours. This time I had road support from John Barrett and two pacers on the fells; Joe Faulkner and Andy Harding.
>
> Conditions were not ideal, with deep snow on the first section to Threlkeld being replaced by icy and misty conditions on the second section. However, I left Dunmail at 3.40am (20 minutes ahead of schedule) having travelled on my own up to that point. I was very pleased to have Joe's company at such an unearthly hour of the morning, but despite his unstinting efforts at trail-breaking through the deep snow we reached the summit of Bowfell about an hour behind schedule, just after dawn. However, the going soon improved and morale was again restored. With 10 hours remaining in which to traverse the remaining 19 summits the race was on for a sub-24 hour finish.
>
> We made good progress over the Scafell range to Wasdale, where we were encouraged to meet John Barrett and Joe's girlfriend, Ruth Taylor, who had driven round from Dunmail in support. After a brief halt at Brackenclose I continued on my own to Honister, where I was met by John Barrett and Andy Harding at about 4pm. For the first time since Bowfell we felt that there was a chance to break 24 hours.
>
> After a few minutes at Honister I ran in Andy's cheerful company on a rapid traverse of Dale Head, Hindscarth and Robinson to Newlands church. A final five-mile race against the darkness along the road took me to Keswick to

---

1 Rucksack Club, December 1986.

finish at the Moot Hall at 6.26pm, 23 hours 26 minutes after starting.

Parr then made some interesting points about winter attempts (remember that this was in 1986 – very early days in terms of winter attempts). First, he reckoned that dates needed to be flexible to take into account the weather and prevailing conditions. He thought, 'a slavish devotion to the 21 December [*shortest day*] can transform a challenging event into a dangerous lottery.' Secondly, he thought up-to-date info on the local conditions, and also a crystal ball for weather predictions as important as organisational skill. Thirdly, he thought contenders had to be able to 'maintain a high level of fitness over a number of weeks and make an attempt with minimal support if one is to use spells of good weather to best advantage.'

The first 'winter' sub-24 round was by **Martin Scrowson** and **Barry Laycock**, with their 22 hours 8 minutes in 1989. Martin Stone noted in *The Fellrunner* (in Jan 1990), 'During a period of unseasonably clear weather, Ambleside AC were out in force on 9/10 December. The moon was full, skies clear and the wind light. There was a dusting of snow on Helvellyn. For Martin [Scrowson] it was especially satisfying as he hadn't already completed a round in summer.'

The first ladies 'winter' round was a supported one by **Alison Crabb** in 1993, with a time of 23 hours 52 minutes. Crabb had also done a summer round earlier that year. She wrote about what must have been an epic winter effort in *The Fellrunner* (Feb 1994):

Two of the pacers did a last-minute recce of the Dunmail to Wasdale section. They phoned in with grim news. Everything was frozen. There were huge areas of ice, which were hard to see even in daylight and there was a lot of snow to run through, rather than over. Broad Stand had ice all over it so we would need to go via Foxes Tarn, where it was likely we would need crampons!

Crabb wavered between going and not going, but went for it, as the moon was promising good navigating conditions. She temporarily lost the pacers on leg one, but things went well as a lot of the ice had disappeared. She fell and hurt her hand on the way via Foxes Tarn, which she said was the hardest part of the day. On Steeple there were gale-force winds, forcing her to fight to stay upright. Before Honister she was convinced it was all to no avail and started wavering, not even recognising her next pacers coming up to meet her. However, her pacers picked her up and pushed her onwards. She noted:

> Wind whipped the tea out of the mug and Dennis and Davey, either side of me, held me down as I drank the last of it. The next section proved to me that it is possible to do something that you believe to be impossible. Looking back over our shoulders, the grey-black outline of the Buttermere fells stood out, magnificent in their boldness. The big bright moon was right there in front of us again, a talisman, leading the way.

The Guidance Notes for the Bob Graham Club (which apply to both summer and winter rounds) state only that 'the contender **must** be accompanied at all times by at least one witness. During darkness it is advisable to have two or more for safety.'

What is a winter round like? Martin Stone gave this eloquent description in the January 1991 *Fellrunner* magazine:

> Fifteen hours of darkness can become tedious and takes its toll mentally, especially when the moon sets and the lights go out. For 24 hours every step is premeditated, the torch kept low as you check for glazed rock and pools of water ice. Each foot placement is with care as you skate across streams which have frozen and spread over large areas of hillside.
>
> The 28,000 feet of jarring descent is unyielding, even frozen earth feels like rock to a tired body. The occasional slip on dodgy ground serves to concentrate the mind after a lapse

into the long distance runner's dream world. Cold air numbs your face and mouth, it also chills the stomach. Freezing water destroys the sense of taste and food loses its attraction. Your feet soon feel numb, no longer providing you with the spring and agility you need.

Is it really worth it? Well, if the weather is good and there are views of the hills capped with a light covering of crisp snow which you can descend in a relaxed way without fear of injury, that all too short period of daylight is one of the most uplifting experiences you can enjoy on the fells. By the time you reach your 42nd peak, Robinson, it is dark again and has been so for two hours. You pause to look around you at 41 snowy peaks lit by a rising moon and you'd be a strange person to not be moved by the beauty and grandeur of the hills you have crossed that day. Before the moon has fully risen you are jogging back to Keswick, the final obstacle to success being a few strips of lethal black ice which send you tumbling.

Martin Stone's solo winter round, way back in 1987, was only the fourth sub-24 winter round recorded. In reviewing the history of winter rounds in *The Fellrunner*, he wrote that he 'set off from Keswick on 7 January 1987 attempting to complete the first solo, unsupported sub-24 hour round. The conditions underfoot were lethal thanks to two weeks of freezing snowy weather. A massive anticyclone was stationary over Britain and there was not a breath of wind. This was fortunate as the temperatures dropped to –15°C on the Helvellyn range and my water bottle froze solid in the sack. The ascents of Fairfield, Bowfell and Scafell provided dangerous moments in the dark on hard, consolidated snow but I finally cracked the round in 23 hours 41 minutes.'

Martin Stone has touched on so many people's Bob Graham efforts that it soon became obvious to me while researching *The Round* that he was a crucial person to talk to.

This turned out to be the final interview in my research, which in some ways was quite appropriate. Martin Stone was part of Billy Bland's iconic record round, did a solo winter round, and recorded many other endurance efforts in his 'Long Distance Round Up' in The Fellrunner since the late 1980s. He is a very busy man, running SPORTident from his home/office on the edge of the Lakes. We sat in the lounge in front of a crackling fire at the end of a Saturday afternoon in January. I only needed to ask a couple of questions and the memories and stories came flooding out – so much so that he got a mild reprimand from his partner Debbie for letting the fire burn down so low. His influence being so wide meant that many of his responses either corroborated or expanded on other rounds, experiences and views that I had already reported through talking to significant players in this Bob Graham story.

In his early life Martin Stone spent a lot of time walking on Dartmoor. He also did cross-country running at school, but admits it was not to a very high standard. 'I got incredibly enthusiastic about distance walking, taking part in Ten Tors, etc.,' he explained to me. 'We also went on what our school CCF called arduous training. Nothing competitive though.' He went to University in London and within a couple of weeks had joined the Rockhoppers Mountaineering Club. There he met Frank Thomas and Chris Dodd, who had both just done a Bob Graham. They were members of the Long Distance Walkers Association (LDWA) and had also done a few fell races. 'I started doing camping and stuff in the Lakes, this was in Autumn 1976. By next spring I was doing LDWA events, up to 25 miles or so, without any more background work. It was hard, but I got better.'

At the end of his second year at University (June 1978, when he would have been 19) he took a trip up to the Lakes, after having already supported on a few BGRs. 'First of all I supported on an annual Dark Peak round,' he said. 'On a really wet weekend I think five out of seven contenders got round. They were all really strong runners, like Martin Hudson. Then I paced John Blair-Fish.' He went back up to Lakes a few weeks later for two weeks, and prepared for his own BGR. 'It was fairly unconventional, but as a youngster you could get away with it,' he laughs. 'I reccied the Langdale, Borrowdale and Wasdale fell race routes, and then watched the Wasdale race and did a few other things. That was all in the first week and a half, before doing the BG on the last weekend. I went anti-clockwise and was supported by people like Boyd Millen and Chris Bland. I think I did 22 hours 54 minutes. I think I had probably overdone it in the weeks before. But I had a great time, was supported by some great friends, and at that time I think I was the second youngest [to Steve Tosh] to have done a BGR. Not bad considering the preparation.'

After finishing University, Martin worked for a firm of consulting actuaries in London for two years. He says it was a fairly tedious job, and that by his second year he was travelling by train to the Lakes most weekends. In 1981 he got a job in Preston, writing CAD software for the Building Design Partner-ship. There he met many fell runners, including Ken Taylor, with whom he later did mountain marathons and yachting/running events. 'I also worked with Ed Hill from Clayton le Moors, so running was very important to the practice,' he noted. He says that at the time he knew of the energy drink Accolade, which became Staminade but then was suddenly not available in the UK. So he found out how to import it from Australia and distributed it to shops involved in running, and directly to runners. 'I used to have a thing where I would be at the bottom of a hill and I would have a bag of the powder and add water from a stream,' he recalls. 'I would say to anyone who was around 'see this, I am going to drink this and in 10 minutes I am going to piss off and leave you'. I don't know whether it was the psychological element but it always worked. Basically I did that for a few years but realised I couldn't make a living out of it.'

In 1979 he made a winter BGR attempt with Pete Simpson.

That was the very first attempt at a winter round, and it was done on the shortest day. He had met Pete Simpson on the Three Peaks Yacht Race and they became friends. Martin described the attempt. 'Pete said he was doing a winter BG and I said 'could I come up from London and come with you?'. Basically, we set off from Keswick and made really good time to Honister. It started getting more snowy on the next section, but we got down to Wasdale on schedule for 24 hours. I started to feel unwell as I had a bug coming on. I accompanied Pete to the top of Scafell. For the guys who were going to fix a rope down Broad Stand something hadn't gone right, and they weren't well set up, and it was only going to work for one of us to go down there. There was a lot of snow and we also knew Foxes Tarn would be bad. I dropped out and walked back down to Wasdale and Pete carried on. The snow got deeper and he got slower and I think he did 26 hours. But still it was a good start to people doing winter Bob Grahams, no doubt.'

I was interested in how Martin had got involved in supporting Billy Bland's record round. He said he already knew Billy a little. 'I thought I wanted to be involved in it because Billy was such a fantastic fell runner,' Martin explained. 'I was going along knowing that we were possibly going to see something spectacular that day. When he showed no sign of slowing down you start projecting forward what he might achieve.'

The runners with Billy were the top runners at the time, like Bob Whitfield. Martin points out that it was the same when Mark McDermott did the 76 peaks, he needed the fastest supporters possible. Martin thinks that Billy wouldn't have done any specific recces to create a schedule. 'I think he just knew he was on phenomenal form, and just set out to do everything as fast as he could. He would have gone at a pace that was just a little below his race pace. I didn't really pace him. I knew I wasn't quick enough, so I mostly did support.' We discussed briefly Billy's comments on coming down to Honister. 'He sat down on Grey Knotts,' Martin recalls. 'I don't remember being influential in anything he did. It may have been subconscious.

Maybe if he had eaten earlier he might have smoothed that out.'

I asked Martin if he thought Billy got the optimum out of himself on that day. 'Where the time was lost, if he had managed to smooth that out by going a bit slower earlier on and doing some eating, there is no doubt he had the potential to go faster,' was Martin's view. 'But obviously in his mind it sounds like he was projecting towards the finish and thinking 'oh yeah under 14 is possible' and that became the overriding thing. He wouldn't have gone that much faster, if he became focussed on going under 14 hours. And 7 minutes under 14 hours is quite large in the grand scheme of things.' We then discussed why no one has beaten that time. 'Because no-one is that good,' came the swift reply, before more considered reasoning followed. 'To do the record you have to be a really good racer. The people who have attempted it since then have not been great racers in the class of Billy. To be able to go for under 14 hours rather than 24 hrs are two completely different things. To do something in 14 hours is more suited to somebody who is a top racer. So somebody who is incredibly agile and good at running down hills and an out and out racer would be the sort of person I would think.' We then discussed anyone who *might* be capable of challenging the record, and covered very similar ground to earlier interviewees.

Martin concluded that topic by saying: 'It was interesting that this was such a light touch BGR and yet it was such a significant one. I take the view that the greatest runs are those that establish and set a record that is so much more outstanding than anyone else has done, and that you couldn't expect them to do in the first place. If you are chipping away at that later then you know what you have to do. But if you are the person who is setting this amazing standard, and you are 3–4 hours faster than anyone before, then that is absolutely stunning.'

Moving on, I mentioned a winter BGR attempt of Martin's that had ended up in the pub. 'It was the Clayton le Moors machine,' he recalled. 'Stan Bradshaw Jr and I decided to have a go at a winter BGR on the shortest day in 1985. We enlisted a load of CLM Harriers as support. It was an incredibly wet night, with gale force winds on the tops. I was younger than Stan and I at least wanted to make a start and do a section to say we had checked out the hills and that they were unsuitable. We assembled in the loos in the car park at the Moot Hall. The CLM people almost pinned me to the wall and said 'you are not going out.' So we went to a pub in Staveley instead to celebrate Christmas. That actually set me thinking that you impinge on everybody's Christmas and it didn't seem fair to get everyone excited, yet mostly they were inevitably doomed to failure. So I was thinking could I do it without involving loads of people, and also give myself more flexibility? At that time I was really fit, and getting more experience at long distance things.'

I presumed that he had found a good day to do it on later. 'No, no,' he laughs, and describes the occasion. 'It was exceptionally snowy. I had a go on the shortest day on my own in December 1986. I set off clockwise at 8.30pm and I knew there was a bad weather forecast. I got the northern section done, going down Hall's Ridge. Halfway along the Helvellyn range this amazing gale came up behind me, and I could hear it roaring. It came with virtually no warning and I was knocked to the ground. I was sitting on the ground and the strength of the wind was pushing me across this water ice. I thought I have got to get off here now, no decision to be made. I am on my own, I have got to get off. I took a bearing off the ridge, down towards Stanah. I knew there were crags but got down to the road. I walked back to Keswick, not too dejected as I realised it wasn't to be that night.'

Martin put it in perspective by recalling that he was there pacing when Selwyn Wright and John Brockbank did the first winter round, which was a few weeks before his. They went in mid-December 1986 with very good conditions, lots of moonlight, a light dusting of snow, and a still night. 'I paced them down the Helvellyn ridge, as part of a large support team, and they got round in under 24 hours,' he noted. Then he described his own round. 'The night after I made my unsuccessful attempt, Steve Parr, who was a great mountaineer as well as fell runner,

got round with a small team in support. I resolved to take the
first period of decent weather after the shortest day. I set mine
up for 7/8 January. This time there was a sustained period of
high pressure. It was really cold, there was snow and ice over the
fells – absolutely classic winter conditions, but lethally slippery.
All the streams were frozen. I felt that if I could go round in that
it would be the most classic winter round. There wasn't much
moon. I made really good progress up until Fairfield. Although
I was going solo, as a precaution two hours after I went through
each road point someone would be along to pick up a card I
had left with times on and they would phone the next person
to let them know. I had about four torches with me which I
dropped off as I went round. So I dropped stuff but didn't pick
anything up.'

As he went on to Fairfield things started getting a bit crazy.
'On Fairfield I went up too steep a line. It was like a Tom and
Jerry cartoon. I didn't have my crampons on and I couldn't go
up and was in danger of slipping down. I had a torch dangling
on a cord from my mouth, the light playing on my feet. Looking
down between my legs to the tarn I really thought I was going to
fall. Then I discovered something I didn't know. I was wearing
a Lifa top and a thin woollen jersey, and I actually lay against
the icy slope and the jumper stuck to it and I cat-crawled up
until I could stand. At the summit I was jumping up and down,
excited that I had survived.'

Hearing what happened on Fairfield I suggested getting
between the Scafells might be his next problem. But Martin
explained that before then he had a problem on Bowfell. It was
just dawn and he was beginning to get weary. 'Stupidly, I had
discarded my crampons at Dunmail, and now I really needed
them. I chose the wrong line on the diagonal. I was having
problems on this snow slope. I sort of climbed and slipped,
losing something like 25 minutes here. I was now down on my
23 hours schedule, and was losing my leeway.' It was lovely
sunshine when he got to Scafell Pike and he looked at Mickledore. 'I had never been round Foxes Tarn, even though I had

done many rounds. So I thought I would have to do the West Wall Traverse and Lord's Rake. I got to the bottom of it and it was just full of snow. I thought, I am not really a climber but set off. I was dusting off steps that had been made by previous walkers with proper kit. Finally I was finding ice axe holes and I was able to put my fingers in them and pull up on them. It was just epic, but it was exciting stuff. I came out on the shoulder of Scafell and I thought, I don't know how I have done that. I thought that if that is the most technical thing I have to do on this round, and if time allows, I have a chance of completing it.' He dropped down to Wasdale and now really began to get very fatigued.

His bottle had been frozen since Helvellyn, he could not find water anywhere, and he felt he was suffering from dehydration. He dropped down to the col and was having terrible problems getting water. 'After Yewbarrow a most remarkable thing happened,' he said. 'Suddenly on Red Pike I came across a single set of studded running shoe prints frozen into the ice. I followed them and I realised that whoever this person was they were taking the perfect line. They were completely clear as it was such crisp conditions. I followed them across Scoat Fell and Pillar. On Kirk Fell they came beautifully in to the col, and they were like a guardian angel, but they disappeared just before Gable. That was very memorable.' He knew he had to make the best of the daylight and go as fast as he could, and that was working really well. When he got to Honister it was completely cut off to vehicles because of the snow and ice.

'I knew I was just about on or just behind a 24-hour schedule. I thought, I have to move as quickly as I could. I had a mountain marathon rucksack and a bumbag with me, and I left the rucksack in the porch of the hostel and put everything I needed in the bumbag.' It was a still, frozen night. 'I set off thinking that rucksack will make its way to Keswick somehow, or not. My nearest to an accident was bizarrely on the road coming towards Little Town. I went skidding on this amazingly long patch of ice. I got to the Moot Hall and there were two people there to meet me – Ralph Stephenson from Keswick, who had picked up my kit at Threlkeld, and Pete Parkin who used to manage the hostel at Longthwaite. Pete said 'interested in this?' and presented me with my rucksack, which I wasn't expecting to see ever again.' In that whole 24 hour period he had seen just one group of people, scouts who he met at Mickledore, and he never met another soul all day. 'It was a fantastic day, and to the best of my knowledge nobody has repeated it to this day. I couldn't have expected it to go better, and was one of the best days out ever.'

We then reminisced about some of the incidents on other people's rounds that occurred when Martin was supporting, some of them included in this book. First, I mentioned that Helene Diamantides, in her report on one of her rounds, said, 'I stood on Martin Stone's shoulders and then hoiked him up Broad Stand'. Furthermore, that she liked to stretch things as well, doing a solo round for instance. 'Absolutely! We were going out together at one point, and we had a falling out. I almost felt she may have done a solo/unsupported round to prove herself. She absolutely nailed it, and at the time, it was the fastest solo round ever. She may have come across as under-confident, but deep down she knew she could deliver.'

I asked Martin if Anne Stentiford lacked confidence, as she mentioned that Martin had set two schedules for her BGR and that he moved her to the faster one after the start. 'That is probably how it was,' he chuckles. 'I think she lacked experience then rather than confidence. It was clear to me that she could do a very fast Bob Graham Round. I devised a schedule based on the previous ladies' schedules. Because it was soon after the Paddy Buckley we decided that we would see how it went and decide on the day.'

I commented that Mark Hartell had said in reference to his fast round preparation that 'Billy's splits were available, probably from Martin Stone'. Martin agreed that he used to keep schedules, and that people used to send him them. 'I would use them to help people I was supporting. I think Mark Hartell set off thinking he could do it [*the record*]. I think it was just a few minutes per leg that he lost. He never really bonked or had anything that went wrong, it was just that the pace was crucifying.'

So, did Martin ever try for the Naylor 24 hour peaks record? 'I never thought I was good enough,' was the immediate reply. 'I didn't have the speed, which a lot of people thought of Mark McDermott too. I never, ever, considered doing it.' Martin then went on to shed some more light on Mark McDermott's 76-peak record round. 'After I had done three good efforts in 1986/7 I was amazed when Mark announced he was going to beat Joss' record. His training was just awesome. No-one believed he could do it, except him, his wife and later myself. After his 76 peaks success all the supporters were gathered for a celebration with some champagne we had bought and hidden in the car. Our team of 22 were all stood around and Mark suddenly said 'right, hands up those who thought I would do it', and only his wife Alison and I were able to raise our hands!'

'The 72-peak run by Joss was an absolute legend and Mark wasn't a well-known fell runner, so it wasn't clear to them how he could possibly do it. On the round he had trouble because he got quite hot during the day, and he was up against the schedule. I said "just get through till it cools down and you will be fine". When he got to Wasdale, with still three sections and some 9 hours to go, he said quietly to me "it's in the bag". How fantastic, to be able to say that. Incidentally, we met Chris Brasher a couple of days later and he wrote a great piece in *The Observer* about Mark McDermott setting such a great record.'

As we wound down, I asked Martin for his best advice for changeovers on a BGR. 'You have got to be a combine harvester. The two Marks were just brilliant at doing it. They wouldn't stop and you would have to be walking alongside them 'servicing' them.'

In conclusion, I asked Martin what his proudest achievement was. 'Perhaps the winter Bob Graham Round, because it was amazingly serious conditions. In terms of inspirational events it would be winning the Dragon's Back race. That was such an amazing journey. I have always said to people that you can't beat a good journey. Helene [*Diamantides*] and I always ran well together as a team. We enjoyed each other's company running in the mountains. Actually, I wasn't supposed to be doing it. I was going to try and break the Lakeland 2500ft record. She would probably not have achieved her potential with her original partner, as it would have been a steadier pace. I came back from the Alps very fit and it was evident from Day 1 that we were both going really well.'

In the course of the conversation we covered a wide range of BGR-related topics. Because of the involvement Martin Stone has had in many of the significant rounds, his comments filled out new dimensions in much of the BGR story narrated in this book. Listening back to the audio files as I transcribed them, I marvelled at both the range of his exploits and the fine art of his storytelling.

Chapter 12

Jim Mann

In 2013, Jim Mann smashed the winter best time, to post the fastest time of all – at least so far. He had attempted a winter Bob Graham Round in February. But after losing time in deep snow, he stopped, commenting: 'I was delighted – I knew there and then that I could do it and promised myself to go on the first day of the following winter with good conditions.' Mann stormed round in a new winter record, coming back in 18 hours and 18 minutes. Shortly afterwards he wrote a detailed report[1] on this spectacular performance, which is included here in edited form:

> Sunday the 1st of December had been on my calendar marked as 'Break Winter BG record' since February but it was always going to be weather dependent. As the date approached the 12-day forecast looked like there was a chance, and I started to taper. With things still looking OK, but not certain, one weekend beforehand I started checking for road and hill support. I desperately tried to get more than my normal four hours sleep, so I had a sleep bank built up. It was not easy, and maybe is not required, but it seems to help and psychologically makes a difference for me.
>
> The weather was a lot worse than forecast – it had looked like I might get still conditions with temperatures above zero

---

1 http://h18-orr.blogspot.co.uk/2013/12/jim-mann-winter-bob-graham-round-report.html

all the way and some mist, but in fact there was a strong breeze and drizzle which I find energy-sapping. I couldn't really delay the start, as I wanted light over the middle section and had to be at work early Monday morning, so we stuck to the 1am plan – eventually setting off at 1.03am. Jules Coleman was pacing and was great company. Skiddaw was windy but OK, and we had a couple of little navigation wobbles in very heavy mist on Blencathra.

My intention was to run straight through the change point, and I had chosen to have the change at the very bottom of the hill, so I could grab a paper cup of pasta and a coffee and consume them on the climb. It worked perfectly – I jogged right on through without breaking stride, only slowing to a power walk when the gradient increased. At that point I started eating the pasta.

Steve Birkinshaw supported me on leg 2. I could feel a small niggle in my right hamstring that had been troubling me since resuming track training a few months earlier, and I was drenched. Despite eating on the climb up Clough Head, we took three minutes out of the schedule and the mist and rain that was causing us some issues on leg 1 had not subsided. We could just about see the path/trod with our head torches. We had a couple of little wanders on the leg, going nearly to the top of Calfhow Crag, and starting down Striding Edge (thankfully not very far before we both realised). Then I got a really bad line up Fairfield. I take a direct line up the side from the tarn outflow, but you need to avoid the boulder scree to get a time saving. I didn't manage to avoid it at all though and dropped about three minutes there.

These tiny, but annoying, navigation errors kept cancelling out the hard work to get a few minutes up on the schedule. Now a rapidly tightening right hamstring was causing me to have a real low point, and I was questioning whether I could continue from Dunmail. I told Steve I was having a bad time, but he highlighted all the positives, and his pep talk was crucial to me getting my spirits back up.

I was now back in fighting mood and I think it showed as we moved into leg 3. We were after another 'rolling stop'. A clean dry base layer was handed to me and my wet hat and gloves were dumped on the verge. The fresh top was going on as I climbed Steel Fell. Carol Morgan, Mark Ruscoe and James Byrne were pacing, and quickly sorted the kit change and re-grouped with me on the way up. Pasta in, coffee in, and with lots of banter we were well on our way. Steel Fell was surprisingly easy after the battle I had just gone through on Seat Sandal – maybe, just maybe, things were turning? The pacers were relentlessly forcing me to eat and drink. When I didn't fancy any of my food on the way through the Langdales they starting trying to tempt me with whatever they had for themselves. Mark found the solution with Kendal mint cake – he had a whole bag of it which I proceeded to consume. I'm pretty sure he stopped eating it himself to ensure there was plenty for me as it was the only thing I was eating for a while. By the time we were at Harrison Stickle I was finding my stride, the day was starting to warm up a bit and my confidence was slowly increasing.

I had reason to be feeling better. The underfoot conditions were OK too for the time of year, although the rocks were wet and very slippery, but there was hardly any ice or snow except a few patches that could be avoided.

John Oldroyd had taken ice axe and crampons up to the col before Bowfell, as the previous weekend there was a good layer of ice and snow on the high fells. My poor pacers were still carrying microspikes with them at this point too. It was great to see John, and the flapjack and coffee he had brought were really nice. We then had the Scafell Pike ridge and then the decision on the route to Scafell. Despite being great conditions I was keen to drop to Foxes Tarn as I had lost 45 minutes on the traverse via Lord's Rake back in February.

The run down from Scafell to Wasdale has never been so easy. We were through on time and I knew I had it cracked. I really like leg 4, and leg 5 is short so can be ground out. At the first view of Wastwater I was aware that I was grinning ear to ear, I had finished the leg in better shape than I started it.

I was delighted when Bill Williamson said he would do leg 4 with me. He's great fun to run with, and as a bonus leg 4 is a bit of speciality of his – he knows all the best lines and on leg 4, more than any other, that can make a big difference. Again we went with a rolling change. Bill caught me up with another cup of pasta, and we then got stuck in to Yewbarrow. It hurt but we were on schedule and Bill was coaxing me along. Red Pike was a fight and I started to worry that I was going into another low (eating had become hard, with a bit of acid burn). However, on the way to Steeple I had a toilet stop and instantly started to feel better. From then on we started to wind it up and from Pillar to the end we were really motoring, or at least it felt like it. My legs felt great – I was going to do this.

Honister was strange. There were quite a few people about, but I had no idea who they were as it was now pitch black again. I just did the same as on all the other road crossings, running right on through letting my pacers switch and catch me with yet another cup of pasta. We just set to trundling round the last three summits – uneventful and for me pretty much on autopilot – just follow Andy Blackett and Helen Skelton and let them do all the work. Martin Stone had hot-footed it over from Dale Head to meet us again up on Robinson and take us down to Newlands church.

Helen tried to feed me and I had a couple of sweets and some more Kendal mint cake, but not a lot else as my stomach was really not good by then. I wasn't concerned as we were pretty close to home. At the church I stopped moving for the first time since leaving the Moot Hall to make a quick change into road shoes. We ran pretty steady but consistent all the way back into Keswick, to finish with a very satisfying time of 18:18.

We went to the Scafell Hotel for some dinner as in the past

they have let me use their toilets in the early hours of the morning before a BG attempt – that sort of service earns you custom. It was delicious but I couldn't eat it with my stomach so trashed, so took it home and had it for breakfast at 5.30am Monday morning, and it was still delicious.

This had been nearly four years in the making and I am really pleased that it came together. So many people have played a part in this, not just those that were there on the day. I wouldn't have even dreamed I could go that fast three years ago. It is deeply satisfying to push yourself to your mental, physical and emotional limits and emerge on the other side.

I had interviewed Jim Mann when writing It's a hill, and he had done some even more impressive endurance efforts since then. He was down in London for work reasons, and we agreed to fit in an interview. It turned out that he would be around on a Tuesday night, so I invited him to join my group of athletes at Allianz Park track for a session. We were doing a 6 x 1000m session, which is typical mid-winter fare for us. After being introduced by me to the squad as a 'fell runner of some note' he fitted in very well, gritting his teeth in the face of some dank weather, and being in the company of Barnet and District's finest track, road and cross country athletes. We repaired to the Three Hammers to dry out and talk about his winter BGR efforts.

I first wanted to establish how many BGRs he has done. 'Six attempts, of which three were successful,' he told me. 'I did my first one a year after I started running. On 17 October 2009 I did my first proper run after starting running again. On 30 September 2010 I did a BGR, with someone who I didn't know, which I would not recommend. He got in trouble on Bowfell and stopped, so we were about halfway. We were an hour and half down on 24-hour pace. I had always said I would stay with him.' When Jim knew he couldn't do it he was still quite comfortable himself, as he had been going quite steady. Having got that far Jim wanted to do it, so he set off like a rocket, and got round. 'On leg three we split the support, some to get him down off the hill, someone to get me round,' he said. 'I had support on the last leg. Leg 4 was crazy fast, 3 hours 43 minutes off the top of my head, which is about 20 minutes outside what Mark Hartell did. That got me back on time, and I did something like 22 hours 8 minutes. I had not done more than a half marathon at that time. It just seemed like a good idea.'

Jim Mann seems to know his BGR history and we discussed different people's splits. 'Billy Bland's leg 1 is ridiculous,' according to Mann. 'I have never got round at that pace, the fastest I have done it is 2 hours 25 minutes. So, you need to be on the top of Skiddaw in 55 minutes to do that, it is just too fast. I believe that Billy went off too fast. I don't think he ran an optimum round, and that is where the weakness is in Billy's round.'

I showed him a splits comparison, which included the four fastest clockwise rounds, plus Steve Birkinshaw's anti-clockwise round. 'You would expect Steve Birkinshaw's to be different because of difference in heights that way round,' explained Mann. 'Mark Palmer's time is under Billy's time later on, but he had gone off much slower.' I commented that Steve Birkinshaw had wondered whether that was a better way of doing it. 'No, that's wrong, it's too cautious,' came back Mann instantly. 'What you should be doing is what Stuart Bland did. I think at 2:30 for leg 1 you have got the right pace. If I was setting pace for someone to do the record they should do leg 1 in 2:30, then probably need to do something like Billy's 2:45 for leg 2, and it is then that you need to be down to 3:45, 3:17, and 1:45.' He then slipped in the view that Ricky Lightfoot is probably the person to do it.

I then put forward the view Billy Bland espouses that considering split times is actually counter-productive. 'I completely disagree', said Mann. He went on to explain that, 'Ricky doesn't work like that as far as I know. He is quite methodical and trains hard. His training has been methodical and has built up year by year. He runs that sort of distance, but Billy didn't really do ultra distances. I think Ricky can do it. He is young and he has got time.' When asked if anyone else was in the frame as far as he was concerned Mann replied, 'The guy who nearly got the 24-hour record recently, Adam Perry. He is absolutely phenomenal.'

Returning to Mann's own performances I asked what happened after his 22:08 round. His own assessment was that it was nothing spectacular. 'I was somehow empty after that, which is why I wanted the winter one,' he explained. 'I don't mean to sound arrogant, it just didn't fulfil me. The other five rounds have all been winter ones. I had three winter fails – one on 10 Dec 2010, and two more in Jan 2012 and Feb 2013.' He did a 20:39 round on 28 Feb 2011 and then a very fast one on 1 Dec 2013.

I asked Mann to talk me through those other rounds. 'The first time I tried to do a winter one it was blizzards and I failed. Ricky Lightfoot was having a go that same night, he went out an hour after me. He overtook me when I went the wrong way and tried to go down Sharp Edge. I didn't know the way and got caught in the blizzard. It was horrific. One of my pacer's eyes got frozen shut. He thought he had lost a contact lens but his eyelashes actually froze.' Then he came back and did 20 hours 39 minutes at the end of Feb 2011. 'I tried to go faster,' he said. 'The first time I got a niggle that got worse. The next failed attempt I got to Wasdale in 12 hours. It wasn't really a failed attempt, it was a conscious decision to stop. I couldn't break the record but was running under the time I had run before. It was at a great pace.' He knew he couldn't break it that day but it gave him confidence that he could another time.

I asked him what he did between February and December 2013 to give him that extra edge. 'Nothing really, it was all done,' he replied. 'I kept doing Skiddaw a lot. I hated Skiddaw, and it is 10% of your climb. It is now my best friend. You need to make friends with it if you want to go fast. I would come back from London and get a train to Lancaster rather than the

Northeast. The last train gets in to Lancaster at around 10pm, and you can be in Keswick by about 11pm, and on the top of Skiddaw by midnight. Back down to the car and back home by 2am.' He reckoned that he had done this 16 or so times in the year, every three weeks or so, and that it was a significant key to his success. It was prior to his February round as it gave him a great deal of confidence in winter. 'When you go up there in snow, gales and blizzards, it makes you 'fell hard',' he explained. 'That is something that I know Billy Bland talks about, 'fell hard' is what you get off that kind of training.'

Doing this surely couldn't have helped much navigationally, as it is too much of a simple path up Skiddaw. 'Don't you believe it,' he retorted. 'If the clag or snow is down you lose the path. It vanishes. Having the confidence to know where you are on that first one, of finding the gap off the fence coming off, it just builds confidence in the round. That is the hard bit of the navigation on leg 1. It is like leg 2, it is the easiest nav in the world in good conditions. In bad conditions it is the worst. It is the easiest place to screw up, and Skiddaw can be a bit like that too.' I suggested that anyone who has walked it in good weather wouldn't believe that. 'Once the snow is down and covers that path it is like a moonscape. When clag is down and you are on the rocky bit at the top you can wander off that path, I have done it loads of times. It gives you confidence to know you can get up there comfortably and that you are holding back.' His meticulous planning and preparation are shown further by his next comments. 'I think it was 67 minutes on my schedule. I know what time I have to be at the first gate, and at the second gate, and at the third gate, and at the top. You are correcting to the minute, and you don't go off too fast. You just know what you are doing. It is psychological as well as physical.'

Moving on, I questioned how much the conditions and way you come off Blencathra affect the outcome in winter. 'I wouldn't say it has the same impact,' he replied. 'You need to know every route off there. I have spent a lot of time on Blencathra, as it is the nearest hill in the Lakes to me. So if I nip over to the Lakes for a run I will often nip up Blencathra, or do leg 1.' He often dumps the car at Threlkeld and goes and does leg 1, often doing it at night, as it fits in with his work. 'I know that leg really well. I have used different routes on the rounds in winter. I used Doddick on the first fast winter one. Then I used my own version of Hall's Fell on the second one.' I queried what his own version was. 'It is a contour route. You drop down the side of it. You drop 100m vertical then contour so that you don't have to go down the slabs. If the conditions are right you can use it, but you don't know till you get up there.'

His target going out on 1 December was to be running on an 18:28 schedule, which was 15 minutes under what was reckoned to be the fastest winter time that had been set. 'Not a comfortable schedule, but I like leg 4 and always think I could pull some back there. I thought if I could get to Wasdale on schedule I could do it. I had done the right training.' But it didn't go evenly all the way. On Helvellyn he made a mistake coming off. At the end of leg 2 he had a bit of a low and didn't know whether he could do it, partly because he hadn't had enough sleep beforehand. I wondered how close he had come to not completing. 'Steve [*Birkinshaw*] just gave me a bit of a talking to, and I came out of it. I don't think you ever know [*how close*], because I got through it. It is really difficult to see. His technique was to threaten to set Helene [*Whitaker*] on me! What he said to me was to push all the positives. He said 'how are you going to tell Helene you were running on schedule, the weather was improving, everything was going perfectly, and you stopped'. I thought, shoot, I can't explain that, and every-thing is right. A lot of people have come out to help me. I have been trying to do this for a long time. I have spent the last seven hours setting all the conditions to do it, and I am going to let all those people down, because I don't feel good just now,' was how Jim put it. He then admitted that one of his pacers he had only met at the Moot Hall. Others were friends he knew well.

I asked him if he had ever thought of doing a solo winter round. 'Yes. Two weekends' time,' he chuckled. 'The weather can do what it wants, I am not going for a time. I am going for the experience. I want to do a mid-winter, I have missed mid-winter by trying to go fast. Solo is a big ask, and I think Martin Stone is the only one to have soloed so far. I will have a tracker on, but am not bothered whether it is recognised by the BG Club.' But he did ask that 'supporters' didn't release the track details until he was past Dunmail, just to reduce the pressure a little. (*He started the round, but it was dreadful and he was 'weathered off'.*)

He then told me a story about being a supporter on Steve Birkinshaw's Wainwrights round. 'There was a time when he got phone calls because people thought he was going the wrong way. Steve was having a kip on one of the tops, and I was trying to draw a picture on top of the fell by moving around with the tracker. I just needed about 6–7 minutes to get it done, but he woke up too soon.'

I pressed Mann about taking his obvious fitness to a super-fast BG round. 'I don't think I have got it in me, I am not sure I am fast enough.' I suggested that maybe doing a 15-hour time wouldn't satisfy him, to which he gave an interesting, but slightly contradictory reply. 'I would like to get in the top ten fastest rounds, I might do that. If I did a round much quicker than I think I can, then I would feel obligated to have a go at the record. But I don't think that I will do a very fast summer one, and even if I do I don't think I can then get near Billy's time to be totally honest. I don't think I am capable, and if you don't think it you won't do it. I would need to be able to run under all of Billy's leg times. I am also at the top of the age bracket. I am 37 now and I would need to do it in the next two or three years. With work like it is that might not happen. I suspect it is beyond me.'

As with all the interviewees, we discussed the ladies' and men's records, and who might tackle them. Jim gave this cautious response: 'I know someone who is going to have a go early next year for the ladies, and it isn't someone you know well. For the men's, Adam Perry has got to be in with a shot.' Then he gave a fascinating insight into both his competitive instincts and his respect for other athletes. 'Kilian Jornet – I am not sure he will do it. If he said he was going to do it I would be there to help. Anyone who is having a go I would want to be part of it. I would help anyone to do a fast winter round too. If they went faster I would try to go faster again.'

He then revealed that he tried to break the Paddy Buckley record twice in 2014, and didn't. He had deliberately kept it low key. What he said next showed both a certain vulnerability and a massive amount of self-confidence. 'The first time I got lost, very embarrassingly. The second time I got halfway in eight hours and stopped. The record is 17:46. It was stupid to stop, in hindsight. I was trying to take two hours off the record. I was trying for 16 hours, which I think is possible. I have spent a lot of time down there. I will run under the record next year, if no-one gets there before me. But I think it is a soft record. I may also do a winter round there. It is harder to get pacers there. The Ramsay is on my radar as well. The summer record there is vulnerable. I don't think it is that fast. I am not shy to say those records are both doable, whereas I think Billy's may be beyond me.'

Mann feels that being self-employed actually hinders rather than helps him, with regard to his endurance efforts, except for one crucial aspect. 'I work too many long hours and nearly all my training in winter is done with a head torch, off-road. Thus I am quite quick across mountains in the dark. I don't have any more difficulty going at the pace I need to go on a winter BG, for example, than I would on a full daylight.'

Doing the track session earlier with my athletes, Mann had been mid-pack. I wondered whether speed training like that, and conditioning, figure in his fell training. He went on to explain the balance of his training, which seems to have changed considerably since I last spoke to him about it. 'Yes. I do quite a lot of conditioning work, for strength,' he explained. 'Because it feels easy on the fells sometimes, I believe that if I get the speed work done I can run at pace for longer. Last year I spent a lot of time with Gateshead Harriers pushing down mile-paced type runs. I then didn't need the hills any more. I still believe in conditioning, and running for eight hours, but also running quicker over short stuff.'

We finished by talking about Mann's navigation technique, a theme I have explored in the various interviews for this book. In particular, I was interested to hear whether his navigation involved good local knowledge, maps, bearings, and/or GPS devices. 'I will expect to not need anything,' he replied. 'But I will have a map and compass. Certainly a compass on my bag strap so it is always accessible. If you are in thick mist it is the quickest way of reassuring yourself that what you are doing is right. I will carry a GPS and have no qualms about using it. My navigation is not the best, although it has got a lot better. Would I carry one on a solo attempt? Probably not, because of the weight. I might just take map and compass. The only reason that I carry a map, if I am totally honest, is because I feel I should. I would feel like an idiot if mountain rescue were involved and I wasn't carrying a map. The map will also show you routes off the fells if you get in trouble. I know the fells pretty well, I could take an escape route off almost any Lakeland fell and get to somewhere safe.'

Chapter 13

Impressions

The fastest runners don't have a monopoly on interesting responses to the challenge that the BGR provides. In this chapter we hear from some worthy completers who were not necessarily even thinking of challenging Billy Bland's time (although some were).

On 17 June 1973 **Stephen Poulton** narrowly failed to complete a solo clockwise round (with road support from his wife Shirley). He was a Flying Officer in the RAF and a member of Gloucestershire Mountaineering Club. He wrote a short report for *History and Records of Notable Fell Walks* and it has been edited down here to cover just the details that may be relevant to his not succeeding in becoming the first to complete a solo round. His report is interspersed with my own comments.

As an all-round mountaineer I tend to appreciate the challenge of the hills in a full sense, be it a particularly demanding climb or a tough walk. The BGR falls into the latter category and is a challenge not to be taken lightly. From the beginning I realised I may have to be obliged by circumstances to make a solo attempt and to this end maximised my planning. Knowledge of the route was achieved during a three-day reconnaissance in which the circuit was walked in its entirety.

The trek proved invaluable in many ways:

a) Carrying a pack of 20 lbs helped me to develop stamina for fast uphill ascent with a lightweight bag

b) I was able to check sections of the route that were completely unfamiliar to me and ascertain efficient routes between summits

c) Completing the route in three days with a pack was a feat in itself and gave me considerable confidence for I occasionally maintained the required 24 hour pace with this pack

d) I was able to determine a section that I thought suitable for the night section

e) A recent reconnaissance meant that the route was fresh in my mind

f) I could work out 'watering' points so that a minimum only need be carried

For the attempt I considered the weekend of 16/17 June to offer the best combination of maximum daylight and a full moon. The weather however can never be trusted and this remained the undetermined factor.

My preparations for the walk were fairly thorough:

a) A support car was arranged to meet me at all road crossings

b) A schedule of the route was prepared, giving me a schedule of distance, ascent height and expected times of arrival on summits, assuming a constant pace. This was based on Naismith's Rule using 3.75 mph plus 3,000 feet per hour ascent

c) I considered the ascent of Skiddaw and the Derwent fells would offer the least reduction in pace for a night section and thus decided on a 1.30am start

d) The early morning start had the effect of reducing the 24-hour day without sleep to just a long day

All went well over Skiddaw, and Poulton gained an hour on his schedule here. The pace was good to Threlkeld, a clear, warm and moonlit night giving him a time of 3 hours 36 minutes for leg one. He took a 20-minute break for breakfast and foot treatment, before heading across the section to Dunmail in 4 hours 6 minutes. He took another rest to take on soup, and honey biscuits, and to dress a small toe blister.

The day now warmed up and he was only just able to keep on schedule. He also developed what he called a 'repulsion' to the high energy foods he was carrying – Mars bars and glucose tablets. This, and the 16 miles and 6000 feet of ascent on leg three, taken with its rocky terrain, caused him to take 7 hours 9 minutes against his scheduled 6 hours 16 minutes. Having a 20 minute break still kept him ahead of schedule, but a painful right knee was causing concerns, and also a slowing down on the descents on the next leg.

Over Kirk Fell the clouds came in, bringing wind and rain. Compass navigation and thoughts of possible time loss now dominated. Soup at Honister was very welcome. Poulton left for Dale Head with extra clothing, a torch and a luminous compass. Hindscarth was located, with no help from the moon, and the fence followed to Robinson. A failing torch caused problems on the ridge to High Snab and time was lost on the minor crags. Poulton's report continues:

Upon arrival at Littletown and the cars at 1.30am I had 18 minutes to cover four miles – an impossible task. The road section was more than a chore. I clocked in at Keswick at 2.41am. I later discovered my watch had gained 5 minutes somewhere on route so that my arrival was at 2.36am. I console myself to the fact that I still could not have run the road section in 23 minutes.

The weather eventually proved to be my downfall, for I lost considerably more time to navigation than I had previously. Many would have considered it complete madness to have attempted the Derwent fells under the conditions that prevailed, especially solo. It is difficult to define what spurred me on – perhaps faith in my mountaincraft, perhaps a foolhardy desire not to give in.

It turned out that he had torn a knee ligament, but a couple of years later Poulton came back to the task, with his determination and fitness honed on long road runs in flat Lincolnshire. He was rewarded with success – a solo round in 23 hours 37 minutes. Modestly putting that achievement into perspective, Poulton is quoted as saying: 'No matter how much I valued my achievement, it was quite belittling to remember that whilst I was relaxing by a quiet bubbling mountain stream the following day Joss Naylor was pounding round the hills on a record attempt of 72 peaks.'[1]

On 28/29 May 1977 **Ken Ledward**[2] completed a clockwise round in 22 hours 57 minutes (including 1:55 rest). He was paced all the way by Joss Naylor, and helped by Chris Brasher. There was short report on the round in Rogerson's *Notable Walks* . . .

I was very unsure of the outcome, indeed at Dunmail Raise I was debating with myself whether I should continue. As things turned out I began to feel better with each peak gained until eventually I found myself really enjoying the 'trip'. Several times I thought of others who'd made a first attempt only to be hindered by bad weather. Torches were needed only for the descent of Hall's Fell, minimal clothing was required also.

This particular attempt was unavoidable as I had been telling fellow runners 'I'll do the Bob Graham when I'm exactly (?) 43, the same age as Bob'. This was the year, so I started early in case of failure! Joss told me to 'pick up your knees' going on to Great Calva. Very difficult when the b----- stuff is thigh high. I bet it wasn't that tall for Bob Graham!

Ledward also remarked on the way Joss paced him: 'He'd race ahead and he'd look at the views and he'd run back and then he'd start away again. So I was on my own for an awful long time!' Chris Brasher had camped out with an alarm set

1   *In quest of the ultimate*, Fred Rogerson, Alpine Journal 1976.
2   Perhaps unique in combining fell running and opera singing

for 5.20am to await Ledward and Naylor's arrival after they completed the Helvellyn range. He described in *The Observer,* in an article entitled *On the peaks of satisfaction,* his feelings about their leaving of Dunmail Raise:

> After a breakfast of bacon butties, hot sweet tea and some tinned pears which created an awful stink later, we were off up Steel Fell into the early morning sunlight. Now I knew why I had driven 250 miles through the night and slept under the stars. Here we are, three friends on the fells, the sun warming our backs as it burnt away the mist of the night, chattering about the distant views and the solitude, thinking of the tourists down in the valleys below sleepily stirring towards breakfast and we, up high, moving freely over the most beautiful land on earth.

Martin Stone was an innovator in many ways and has been involved in rounds many times over the years. He did an anti-clockwise round on 5/6 July 1978 in 22 hours 54 minutes, with 1:39 rest. He wrote a short report for *Notable Walks* . . .

> Prior to my attempt I spent a fortnight in the Lakes doing a recce of the Bob Graham in addition to various fell race routes and generally trying to attain some semblance of fitness. After a three day 'rest' period I felt that I was ready to make the attempt.
>
> I set off from Moot Hall at 8.00 in perfect weather conditions being paced by Frank Thomas. We jogged easily up Newlands Valley and encountered a little mist on the summit of Robinson. Honister was reached in 2 hrs 11 mins and it was then that I realised the full value of a well organised support group. After a short break we attacked Grey Knotts with an additional pacer, Chris Dodd. The correct line was found off Yewbarrow and a very fast descent was made to the campsite in 15 minutes. Having completed that section in 3 hrs 45 mins we were now 20 mins up on schedule.

After a welcome break of 30 minutes Frank, who was now pacing his third consecutive section, and I started the long ascent of Scafell which was completed in just under an hour. Meanwhile Sandra [*Wright*] had walked up to Mickledore where she gave me some assistance on the descent of Broad Stand.

A few minutes were lost on Broad Crag and Ill Crag due to the mist but good time was made towards Bowfell. It was at this stage that Frank realised that he had dropped the map on one of the previous summits. Fortunately we met some backpackers at the foot of Rossett Pike and they gave us one of theirs. Fast running to Steel Fell was followed by a good descent on grass to Dunmail Raise and another 30-minute break. At this stage Frank had completed his pacing and decided to join me as a contender and thus attempt his second round of the 42.

Chris Bland was to be our pacer for the last two sections. Dunmail was left at 20.30, an hour up on schedule, and good time was made as far as Dollywagon. By now it was almost dark, very cold and windy on the exposed ridges and the cloud base was at about 2,500 feet. We were now aiming for a rendezvous at Sticks Pass with Jon Broxap for hot drinks. We arrived there at 23.30 to find him installed in a large tent belonging to an American who had unwittingly pitched at just the right spot and now found himself part of the support for a Bob Graham attempt. After some tricky navigation in mist and low cloud Threlkeld was reached at 01.45.

We left Threlkeld after a 30-minute rest and the summit of Blencathra was attained within the hour. Slow progress (due mainly to tiredness) across Calva to Skiddaw was followed by a fast jog down to the Moot Hall. We arrived at 06.54 to a warm welcome from the support group, feeling tired but happy.

In 1987 **Mark McDermott** had done a standard BGR in 18 hours 14 minutes with Adrian Belton. Then in February he resolved to attempt the 24 hour peaks record. The following are some extracts from his own report, which appeared in the September 1988 issue of *The Fellrunner*, recording his feelings on the lead-in to the attempt. He called the article *Fat Man in Cuckoo Land*, a nice little in-joke that was prompted by reactions to his setting a fine new record.

February 1988, the usual round of curries and beer signalling another birthday, but this time it was my 29th and the mid-twenties I had been languishing in had come to an abrupt end. I decided it was time to do something while I still can, but what?

I vaguely remembered a conversation with Martin Stone about the Lakeland 24 Hour Record; the record set by Joss Naylor in 1975 consisted of 72 peaks involving 105 miles and 37,000 feet of climb. I did some rough calculations and realised this was an equivalent pace to running the Bob Graham Round in 17 hours. The previous summer I had struggled round in just over 18 hours, so I figured that if I could get fit I would be able to run a Bob Graham at that pace, but would I be able to keep going for the extra time, and how could I cope in the dark?

At the next training night, after a few pints, I boldly announced my intentions – much to everyone's amusement. But the commitment had been made and I started to train. The house became littered with scribbled notes and maps and gradually a list of peaks and a rough schedule took shape. I decided to adopt 75 peaks suggested by Fred Rogerson (and attempted by several people over the years) to avoid any controversy (!).

My weekends were spent checking the route and training, refining the times on the schedule. I even resorted to spending a foul night running the proposed night section to see how I coped. The real night section was infinitely more pleasant than the (sic) 'dry run'! Eventually I could delay no longer and started asking people if they would be willing to act as pacers. Why did everybody volunteer for the later sections? After some serious arm twisting I had enough gullible people and, after an anxious week watching the weather, the day arrived dry and warm.

Mark's report continues with an amusing description of the round, listing many of the support team on the day. Covering the north-western fells section he was 'preoccupied with the question of how many of my scheduled peaks I would have time for and struggled terribly with the mental arithmetic – I'll have to get a portable PC for next time'. He completed the 76 chosen peaks, adding four to Joss's total, coming back in to Braithwaite at 4.26am, 23 hours 26 minutes after setting out from there.[1] Although his standard BGR was merely a good time, this was something special, and I wanted to hear him tell the fuller story.

My interview with Mark McDermott was set to happen on my way up to the Lakes for a weekend. As he works in Wythenshawe he suggested an easy place to meet would be a pub near Manchester Airport. As the Friday after-work crowd assembled we found a quiet-ish corner and Mark ran through some of his exploits on the fells. It was fascinating not just to hear these stories, but also to talk to someone who had summited Everest. Some of his stories about the chaos of 'organised' Everest expeditions could fill another book (now there's an idea). An unassuming guy, he has some impressive achievements, and has also helped, encouraged, trained with and competed with some of the other characters in this book. At the end of the Everest story we wound up and I carried on north, reflecting that he deserved more respect from his peers than he has sometimes been given in the past.

1   Fred Rogerson said of Mark McDermott's scientifically-planned record of 76 Peaks in 1988: "Never under-estimate a man's determination. Here was an 'unknown' whose schedule and actual times never varied by more than two minutes over 24 hours."

Mark McDermott got interested in outdoor sports when he was in the Scouts. He grew up in Leyland (Lancashire) and used to go up to the Lakes 'just because it was a nice place to go'. He started doing things like walking the Three Peaks of Yorkshire. 'I went on a week's organised climbing holiday in Wales, and ended up walking the Welsh 3000s on my day off, when I was 16 or so', he said. 'I was always keen on doing hard walks. I used to read Harry Griffin's books, and got interested in the Lake District 3000s, which I think he had written about.' He got it into his head that he wanted to have a go, so decided he needed to toughen himself up a bit. 'I can remember I went out for a training run once when I was 16 or 17. I had not done any serious running before. I did an 18-mile run over rough ground. A bit of a shock from 0 to 18! Running back my head was spinning.' His brother was interested in orienteering, and he used to tag along with him. They ended up doing a Karrimor in the mid-1970s.

McDermott wasn't a fell runner in those days, but says that he gradually drifted into it. 'I didn't really run, I was more into climbing as a teenager,' he noted. He then expanded on his early days. 'I went to Oxford and then stayed on to do a DPhil. I didn't really compete at University, except in inter-college cross-countries, which I found I was reasonably good at. The marathon thing took off in the early 1980s and I did a couple of Abingdon marathons, finishing in 2:50 and then in 2:36. Then I moved to the Lakes and worked for K Shoes in Kendal. I realised it wasn't the best career choice, so I got a job with Shell, and have been working in IT ever since, now as a freelancer for nearly 20 years. It gave me the freedom to go off and do the other things I have done. I have always been keen on skiing since I discovered it in my late 20s. I also climbed to E1 standard as well, which is nothing by today's standards.'

Mark remembers speaking to his elder brother on the phone when he was at Oxford and he was doing the Blisco Dash, and Mark thought he would enjoy that. 'I followed him into it really. I found that the longer the event the better I seemed to do.' I asked Mark if the 18:14 with Adrian Belton was the only standard BG round he had done. 'No, I had done one before that, just tagging along with Dave Hall and Geoff Reade,' he replied. 'I had ambitions of doing some fast rounds, but they remained just ambitions. I once set off to do a fast Paddy Buckley, but the heat got to me. I did the 76 peaks record in 1988, and after it I was keen to have a go at breaking the record for the fastest BGR or something equivalent. I realised I was still recovering from the 24 hour run in 1988, and in 1989 pretty much every weekend I was in Wales with Adrian Belton, and my girlfriend Alison Wright, training and recceing on the route of the Paddy Buckley [PBR].' After spending so much time in the Lakes the previous year, they were having some variety by going to Wales. Mark takes up the story from there:

> People reckon a PBR is about an hour slower than a BGR, so I had ideas of trying to do it in sub 15 hours – and I think I had run round all the sections at that sort of pace. Unfortunately, I turned my ankle in June 1989 so that ruled it out that year. I think I had a go in 1990, but I had difficulty finding enough pacers to make a proper attempt. I think the patience of quite a few pacers had been worn thin by the various rounds Adrian Belton and others kept doing! So I decided to go for minimal support and a 16-hour schedule, but unfortunately it was quite a hot day and the heat got to me by Rydd Dhu.
>
> I was also keen to have a go at Adrian's Ramsay record, but again never quite contrived to have the fitness, the weather and the pacers available at the same time. I can recall one weekend with Adrian, where he was having a go at a Munros record and Andrew Addis had driven us up to Fort William on Friday evening. We set off at either 11pm or midnight from Glen Nevis, and I was meant to be navigating and pacing for Adrian along the Mamores in the wind and rain, down to a tent at Loch Eilde Mor where he had fresh pacers. I had this cunning plan to continue on solo unsupported up Beinn na Lap and the rest of the Ramsay route, on a sub-18 hour

schedule, but when we got down to the tent I'd had enough and I made a beeline for Corrour railway station.

I finally contrived to have a go at a fast BGR late in 1992, after coming back from a fantastic Alpine holiday where we'd made fast ascents of some easy 4,000m peaks and I'd also had a good run at the La Plagne 6000D where I'd finished 10 minutes behind the then World Mountain Running Champion in a five-hour race. Unfortunately, I was short of pacers again. The rain and wind on the tent had made it hard to sleep the night before, and conditions weren't great when I/we set off. I went OK along to Fairfield but I knew my body well enough to know it was all over, as I hadn't been taking in food and drink continuously.

It was galling (having been so short of pacers) to come down to Dunmail Raise and see one or two cars of very fit Lakes fell runners who had apparently come along to keep an eye on my attempt – word had travelled. At any rate, once they realised I had packed in they drove away.

Alison Wright had already been involved with the BGR – being the youngest lady [still?], in 1990 she attempted to break Helene's record (which I think was 19:11), and achieved a time of 19:18, and was making an attempt on Anne's record on the same day as my attempt – I believe she too retired after Esk Pike owing to indifferent weather conditions.

I suggested that Mark's 18:14 BGR in 1987 was actually a pointer to bigger things to come. 'I suppose so,' he mused. 'On the round there were four of us. Rex [Stickland] got left behind first, and then Andrew [Addis] did too. It sounds terrible really abandoning our mates like that! Adrian and I went on and finished, but we weren't trying for anything except a fast-ish time. It was late in the season and not brilliant weather. I thought if I sharpened up I could knock a couple of hours off. It set me thinking by looking at the numbers that I could maybe have a go at the 24-hour record.'

I pointed out that Mark Hartell had told me that Mark

McDermott trained hard and that he had (semi seriously) said that he had 'followed him' to his own detriment. 'Mark and I used to work together at one point, and we became close friends,' McDermott said. 'I flew back from Oman on the Friday and went up on the Saturday to help him [*on his big round*], with some of the others. Shortly after that we were flying out to the States to do the Hardrock Hundred Miler.'

After returning from Oman, McDermott lost interest in fell running for a while, not least because he had injured his knee skiing, which didn't recover for a year or two. 'I liked trail running, almost more than fell running. I like the concept of going from A to B, traversing through the landscapes. I remember being fascinated by Mike Cudahy's book about his long runs.'

Mark McDermott tagged along with Adrian Belton and Andrew Addis, when they set a record for the South Wales Traverse in 1988. 'We did it on a May Bank Holiday weekend, and I went along as I thought it would be a good training run,' he said. 'They went on to attempt the other rounds later in the year but I gave those a miss as I was focussed on the 24 hour Peaks record.'

I was interested in Mark's thoughts on why Billy Bland's record still stands. 'Not many have tried it except Mark Hartell (and myself) – I don't know if it is a fair observation, but perhaps people are frightened of having a go in case they are not up to the mark.'

I then asked Mark to expand on why he thought he could take on Joss Naylor's 72 peaks record. 'Martin Stone, as ever, had a schedule for it,' he noted, before explaining where one of the advantages he had lay. 'Looking at Joss's times I realised he had run more quickly over the ground than I would wish to, but had spent a fair amount of time at road crossings eating and drinking – my strategy was to keep moving and take on food and drink while climbing the big ascents. I've always been good at that, and it's something that is less important for a 3–4 hour fell race than it is for a longer 'ultra' event. Mark [*Hartell*] and I became involved in supporting one of Steve Birkinshaw's attempts at the 24 hour peaks record. He seemed to be struggling to take on board much food while on the move. I can recall climbing up Steel Fell and Pike o'Blisco trying to coax him to eat food as we had done.'

Mark McDermott said he had done most long classic fell races, and I wondered which he thought may have been his best result. He thought for a while, before replying. 'I was not particularly satisfied with any of the results. I always wanted to get under four hours for the Wasdale race, but never quite managed it.' He said he thought that I was probably asking the wrong question. 'I used to enjoy competing in the long races, but as mentioned I was better at longer events – mountain marathons etc.'

So, I asked him what he saw as his greatest endurance running achievement. 'Probably the 76 peaks record,' he suggested. 'When I moved up to the Lakes from Oxford, I was living about 12 miles from Kendal and used to run to and from work on alternate days. I remember doing the Tour of Pendle in 1984 and finishing fourth – ahead of some respectable runners – and Martin Stone was joking with me afterwards that he had thought 'who the hell is Mark McDermott'. I then got to know him really well. I went up a notch in fitness really. Martin and I did a few events together, such as the Scottish Islands/Peaks race for instance.'

We ended by talking of mountain marathons. I asked Mark if he ever won an Elite Karrimor, and he replied brightly. 'Yes, Adrian Belton and I won one year. My navigation used to be pretty good.' So, finally, does Mark have any ambitions still? 'I have just had a hip replacement – but I had the sports model,' he chuckled. 'I'd like to get back to skiing and have a jog with my lad. Just getting back on the hills really.'

I left wishing all the best to a man who had enthralled me for over an hour, reliving some fantastic achievements which include the Mt Kinabalu race, the Hardrock, Wasatch and Western States races in America, and the Breithorn Sky Race in the Alps, plus several Himalayan and South American mountain adventures.

In his book *Running High* **Hugh Symonds** tells the story of completing 'the first continuous traverse of the 303 mountains of Britain and Ireland' in 1990. He had previously won the Ben Nevis race in 1985, and the Three Peaks in 1984, 1985 and 1987. This was all on the back of an impressive training regime while a maths teacher at Sedbergh School. For years Symonds had meant to have a go at a Bob Graham Round, but had never got round to it. He finally agreed to do it with another teacher from the school, Mark Higginbottom who was in his last week at Sedbergh, before moving to Scotland to work at Strathallan School. This short report appeared in the school's *Sedberghian Magazine*, and shows the different, extra-curricular life some teachers lead:

On the penultimate weekend of the summer term we left the Moot Hall at 4.47am on Sunday morning. Thick cloud and heavy mist covered the Northern peaks, slowing the pace as careful navigation was called for in this wild and empty space. Then as we descended the rocky ridge of Hall's Fell, the sweeping fog thinned in shafts of sunlight, giving us a rare glimpse of our own two shadows in a rainbow halo – a Brocken Spectre – this freezing our pace for 20 seconds of visionary delight. At Threlkeld we enjoyed a restful 15 minutes breakfast in warm sunshine as Pauline and Jackie delivered us deck chairs, bananas and clean socks.

As we climbed the Dodds, the day now intensified in heat, and the sky revealed a clear blue which remained with us till dusk on Great Gable. Through the early afternoon the heat had given us insatiable thirsts as we slowed the pace in crossing the highest peaks from Dunmail to Wasdale. The intention had been to return to Keswick within daylight hours and to get a few hours' sleep before maths and classics lessons on Monday morning. The heat, however, had got the better of us and the run had slowed to a walk over the Western fells around Pillar.

Night had fallen before Honister and dawn broke just south of Keswick. We touched the Moot Hall at 3.30am, having completed the round in 22 hours 43 minutes. We rushed back to Sedbergh in time for two hours sleep before lessons.

More was to come from other runners. *The Fellrunner* magazine had a note in Martin Stone's column saying that in June 1991 **Colin Donnelly** did a solo, unsupported Bob Graham Round. This intrigued me for two reasons. First, I had seen no other reference to this round. Secondly, Colin Donnelly has a hugely impressive record of endurance achievements, often achieved either solo or lightly equipped and/or unsupported. I set about trying to find out more about this feat. Being solo and unsupported it would not be 'counted' as a round by the Bob Graham Club, who insist on evidence from supporters.[1] There are obviously quite a few who just do the round for the challenge it represents, and have no intention of joining such a club. As noted, solo rounds would not qualify for membership, and checking the membership list on the website duly shows no entry for Colin Donnelly.

Colin Donnelly is one of a small band of fell runners who have achieved exceptional performances over an impressive number of years. During his early career he set a new record for the Bob Baxter Round on the Isle of Man – 11 hours 34 minutes in 1982. He also set fast times for other rounds such as the Grey Corries 12 3000-footers and the 16 Mamores 3000-footers, which have never achieved the same status as other major rounds. In 1988 Donnelly set the record of 4 hours 19 minutes for the Welsh 3000s Challenge, which still stands. He was British Fell Champion in 1987, 1988 and 1989, whilst competing for Eryri Harriers. Nearly three decades on he was still running well enough to win the Two Breweries Hill Race in 2013, and come second in the Welsh 1000m Race in 2014 – both times as an over-50 veteran runner.

1   The Bob Graham Club has the very rigid statement on its website: 'Applicants must register with the Membership Secretary before an attempt and must be accompanied at every summit for verification purposes'.

Through a contact on the FRA forum I managed to get to speak to Colin about his BGR achievement. In fact, he phoned me out of the blue one day, as he had been passed my contact details by a forumite. Colin told me he was working in Wales at the time, and had already done a Paddy Buckley Round in around 23½ hours, and also a Charlie Ramsay Round. He said he just wanted a good day in the hills when he did the BGR. He didn't know some of the Bob Graham route especially well, which showed at times. He claims his navigation technique was just to have an instinctive idea of where he was going.

In the ensuing discussion I complimented him on running so well as a Veteran, which prompted Donnelly to make two points about Billy Bland, whom Donnelly had been quoted as saying (in a couple of *Fellrunner* interviews) was someone he hugely admired. He once asked Billy what he was doing now that he was 40, only to get the reply 'just playing golf'. That was hardly the case though, as Billy Bland was still winning races outright as a Vet. For instance, in 1988 Billy won the Wasdale race from a class field as a Vet, with that year's British Fell Champion (Colin Donnelly!) a distant third. However, Donnelly reckoned that eventually Billy couldn't get adjusted to NOT being at the very top. He then laid out Billy's take on this, which was: 'First is first, second is nowhere'.

The following summary report is from Colin's own diary, which he kindly copied for me to use here. Before describing his solo round he records his Friday morning's work at the hospital, where he was working on cardiac arrest procedures. He then went for a five mile run at lunchtime, using that time to marshal his thoughts, as he described it, towards 'the idea of going to the Lakes tonight to do this Bob Graham Round.' He needed to 'get it out of his system', as he had put it to his partner earlier. He decided to go for it, had some tea and carbo-loaded with macaroni. Despite feeling tired he set off on the four-hour drive to Keswick. Going over Dunmail Raise he hid two tins of fruit and one of evaporated milk under some stones. He packed his sac, had some more tea, changed and was off at 42 minutes after midnight, hardly being noticed by the late night revellers as he left Moot Hall. He gives a fascinating account of the round in his training diary (which is transcribed in the shorthand it was written in, as I think it gives a real idea of how things went for him, and his feelings).

After 100m made my first mistake, taking the Borrowdale Rd & losing couple mins! Soon discovered the head-torch not so effective – had to keep propping up the falling head-piece with one hand. Careful nav needed to negotiate the wee lanes to the bottom of Robinson by High Snab farm. That took 50 minutes. Up the valley for a bit before angling up the screes to ridge. Good views to lighted towns to coast. By time I got to Dale Head it was light enough to see what's doing (2.58am). A cool (not cold) night – running in cycling jersey. Had worn cag for Newlands Valley lanes – and got too hot!

Had a crap at Honister and head torch into sac. Went to YH for water but it was locked. Slogged up Grey Knotts and on to Great Gable. Took some looking around to find the gully off Kirk Fell. No drinks so far – no burns had been crossed. The hills are very dry. Eating enough since Honister. Strange thing am producing so much urine.

Yewbarrow (via Stirrup Crag). Managed to find a scree-descending path. Then a spring!

Mixed some Staminade. Had 9 mins at Wasdale, removed tights. 65 min slog to gain summit of Scafell. Descended via Lord's Rake – dangerous at top. Crumbly. Ill Crag, Broad Crag, Great End. About 9am. Surprising to see walkers (and some runners) up & around here. Esk Pike. I'd been going 9¾ hrs. Walking uphill, shuffling flat and downhill. Came off Bowfell by a silly route – rough and rocky. Up and down climbers' traverse. Bowfell a brilliant viewpoint – esp for Scafells. Rossett Pike [took] what I think is a bob-graham path taking me most of way up Pike of Stickle. A runner seen on Bowfell is taking the same direction as me. After slogging up Harrison Stickle (felt rough – going through a rough patch) he waited for me at the top. He was looking over a BG section. Told him I was actually soloing it. He asked if he could jog along as far as Dunmail. Although it's officially solo I couldn't see harm in this, nor wanted to offend him. Yes. Helped the section pass fast. 12:42 to Dunmail.

The early morning's sunny weather has been replaced by cloud and a strengthening SW wind. Scoffed my grub which filled a hole. 16 mins rest. Seat Sandal was 39 mins pure slog for 500m. 1st of 3 big climbs, Fairfield and Dollywagon the next ones. What impressed me most about Fairfield was its huge immense bulk. Water bottle filled with acidic water of Grisedale Tarn. Dollywagon (good steeple-ish summit), Nethermost (boring), Helvellyn & Little Man (boring), Whiteside. Rain thickening now. Consciously speeded up a bit as if to get away from it! Raise, Stybarrow, Watson's. Put on extra top (cag already on since Little Man) & leggings. Strong winds, lots of rain. Great Dodd, Clough Head.

By Threlkeld the weather had improved enough to remove cag, top & leggings – just cycle jersey. Soon had to put cag back on when weather closed in on way up Hall's Fell to ridge. Had plenty of time in hand. This section [usually] 3½–4½ hrs so hoping I could maybe break 22 hrs. Mungrisdale Common free of mist. Phew! Could see Gt Calva. Had some tinned fish halfway there and refilled water bottle. Calva never-ending heather slog. Here to Skiddaw took 70 mins. Atrocious weather on top. Mist, shrieking winds, heavy rain. Took me 73 mins of shuffling descent. Out of mist but didn't put head torch on – wouldn't have got me going much faster. 22:32 to Moot Hall.

Colin Donnelly also completed the Scottish 4000s and the South Wales 2000ft challenges. He described these to me as real challenges, commenting that, 'I never knew whether I'd succeed with these big rounds (one reason for not bothering with a recce was so it felt unexplored).' You have got to admire the approach Colin has. He is also such a natural runner. I still marvel at his speed of movement, over Crib Goch for instance, in the video of his Welsh 3000s record.[1]

In Martin Stone's *Fellrunner* column in October 2003 there was a comment that not many solo/unsupported rounds take place. He noted this one by **Rob Blyth,** however: 'I completed a solo/unsupported BG on 9/10 August in 23:34. I was on a 22-hour schedule but got confused in the clag at Steeple and when I saw it in a patch of sunlight from Gable I wasn't sure any more if I had been to Steeple or the promontory off Mirk Cove, which also has a cairn (tired and confused state of mind). I decided I had to go back to be sure, so I did that and that put me back to a 23-hour schedule, which once I knew by Dale Head that I'd be over 23 and under 24 I just relaxed and didn't run much on the road to save my legs. I really enjoyed it, especially the night section alone. I hadn't reccied anything after Scafell Pike and this certainly cost me a lot of time. Still one to do again now I know it.'

Steve Birkinshaw had first attempted the Bob Graham Round in the 1990s, but had to give up with a sore knee just over halfway round a clockwise attempt. In 2005 he tried it in the other direction, aiming for a fast time of around 18 hours. He set off with Morgan Donnelly and with enough supporters so they could split up if need be. He was keen on doing it anticlockwise as he wanted to get the road section and then the rocky section over as soon as possible. This is his report:

The weather forecast all week had not looked great but with all our supporters assembled we decided to go for it. As we drove to Keswick for a 6am start the heavens opened and we wondered whether it was a good idea. But we could not back out then, so off we set for a leisurely five mile run down the road to the Newlands Valley with our first pacer John Deegan. The first three hills flew by and we reached Honister Pass 10 minutes up on schedule, to find our superb support crew of

1   https://vimeo.com/79447455

Jon and Joel Bardgett. The weather was getting even worse and we were joined by Nic Davies and Dave Armstrong who were both looking very cold. The next few summits went well but as we were coming off Great Gable I was going at my own speed down the wet greasy rocks, and about half way down I looked back and the others had vanished. I waited a short while but was getting cold but there was still no sign. I did not really know what to do as there are a variety of different routes down and they could easily have passed me without me seeing. I knew this section really well and the others were expecting to follow me, but I knew they had a map and Nic Davies knew the route a bit. So I carried on slowly down to the col and up Kirk Fell. There was still no sign of the others by the time I had reached Kirk Fell and by then I had decided to carry on and probably finish the section to Wasdale by myself. This meant no food or drink for two hours.

By the time I reached Red Pike I was no longer thinking clearly and I did not think of asking some Bob Graham Round people going the other way (whom I knew) for some food. I reached Wasdale 25 minutes up on schedule feeling a bit wobbly. Tim Wylie joined me on the next section and my wife Emma fed me as we started the long drag up to Scafell. Emma went back down after 20 minutes and I started struggling up the second half of this climb, but the weather suddenly cleared and it stayed almost perfect from then on. Emma's dad had put a rope down Broad Stand for us to take the shortest route to Scafell Pike. We found the rope but missed Emma's dad. It was great to see lots of familiar faces doing the Old County Tops race on the next section. There were also lots of people who had come up to see us around the Langdale Pikes and the section to Dunmail seemed to fly by.

I was dreading the next section with three big climbs before you reach the main Helvellyn ridge. Sure enough I really struggled up Seat Sandal, but with the encouragement of Brendan Bolland and Steve Walker on this leg I made reasonable progress. Up Fairfield and then Dollywagon Pike the trekking poles seemed to help climbing on the nice stony tracks. Then it was mainly downhill with the light wind behind all the way to Threlkeld. I felt really good and was running strongly, especially downhill. However, I knew there were three big climbs to come and I was worried about them. After a bit of a rest in Threlkeld, the first climb up Blencathra did not seem too bad and I had a nice chat with my pacer Charlie Stead up this section.

I enjoyed the long run down but struggled up Great Calva. It was the last climb up Skiddaw where I completely blew out. It was one of those times when however hard you try you cannot seem to make any progress up the hill. But with the weather turning horrible and becoming dark I carried on. I knew it was all downhill from the summit of Skiddaw and I might make it back to Keswick in time for last orders. Eventually we reached the summit cairn and we had a cold run down into Keswick to finish at the Moot Hall in 17 hours 9 minutes. I had missed last orders, but all I could do is manage a small sip of the bottle given to me. Morgan finished just 15 minutes behind having been catching me up ever since Wasdale.

The evidence of Birkinshaw's problems in the latter stages is there for all to see in his split times. The following table gives his leg splits, and for comparison some of the early anti-clockwise completers from the 1960s and 1970s (when anti-clockwise was much more prevalent).

Leg	A Heaton 1960	D Talbot 1971	P Walkington 1971	M Meath 1971	K Brooks 1972	S Birkinshaw 2005
1	2:30	2:29	2:29	**2:14**	2:15	1:47
2	4:30	4:02	**3:51**	4:30	4:19	3:05
3	6:35	6:23	**5:54**	6:30	6:37	4:46
4	5:00	5:03	**4:53**	5:50	6:04	3:41
5	3:43	4:20	**3:36**	3:50	4:28	3:48
TOT.	22:18	22:17	20:43	22:44	23:43	17:09

NB: all with rests added in to the time for leg prior to the break. Bold entries are fastest anti-clockwise leg times from the early rounds (ie BEFORE Steve Birkinshaw)

The difference in minutes between Steve Birkinshaw's leg times and the **fastest** leg from the 1970s (in minutes) for each leg is as follows: 27, 46, 68, 72, and -12. The conclusion is that either Pete Walkington had a very good finish (but he was only 7 minutes faster than next best split) OR Steve Birkinshaw had a poor finish, as despite being 3 hours 34 minutes faster than the next fastest he was slower than two of the contenders who were going much slower overall.

Steve Birkinshaw went on to set a new time for the 'Wainwrights Round',[1] taking out one of Joss Naylor's long-standing records in the process. I wanted to know more about this obviously hugely talented endurance athlete.

As I made my way down the farm track to Steve Birkinshaw's remote house in the Northern Lakes I had the thought that here was another amazing fell endurance athlete living in real close proximity to fell running legends Kenny and Pauline Stuart. They are fortunate to have the arena in which they perform right outside their respective doors/windows. I was there to also talk about Steve's recent Wainwrights effort, as I was interviewing him on stage shortly about this amazing achievement at the Buxton Adventure Festival. We then went on to talk through his own Bob Graham Rounds. I was really pleased that Steve came to the paperback launch of 'It's a hill, get over it' later that day, as in fact did Kenny and Pauline Stuart. It says something about fell running that such luminaries of the sport could just be part of the crowd at such an event and chat freely and modestly with fell(ow) enthusiasts.

Sitting in his back garden, Steve Birkinshaw and I agreed the points of interest for the Buxton Adventure Festival gig, and shared some laughs about hill incidents, then got down to

---

1 The round consists of all the 214 Wainwright summits in the Lake District, which Steve Birkinshaw covered in one continuous run lasting 6 days 12 hrs 58 mins.

looking back at Steve's Bob Graham Round, which is still the sixth fastest.

From somewhere I got the idea that Steve's BGR in 2005 was really just a lead-in to the Lowe Alpine Mountain Marathon (LAMM) that year. But Steve said this was not really the case, although it had been reported as that. Really it was just to see how fast he could go. 'Obviously I was getting very fit,' he said. 'I don't remember saying it was a lead in to the LAMM. Morgan [*Donnelly*] and I did do the LAMM, and we won it. But I remember being a little tired still, so this may have not been ideal preparation.' He was doing it anti-clockwise for two reasons. He didn't want to do the road at the end, and he wanted to get the rough stuff done on early, by which he means up to Rossett Pike really. 'I know there are bad things like the big climbs towards the end,' Steve explained. 'There is an advantage to be going *up* Hall's Ridge. Because I was navigating myself I didn't have to worry about anyone else, and I chose whichever route I wanted to go on. Every leg I had someone with me, carrying stuff, but I was navigating all the way.'

This led to some discussion about why he had a 6am start. 'It is fine if you are going anti-clockwise at 18 hours pace,' he thought. 'It was dark coming off Skiddaw, but it is the tourist path. Doing it that way you can get a full night's sleep beforehand. In many ways doing it in 18 hours is easier than 24 hours.' I wondered what his thoughts were on Broad Stand, knowing it would have to be down-climbed if using that route on an anti-clockwise round. 'Yes, I went down it,' Steve confirmed, although Morgan Donnelly was 15 minutes behind, and he went round via Foxes Tarn. 'My father-in-law had a rope on it. Going down is easy, the rope is just a help. It was a reasonably dry day. On one of 24hr record attempts I went up it and I completely lost it as it was pouring with water. I got really scared on it.' Luckily he had a good climber with him who helped him over it.

Considering that this was fairly early in Steve's career it begs the question whether that represents his optimum performance for the BGR challenge. 'No, I reckon a perfect run for me would be about 15 hours,' was his answer. 'That was the first really long effort I had done. Things like getting the food wrong, and only having one support person per leg, which was fine, but two would allow more food for instance.' Noting that his food strategy was perhaps not perfect, as it consisted of 'bits and pieces all round', he said that he couldn't remember exactly what he had eaten. 'The food went down OK, I wasn't sick or anything,' he said. 'I probably just didn't eat enough. By the time I got to going up Hall's Fell I was probably suffering from lack of food. That took me a lot longer than normal, probably an hour rather than the expected 40 minutes.' He was well prepared, having reccied it all, and knew it pretty well. He had not done a huge number of long days beforehand, though he had done some long fell races. One weekend he had done a half BGR on Saturday, rested Sunday and did the other half on the Monday.

With his undoubted endurance I suggested that making it harder for himself, by doing a solo and/or winter round, must have crossed his mind. 'I keep thinking about that, and then think phew,' he laughed. 'They are possible future activities. A solo winter round by myself maybe. Martin Stone did that. It is a hard mental challenge. I did the Ramsay round by myself and had some really low times during the night – and that was in summer. The advantage is that you can pick a nice day and just do it.'

We talked about Billy Bland's time, which some put way up on an unreachable pedestal. 'I agree with Billy about it not sitting on a pedestal, I am one of the few people who say the same as him,' he commented. 'His Wasdale race time I can never get close to, but the BGR I could get within an hour I reckon.' Steve commented that there are only a few people who have been good long distance fell runners who have had a go at it and done well. 'I am sure there are plenty of other people who could do 15 hours or so. Ricky Lightfoot is good enough, he would be ideal. If he got a perfect day, because that makes such a difference.' Steve concluded that with Ricky living in the Lakes he should know it really well, and that if he is interested he is a very likely candidate.

Responding to Billy Bland's assertion that challengers should 'just do best they can – don't be chasing a schedule', Steve Birkinshaw commented that, 'They do say in any race you shouldn't focus on other people but on yourself and what you can do.' Mark Palmer had a very good second half on his sub-15 hrs round in 2011, and Steve (who was a pacer for him) revealed that he had analysed the round with Mark after he finished. 'His spreadsheet times are not right,' said Steve. 'If you look at the finish time for each leg he is mostly five minutes down on Billy on each. He has a faster time than Billy from Wasdale to the finish. If you look, he was stopped beside the road for about 30 minutes. So, his running time is only 30 minutes or so behind. Mark is a brilliant runner but not of Billy's standard.'

But Steve thinks someone could do it. Who else other than Ricky Lightfoot? 'People say Simon Booth would have had a good chance of breaking it,' replied Steve. 'I also thought Andy or Joe Symonds, or Tom Owens might have been candidates. You have to be at home running over rough stuff.' He also felt that Kilian Jornet could do it on the right day with the right support. 'I have heard he might be thinking of coming over in 2015,' he revealed. 'He is someone who can race frequently and do it. He would have to get buy-in from the locals, he would never do it on his own. I was out there with Ricky Lightfoot helping Scott Jurek when he did a round and he struggled towards the end (it was the slowest leg 4 I had ever done!). Scott is more of a trail runner, whereas Kilian is a mountain runner.'

Steve Birkinshaw actually had a crack at beating Mark Hartell's 77 peaks in 24 hours record in 2010. He set off at 3am on a Saturday, but had to pull out before Honister Hause, after falling behind schedule around 10pm (with 23 peaks to go). He had been paced by Hartell. Birkinshaw commented, 'The weather was as good as you could hope for on the day but I got my eating and drinking wrong. Once I knew the record was out of reach I lost all motivation, I started to feel all dizzy.' He described the difficulty of getting the energy intake right. 'After five hours my stomach was really bloated and I felt sick. I was getting sweet stuff down but anything else was just sitting there. Eventually after 12 hours it all came up: around three pints of liquid and food. I felt lighter but by then the damage was done.'

As indicated above, I had the pleasure of interviewing Steve on stage at the 2014 Buxton Adventure Festival, an event at which we showed a few clips from the film of his Wainwrights record. These showed Steve dealing with some of the absolute lows of those six days, knowing he had to get out each day for more pain, particularly to his already badly blistered feet. While one of the toughest moments from these clips was showing, I looked across at Steve and just for a moment saw him welling up at the memory of what he had put himself through, both physically and mentally, in reaching that particular goal.

Chapter 14

Pacers: the Unsung Heroes

For many people attempting the BGR a skilled pacer can make the crucial difference between success and failure. I discussed this aspect with **Roger Smith**, co-author of *42 Peaks* and former editor of *The Great Outdoors* magazine. He related his own experiences as both a pacer and contender.

My BGR was in June 1989, to mark my turning 40. I wanted to do something very special that encompassed a serious physical challenge and also took in my great love of the fells. The BGR was ideal, but I knew it would stretch me to the limit. I joined three orienteering friends from Yorkshire – Jack Bloor, Malcolm Cox and Dick Courchee – and between us we felt we had more than adequate support. In the event, all of it was needed.

Conditions were good and we set off from Keswick at 8.30am on an anti-clockwise round. As far as Wasdale Head all went well, but then, as can happen, the group started to fragment. Dick dropped off the pace (and later had to retire) while Jack, Malcolm and I pushed on. We stayed together to Threlkeld and up Blencathra, but then Jack and Malcolm forged ahead, leaving me to tackle the final miles with Mike Gilbert for company.

I knew that I didn't have a lot of time in hand but felt the target was achievable. Mike told me later that he had serious doubts about this. Crucially, he never once conveyed those doubts to me. All the way down Mungrisdale Common and over Great Calva to Skiddaw he was quietly encouraging, trying to keep me focussed and above all trying to keep not just moving but moving at a fast enough pace. I was desperately tired and the heather was awful.

As we were going up Skiddaw, there was a small cloud rolling up the hill beside us – an amazing sight. I am convinced it was a guardian angel ensuring I got round! Mike kept encouraging me, giving me sips of Accolade, not letting me stop. It must have been tedious for him, but it helped me more than he could know. We reached the summit of Skiddaw with 90 minutes left. Keswick looked a long way down, but I knew the prize was mine if I kept going. It was at that point that I realised what a priceless help Mike had been. He had carried out the role of pacer to perfection.

On Latrigg I saw two familiar figures coming up. It was Jack and Malcolm. Having finished a little earlier they had come out to see if I needed any help. We jogged happily through the park and up to the Moot Hall. I had 23 minutes to spare, and all of those minutes were due to Mike's outstanding pacing.

A month later, Dick Courchee decided to try again, supported by Jack, Malcolm and Roger. It fell to Roger to take him over the final section from Threlkeld. Roger describes the conclusion to the round.

When Dick got to Threlkeld I could see he was almost done. He didn't want to stop so after a brief pause for a drink, we set off. The time was very tight. Dick was a good climber and we got up Blencathra not too badly, but then my problems started. Basically, he wouldn't run.

I was aware of the fight he was having between his body crying out for him to stop and his mind urging it to keep going. I recalled the way Mike had been with me a few weeks earlier and, like him, tried to keep everything positive, assuring Dick that we were ok for time as long as he kept moving. The best we managed was a shambling jog. The sense of responsibility

I felt was huge. I knew how disappointed Dick had been a month earlier and I felt a second failure would be a crushing blow to him – and his wife Sue, anxiously waiting down in Keswick.

I was sure we were moving too slowly and was constantly if surreptitiously checking my watch. At last Great Calva was behind us. Dick seemed to rally a bit and we trundled our way up Skiddaw. Just over an hour left. No time to stop. I almost pulled Dick away from the cairn and pointed out Keswick below. 'Right, one last effort and you're there' I said. He nodded. 'I'm ok, thanks'.

Our pace seemed barely adequate but halfway down, with a strong sense of déjà vu, there were those two familiar figures again. Jack and Malcolm were very aware of how tight the time was and had come up to see if they could help. I was mightily relieved to see them. We made a sort of phalanx round Dick and almost carried him off the hill and through the streets to the Moot Hall. He had ten minutes to spare. I was absolutely shattered but enormously happy to have helped my friend achieve his aim.

There will be those who sweep through their Rounds with no trouble at all. But I suspect there will be many more whose stories are like mine, and who owe their pacers a similar debt. Every pacer is truly an unsung hero and it is right that we should salute them here.

A Bob Graham Round can seem a lot different to a pacer than it does to a contender. These next paragraphs, for example, are the thoughts of **Jonny Muir** on a round he helped some friends on in 2014. The following is an edited version of his blog.[1] The entry was captioned '. . . *as seen from the water-carrier's corner*', and is a fine example of good blogging. I have read a few while researching this book, and it is rare to see such well-crafted writing in this genre.

---

1 http://heightsofmadness.com/

High above, the jagged, dark silhouette of Blencathra deco-
rated an oppressive sky. There were no stars. An incessant
rain pounded the car roof. We fretted. Marc and Nayth (and
their water-carriers) had left the Moot Hall at midnight. Time
was winning. Blundering off Skiddaw, the fivesome had been
bamboozled by what is elemental in daylight. Time seized her
moment.

A star came out. A yellow, blinking beam. Then another.
And another, until we could count five precious beacons. They
were descending Hall's Fell, presumably slick and slippery
with water. Slowly, the stars brightened, gingerly descended
Hall's Fell, swept across a mountainside, and plunged down
a road until they were shining in our faces.

You do not run on the Bob Graham Round. You do not
walk. You move. And if you keep moving, keep progressing,
keep going, Time will relinquish her willing grip. And that is
all a Bob Graham pacer – call us what you will: water-carrier,
mule, motivator, navigator, force-feeder, split-taker – can ask
from those he paces. Just keep moving. We – Marc, Nayth and
two new water-carriers – kept moving into the dawn, relentlessly up and up and up Clough Head, over the trio of Dodds
towards Helvellyn. Nothing happened, but nothing is what
you desire. Something is what you fear. We were descending
in clag when my right foot clung to a boulder. I was in the
air. I was skidding on a carpet of rocks. I sensed the others
freezing. Dread. The moment, the something, the horribly
unplanned that can ruin everything. 'I think I'm okay,' I said
breathlessly. There was blood, grazes and throbbing, but it
was not *that* moment. We resumed movement.

Fairfield. A towering monument to hardness. We slogged
up, zigzagging through scree, tapped the summit and escaped
to Seat Sandal. A ripple of applause greeted the runners at
Dunmail Raise. Time's grip was loosening. Steel Fell beck-
oned. We climbed forever. Leg three stretches implausibly
far. Wasdale was the objective, six hours away. Nayth and
Marc kept moving. *'I know what you are thinking. You are*

hating this. You are wondering why you are here. You do not believe you can do this. You can', I wanted to shout, but the epiphany of belief, of wondrous realisation was theirs to accomplish.

Once on Bowfell, Great End, Scafell Pike, Broad Stand and Scafell gathered menacingly. Leg three was transformed. Gone were the bogs and tussocks; rocks rule here. The pounding takes its toll. Marc and Nayth kept moving. They paused momentarily on summits to record a split before they moved off. Scafell Pike was heaving. *'You're nearly there,'* a walker remarked. They weren't.

Broad Stand gesticulated. Ropes had been strung along the wall. One-by-one we were ferried upwards, three of the four of us non-climbers. Marc howled as cramp seized a leg as he hoisted himself away from the hideous ledge where Coleridge knew a fall would have 'of course killed him'. I went up last, flapping and flailing tired arms and legs in unpretty fashion. It was emotionally exhausting. My knees throbbed. Above was a great staircase of vast ledges and boulders, and further up the summit of Scafell. The descent to Wasdale is the longest of the round: a steep wall of rubble and grass, a sweeping moor, a scree shoot, a murderously sharp field, a wade through a gushing white river, a meandering footpath to the National Trust car park. Marc and Nayth's support crew were waiting, a feast laid out.

My job was done. I stopped. I had spent 10 hours on the fells, covering some 28 miles. The relief was crushing; I could have cried. Slowly but surely, the water-carriers had helped Marc and Nayth claw back Time. They were on course to finish in 23-and-a-half hours, having drifted outside 24-hour pace on leg one. They just had to keep moving. I watched Nayth vomit profusely as he left the car park and craned my neck skywards as the group processed up Yewbarrow. Momentarily, 45 minutes later, they were silhouetted on the skyline, then they were gone, swallowed by Yewbarrow. I got into a sun-baked car and closed my eyes.

The silhouetted stars reappeared four hours later, scuttling into Honister. Marc ran past like he was finishing a 10k. Dangerous thoughts had been racing through my mind since my Yewbarrow-gazing. I was going to run again, run leg five from Honister back to the Moot Hall in Keswick. I couldn't not be part of this.

A pack surged up Dale Head. What belief does to a man. Marc and Nayth, in particular, believed. Their stride and their body language expressed the decisive compulsion of a human who is going to complete a Bob Graham Round. There was magic in the air in those hours. Dusk began to fall as we bounded off Dale Head. Mountains gradually faded into the sky. Rain began, rain that I have never minded less. Marc and Nayth embraced on Robinson, summit number 42. Nayth's mother – who had run with us from Honister – was over-whelmed with enthusiastic pride. Time, of course, would not stop. We had to keep moving. The hills were still and silent; Hindscarth appeared impossibly vast from the west. Keswick was a bright smudge. Marc shuffled down Robinson, a man who did not seem able to bend his legs any longer. Darkness. We were stars again: seven head torches inching closer to the steps of the Moot Hall with every step, every shuffle, every movement. Rain fell harder. Little was said. Water-carriers burst forward to open gates. It was very dark. Time had slipped beyond 11pm. '*How far?*' Nayth asked. '*Not far,*' I replied, knowing that after 65 miles, a step can be too far.

We were in Keswick, over the river, over the roundabout, past the shops. The Market Square was ahead. Cigarette smoke wafted across the road. Scafell Pike walker, they were 'nearly there'. At 11.21pm, Marc and Nayth scaled the last two metres of the Bob Graham round and stood atop the stone staircase of the Moot Hall. Relief. Joy. Disbelief. Time stopped.

Those are just two examples of rounds from the point of view of a pacer. As Roger Smith notes, most Bob Graham contenders agree that good pacers are vital to their success, and duly acknowledge that fact afterwards. There are of course those that take the view that they are a necessary encumbrance, required for not much more than carrying stuff, and verifying the round. In my research I came across many, many, different stories of how pacers had been vital to the contenders, and even some where they had been a real hindrance.

It is worth remembering that Bob Graham himself was massively helped by pacers, with whom he retired to his own guest house for a meal and a rest after completing his round. Like the good host he was, he then got up early to cook them breakfast, before they all went off to their respective jobs. Others' experiences have varied, as shown by the following selection of thoughts and attitudes.

Bill Smith reported on his own round in *Fellrunner* magazine, where he commented on how the pacers did their job with regard to keeping the attempt on schedule:

> I remarked that the pace was too slow. "Don't worry", said Eric [Roberts], "You're moving on a 22-hour schedule. If anything you are going too fast". He constantly emphasised the need for concentration, and for making every movement count as a step towards Keswick.

Others also have felt that the pace has seemed wrong, and have even reprimanded their pacers on that point. The report on John North's round in *Notable Walks* . . . includes an explanation of one such incident:

> Robin Price was North's pacer from Dunmail, and they set off into heavy rain, thick mist and a gale which was blowing straight into their faces. Things went well until coming off Helvellyn, where they strayed down towards the Glenridding valley. At this point North lost his temper with his pacer, but soon realised it may have been because he was pushing too hard.

Of course, the set schedule can turn out to be too conservative, and things can change as the round progresses. Billy Bland noted that on his own 1976 round. 'We were now so far ahead of schedule that the pacers hadn't arrived for the next section so Mike Nicholson kindly volunteered to do the next section with me instead of wasting time waiting.' After Mike Nicholson had been a pacer on Billy Bland's round that year (which took 18 hours 50 minutes) he gained the confidence to go for his own round the year after, for which he set an ambitious 17 hours 30 minutes schedule, and came home with a new BGR record of 17 hours 45 minutes.

Good pacers are often able to move at a faster pace than the contender, mostly by dint of them doing shorter sections rather than the whole round. Many take advantage of this capability, as Mark Hartell notes: 'Pacers would sometimes summit hop via cols to get ahead. At a road crossing the pacers run in 30 seconds ahead and say what I am asking for.'

Pacers have a vital role to play in the tricky area of the state of mind of the BG contender, which as can be seen from Jonny Muir's reports can take huge swings within a round – from strong positives to deep negatives. For example, Jim Mann told me how on one of his rounds he told Steve Birkinshaw, who was pacing the leg, that he was having a bad time mentally. Jim noted that Steve, 'highlighted all the positives. We were on schedule, give or take a bit in horrible weather, the forecast was for it to improve, it was getting light and the relentless pace in those conditions was bound to make me feel tired. He lifted my spirits and as I came into Dunmail I was ready to at least try and give as good back as the course was giving me. I can't stress how important Steve's pep talk was at this point in the round – great pacers like him can genuinely change the fortunes of a round.'

Jim Mann obviously has a well-established relationship with Steve Birkinshaw, but freely admits that he has used pacers that he has never met before, a chance that many BGR contenders take, and which often works out fine. There are often calls on the FRA Forum for pacers to help out contenders who, for whatever reason, can't raise a full complement of friends for their round. Mind you, these impromptu arrangements don't always deliver good results. Mark McDermott told me a story of his pacer difficulties on his fast BG attempt in 1992:

> I only had one pacer on the first section, and I left him halfway up Skiddaw. So I arrived down at Threlkeld in 2 hrs 17 mins without having had anything much to eat or drink. Halfway up Clough Head I said to the next pacer 'I'll have a drink now if you don't mind'. He said 'there should be a puddle at the top', which was not really what I wanted to hear.

Many experienced fell runners will use pacers, but often within strict pre-determined limits. Nicky Spinks remarked that she normally classified her pacers as mostly carriers, more than anything. 'I like navigating myself mostly,' she noted. 'But, it is a joint thing.' However, being a pacer can be a tough ask. Helene Diamantides/Whitaker is a person who pushed herself very hard, and expected the same level of commitment from her pacers, whom she noted at one point were thinking of taking union action and 'running to rule'. Helene also commented that inexperienced pacers were often the reason that she has seen many people go wrong with their round pacing. Her view is that people can tend to go faster at the wrong time, for instance. She very much liked being in control of all aspects of pace, stopping, etc. 'I still think that I enjoyed my solo round the most,' was her take on it.

An interesting approach was shown by Martin Stone, who described some of his pacing as 'good kit-testing opportunities'. This was particular pertinent as he built towards a planned solo attempt. On a solo round you are not able to rely on anyone else for psychological boosts. On his solo round in January 1987 Martin went up Yewbarrow very steadily and sluggishly with a few sit-downs. 'Your pacers can give you a boost here, but if you are on your own it you are absolutely at the mercy of your psyche and your desire to succeed,' he said.

Finally, there is the fantastic camaraderie that contenders can generate, through training and suffering together. Adrian Belton commented on this when referring to a recent round:

> Pacers more than willingly appeared, naively I thought to enjoy and appreciate a day in the hills 'for old times sake'. The reality was that the b......s wanted their revenge, in making me, and watching me, suffer.

After reading his account (noted above), I wanted to get Jonny Muir's thoughts directly as he had made some interesting observations about the mental aspects of the challenge when reporting on his own round on his blog. He had completed his own BGR in June 2012, finishing in a very respectable 19 hours 33 minutes.

> *It was a poor choice of meeting place. Costa Coffee at Euston station is small, hot and noisy. I was meeting Jonny Muir and it seemed a good location when I arranged it. I got a call to say he was on the concourse, as he couldn't find the meeting place. I knew we would get on fine when the first thing he said was that he could navigate his way round the BGR but not to a coffee bar! By a strange coincidence it was the day before Jonny set out on his latest 'adventure'. This was what he called the 'Little Twelve' – a cheeky reference to Andrew Murray's Big Ten adventure. His was a trek round the highest points in the 12 inner London Boroughs, a sort of urban version of his Heights of Madness effort. As he pointed out: "Together, these summits add up to 957m – a slouching Scafell Pike. Think of the whole thing as a satire on the Bob Graham Round. Utterly pointless. But then, is not that the point?"*

I first asked Jonny Muir what had inspired him to write *Heights of Madness*. His answer was that he had been working, and had been a journalist for two years, and was bored. 'As a journalist you write about other people's great challenges and stuff they are doing,' he said. 'I wanted to do my own adventure, but I didn't have much money or time. I gave myself three months and decided to climb the highest point in each historical county of the UK.' Then he did the linear Hebrides trip which he wrote about in *Isles at the Edge of the Sea*.

It seems those trips naturally led to the Bob Graham Round. He was one of the thousands of people who had read Richard Askwith's book, and he thought he could do it too. Then at his running club (Herne Hill Harriers) a friend said he was doing the BGR that summer. He asked if he could come on a recce with him. 'I felt that I had to justify my right to go on a recce,' he noted. 'I had to say I have done the Ben Nevis fell race and done Jura, and lived in Inverness a couple of years doing hill running. We had a great day running from Seathwaite. The boys were taking it quite easy, I was trotting ahead and wondering why they were taking it so easy. We dropped down to Wasdale and then we went straight up Yewbarrow.' He was carrying a bag with some spare kit and food in, but hadn't put his clothes in a waterproof bag. As they came over Red Pike it was hailing and heavy rain. Coming over Great Gable it was horrible, and as they dropped down slowly to Honister he had become a shivering wreck.

Maybe this was good experience for the future. 'I had to be rescued from under the hand dryer in the toilets. I was embarrassed more than anything else,' concluded Muir. 'I had gone out in the hills with these boys. I was a good standard runner. I had done marathons, done trail stuff, big mountain days as a walker and a runner, and just got totally humiliated.' It was not a particularly big run, although they were out for six hours. But he was hooked, and felt he had to have a go and do more.

That turned into an ambition to do the BGR. It was 2011 when he did that first recce. His friends did it in that summer, but he couldn't do it as he was getting married. The friends failed, having had terrible weather over the Dodds, and they had split up – a classic way to get it wrong. 'One got to Wasdale, a long way to go and fail. Once you have had the window, if you are southern-based, that is probably it for the year,' said Muir. The three who failed attempted again 10 months later (May 2012) and they all got round. One completed in 19½ hours, and the other two in just over 20 hours. Muir paced some of it and thought 'I am as good as those guys'. Therefore sub-20 was the aim he gave himself – given the same kind of weather.

Surely there must be a huge disadvantage to being based in the south? Muir's response was, 'obviously we were not as hill hardy as some others. But I think two things were to my advantage. One, ignorance is bliss. Sometimes, the more you go up there, the more the weather is bad, the more confusing it becomes, and the more problems you present your mind with. The second thing is, I was very fit. I am light, small and determined – those combined factors helped.' He did as much hill training as he could. In January 2012 he had not run further than a marathon. He completed a 30-mile LDWA event in Surrey in January, and did the Fellsman at the end of April (61 miles). He felt he had been in a fight, saying that, 'in some ways it was harder than the BG. I finished that [*Fellsman*] and I remember sitting on a seat and being blown out. I had finished 10th, and am very proud of it. That was the year they had to abandon the Fellsman. We were in, but three hours later they abandoned because people were getting hypothermia.'

I asked Muir about the quote he had used in his blog about a suggested figure of 10,000ft of ascent in a week's training, and where that quote was from. He couldn't remember where it comes from [*I couldn't find it anywhere on the web*[1]], and I wondered if he ever did that in a week. 'The week of the Fellsman, yeah, so once. It is huge, and to try and find that ascent down here is counter-productive,' he replied. Later, Muir came back to me to point out that he thought it was courtesy of Bob Wightman,[2] who had clearly got this figure from elsewhere too.

---

1   There was a thread on the FRA forum in 2008, which noted that: Mike Sadula says, "Some say that you need to climb 10,000 ft a week." – http://forum.fellrunner.org.uk/showthread.php?5988-10-000ft-a-week

2   http://bobwightman.co.uk/run/bgr_training_for_runners.php

Part of his build-up was pacing others, and he ran legs 4 and 5 just before his own round, but he pulled a muscle in his Achilles and it was seven hours of pain. But, in his view, 'it was a good move, seeing where I was going to go. Knowing how Yewbarrow would go, and getting a sense of the end. A lot of people see the end as leg 5. I see the end as leg 4. What I learnt from that round is that my ankle was really hurting, but that I could carry on.' It was an injury that stemmed from the Fellsman. 'What I realised that day is that I'd kill myself for my mates to get round, because I could see how it important it was for them. It made me realise what my friends would do for me to get me round. I had three very good runners and my dad giving me great support, and they were fantastic.' On his round on leg 1 and 2 he felt awful, and apparently moaned and groaned. He wasn't enjoying it, and couldn't see the point, and it was misery. He said 'I can't do this' coming down to Dunmail. His pacer just ignored him, just saying 'fine, you are on schedule'. He then said, 'I haven't run seven hours with you just to see you pack it in. You are going to carry on up Steel Fell and just keep going'. A good running friend!

Like many others, Muir has a clear idea of the role of pacers, depending on the speed of the round. For him, 'it felt quick on legs 4 and 5, really exciting – bouncing from summit to summit. Then, I felt my pacers were there to point me in the right direction and to remind me of the line, and crucially for me for the feeding. Like a lot of rounds you wouldn't eat properly. One guy set an alarm on his watch for every 30 minutes to beep to make me drink and eat. I didn't want to, and a couple of times I just flung the food away. I couldn't stomach it.' For them navigation wasn't a huge issue. They knew where they were going and it was reasonable weather.

Muir had to have physiotherapy treatment beforehand, and I questioned whether this was real or psychological. He replied, 'I saw a physio in London, she is a runner and she told me what I wanted to hear, *yeah you are fine*'. I also have a friend in Inverness who is also a physio. She was taking me through a diagnosis over the phone and put my mind at ease.' On the day it turned out fine. He remembers feeling it later in the day. 'If you are descending Blencathra at speed and it is wet and dark it is quite possibly going to be awkward. It is not meant to be easy.'

He thinks he did three proper recces, and remembers the first one as being disastrous. He had done each leg once or twice. He had done each summit at least twice, maybe three to five on some summits. 'I had only done leg 1 once, leg 5 once. I had never done leg 3 in its entirety,' he recalls. 'I was up there to do the Coniston Trail Marathon, and a couple of days later did leg 2 on my own in 4 hours 2 minutes and was desperate to get under 4 hours. I looked at the data and it said that 4 hours 20 minutes was equivalent to a sub-20 round.'

On Muir's round he had a night start and a full moon. 'I think it was a full moon but it was accidental. I am a teacher, so it fell in half term,' he said. 'It was the day of the Queen's 60th year celebration, 3 June. You can have a full moon, yet get clag. Half way up Skiddaw we went into clag and it was miserable from there to Dunmail.'

His pacing arrangements were fairly minimal. 'Someone did leg 1, 2 and 5. Then I had one more do 3, 4 and 5, and someone else did 4 and 5. My father supported me all through the round.' He reflected on his food choices, 'I took bread with me which was a massive mistake. Anything dry is not good. People like me who are quite slight, there is no fat to burn, you have to keep eating. Towards the end I did start going a bit funny, feeling dizzy and hazy, with the odd wobble.'

Interestingly, his times got better in the later stages, which certainly isn't the case with everyone.

He was on 22 to 23 hour pace and had written out splits for 22 hours. The weather was poor earlier, wind in their faces, and clag. They had issues in finding the best way on Dolly-wagon Pike and Nethermost. 'I felt awful on Fairfield. Pretty bad for the next two hours on the next leg,' he recalls. 'I was climbing the steep bit on Bowfell from Rossett Pike and almost falling backwards – it was sleep deprivation, I was so tired. Something clicked though, and coming off Bowfell I felt great and I looked back and suddenly the pacers couldn't keep up with me. Something in my head had clicked. There is a tipping point somewhere on the BGR where you realise you are going to do it. It could be Robinson, Yewbarrow, Great Gable, somewhere. That is the Holy Grail – to find the tipping point.' He remembered pacing two others pretty recently and was running legs 2 and 3 with them. He could tell that they didn't believe they were going to do it. It wasn't until he saw them leaving the car park for Yewbarrow that he could see they believed. He met them again to run leg 5 with them and they were different people [*see report above*].

On his own round they didn't do Broad Stand. 'I have been up Broad Stand since, while pacing, but for my round we did Lord's Rake,' he noted. 'I would have been worried about it, but I had reccied it and decided on Lord's Rake. It wasn't bad. The challenge is getting that huge long descent to Wasdale done. That is where you can win and lose time.'

His total rest time was 22 minutes. 'One of the guys who paced me had run the Fellsman with me, and I adopted his strategy, which was to hardly stop. You look forward to the stop so much, but you are not going to feel better for a 10 minute stop and sit down. You may feel worse for resting.' He became great at eating on the move.

I asked if he felt he got the optimum outcome for his fitness at that time. 'On that day, yes,' he thought. 'Runners are inherently greedy. There have not been that many races that I have finished and I have thought, I am really happy with that and not had a shred of a thought that I could have gone quicker. The Bob Graham time was as well as I could have done. I knew that it was one of the quickest times of the year. I found it strange that here I was, this guy from London, who was training on paltry hills, barely could find a 100m climb in one go, and I was finishing the BGR in 19 hours something. It was incredible.' He also reflected on the way the momentum in his round shifted. The way it had been so awful at the start, and had felt so slow, then the way it turned into a negative split. 'I don't think I ever felt so powerful as a runner as when I was moving over leg 4. I think I did 3:45 or 3:50 for leg 4. I just felt so extraordinarily strong, and fit, and joyous,' was how he put it. 'The best few hours running of my entire life. I remember coming off Robinson and feeling like we were flying. One of my pacers said '*look back, you own these hills, today they are yours*', and we did look back.' He noted that it was a beautiful evening and remembers getting to the road and changing shoes and absolutely flying, someone had said 6-minute miling. 'I remember thinking '*tomorrow I won't be able to walk, but right now I am running 6-minute miles*'. The most incredible day. The best bit was pulling in and out of Honister.' He then remembered having being there in a much more shambolic state, as described earlier. 'This time my wife was there and her family, my dad and all the pacers. You know you have done it. I was blown over, as we were half an hour before they expected. The joy comes from the journey though, not the end.'

The downside was that the round ruined his whole season. He decided to give himself a month off, no running at all. He couldn't resist though, and tried to run after 11 days and got to the end of the road and came back in tears. 'My legs just didn't work, everything hurt. I did the Saunders Mountain Marathon six weeks later and my feet were on fire, and felt terrible. It wasn't till the end of September that I was running normally again. It just wiped me out. It was really quite emotional. The Bob Graham Blues, I called it afterwards. It was such a big day, I had focussed on it for 15 months.'

Muir gave me his thoughts on Billy Bland's record, and whether anyone could challenge the 13 hours 53 minutes time. He thought people may have got a lot of 'pleasure' in seeing Scott Jurek come over and struggle on his round. 'I would love to know the reasons why, because I think they were flying. It seems strange to take pleasure,' he explained. 'But people who have done the BGR are proud of it and want to protect its reputation for being something hard and tough, and that you have to fight to be a member of the club.' When I asked about Kilian Jornet, he responded that, 'there is no doubt that he has the capability. But, the knowledge of the ground is everything.' He thinks he would also have to find the best pacers in the country. 'I am very proud of my time, but it is not meant to be about the best American, or whatever, runners doing it,' he concluded. 'But it just feels right that Billy Bland has the record.' As to anyone to take the record, I asked if he thought Ricky Lightfoot was good enough to challenge for it. 'Everything has got to go right. Maybe four or five guys should go for it in one year and get some focus.'[1]

I asked Muir why he thought the BGR was so iconic, as compared with the other big Rounds (Ramsay and Buckley). He laughed and said, 'If someone wrote a book about either of them would that make a difference? Richard Askwith's book made a difference to fell running. Remember he was not that good an athlete. That is not meant to be nasty, but he makes the BGR seem harder than it actually is because he is not in the same class as Billy Bland.' Muir felt that Askwith did show it can be done with the right dedication. 'With the Ramsay Round, don't you think if someone wrote a book, the romantic outlook, and about doing it, that would perhaps make a difference?'

On sending him a transcript of the interview to check, Muir replied with some minor comments but also added that, 'not a day goes by when I don't think about *that* day, the day I

---

1   Not long after I interviewed Muir, a project aiming to focus on achieving the first sub-2 hour marathon was launched (http://www.sub2hrs.com/). It claimed that it was: 'The first dedicated international research initiative made up of specialist multidisciplinary scientists from academia, elite athletes and strategic industry partners'. It may seem like an academic/commercial venture, but the reason for mentioning it here is that one of the group, Prof Ron Maughan, suggested: 'Offer that sum of money [$5m] to each of the top five athletes to pace and draft each other throughout the race in the hope that just one athlete will achieve the fantastic target!'. i.e. The same four or five guys focussing approach that Muir suggested.

completed my round. The memory is a perpetual source of inspiration. I will, I hope, achieve many more things in life – athletic and otherwise – but I know that the Bob Graham will remain one of the crowning moments of my existence. I am envious of those who have it all to come.'

Chapter 15

The Bob Graham network

There are several people who over time have had a huge influence in supporting challengers on the round, providing information,[1] and in documenting the various successes and failures.

Fred Rogerson was very much the driving force behind the establishment of the Bob Graham Club in 1971, when only a handful of people were known to have completed the round. In *Notable Walks* . . . he writes:

> I was sure that there were quite a number of dedicated Fell Runners with the ability to achieve Bob Graham's round of 42. With this in mind, I called a meeting of interested and knowledgeable friends, namely, A.H. Griffin, S. Bradshaw, A. Heaton and K. Heaton. The meeting was very construc-tive. Subsequently a Re-union Dinner and Social Evening at the Old Dungeon Ghyll was held on 22 January 1971 with 50 people closely associated with the Fell Record attending. The attendance was so fully representative that I moved that a Club/Association be formed and requested Official and Committee Members be elected from the floor.

That first committee was elected and consisted of Fred Rogerson (Chair), Ken Heaton (Secretary/Treasurer), and Stan Bradshaw, Maurice Collett, Harry Griffin, Alan Heaton, Des Oliver and

---

1   The FRA Forum is a great place for finding information, and like-minded individuals, especially within its Bob Graham thread: http://forum.fell-runner.org.uk/forum.php

Paul Stewart (Committee members). They approved the title of the 'Bob Graham 24 Hour Club', with permission to use Bob Graham's name being granted by his niece, Miss Eva Graham, with the proviso that Phil Davidson (one of Graham's pacers) approved, which he did.

The Objectives of the club were:

a) To specify and define the 42 summits traversed by Bob Graham during his round of the fells within 24 hours
b) To provide interested qualifying members with all details and relevant information
c) To encourage and advise intending members before and possibly during events
d) To record in detail all registered attempts

The original definition of membership was:

The Bob Graham 24 Hour Club certificate will be awarded to anybody who completes Bob Graham's round of 42 peaks within 24 hours, starting and finishing at the Moot Hall Keswick (in either clockwise or anti-clockwise direction) or who completes a round within 24 hours based on the Graham Round, but including other peaks which at the discretion of the committee constitutes a more meritorious achievement either by reasons of extra peaks climbed, height ascended, or time taken.

Fred Rogerson was born at Staveley Head Farm in the Kentmere valley on 26 January 1921. He lived near Windermere with his wife Margaret and earned his living as a Master Builder. Double pneumonia when he was young left Fred with a weak chest. His grandfather Robert was a guides racer and miler, and he encouraged Fred to walk and run on the fells. Robert finished second in the 1900 Grasmere Guides Race and fourth in 1902, at which time it was run up Silver Howe.

'I joined the T.A. as a boy soldier,' Fred recalled to Bill Smith, 'primarily to learn how to use a map and compass as I'd often got myself lost on the high fells. My first competitive year as a guides racer was to have been 1940 as it had been thought that I was not strong enough to run in junior or youth events. However, mobilisation on 1 September 1939 put paid to all plans for guides races and the mile, my trainer having thought I showed promise as a miler.'

Later Fred took up orienteering, founded the first orienteering club in the Lakes (Phoenix OC) during the mid-1960s at Windermere and started organising events. He had many other interests. These included fox hunting, fell running, athletics and photography. One of his most visible legacies was his compilation of *Notable Walks* ... which has provided much of the early detail reported in this book. His volume brings together detailed reports of the exploits of the earlier BGR pioneers. Ken Heaton wrote in the Foreword to this mammoth (typescript) compilation: 'all who are interested in our Lakeland Mountain Heritage will understand Fred's desire to perpetuate all that is known of Notable Fell Walks, his insatiable enthusiasm and strength of purpose for all he loves and believes in is personified by this unique publication.'[1]

He was not able to be there when Alan Heaton completed Graham's round in a faster time (22 hours 18 minutes) in 1960, as he was busy elsewhere. But he and Margaret were there to offer assistance when Alan's Clayton-le-Moors Harriers[2] clubmate, 48-year-old Stan Bradshaw, became the second man to break the record a fortnight later (23 hours 25 minutes). Both Fred and Margaret have been present on many people's rounds, providing food and shelter in their campervan, and always plenty of encouragement.

Having founded the Bob Graham Club in 1971, Fred retired

1   A copy of the publication was offered on eBay recently. I made an unsuccessful offer, and was informed later that it had gone but not for the asking price of £200.

2   Fred Rogerson was at one time president of Clayton-le-Moors Harriers.

from the Chair of the club in 1998 (after 28 years). He also co-founded the Lake District Mountain Trial Association, and under its guise organised the Fairfield race for 25 years.

Fred Rogerson died, aged 89, on 23 Oct 2010. *The Westmorland Gazette*, on 29 July 2011, noted that fell runners had honoured him thus:

> The athletes paid their respects to the late Fred Rogerson, of Windermere, by escorting his ashes around the Bob Graham Round – a 72-mile fell run visiting 42 of the Lake District's highest peaks in under 24 hours. They ran in relays, starting and finishing at Keswick's Moot Hall with changeovers at Threlkeld, Dunmail, Wasdale and Honister. Mr Rogerson's ashes were carried in a pocket watch case presented by Bob Graham to his pacer Phil Davidson in 1927.
>
> Although Mr Rogerson, who died last year at the age of 89, never completed the round himself, he was instrumental in the foundation of the Bob Graham Club in 1971 and a regular supporter of runners who set out to complete the gruelling round. The athletes completed the round in 22 hours and 40 minutes. The pace slowed to a walk at Portinscale where the runners were joined by a dozen members of Mr Rogerson's family and some fell running notables.
>
> Among them was 83-year-old Alan Heaton, the first person to repeat Bob Graham's 42 peaks back in 1960, and later pushed the 24 hour fell record up to 60 peaks. Also paying his respects was Bill Smith, writer of the iconic 'Stud marks on the summits' who himself ran a 55-peak round in 1976. He travelled to Honister from his Liverpool home entirely by public transport although well over 70.

One of the greatest chroniclers of the BGR (and almost any aspect of fell running) has been **Bill Smith**. Back in the 1970s he was regularly running 80–100 miles per week. As already noted, he set the fastest time for the BGR with Boyd Millen in 1973, and later traversed 55 peaks within 24 hours, and increased that to 63 peaks in five minutes under 24 hours in 1976. In his ways he was definitely an individual, usually using public transport to get to events. Nominally an amateur, he used to enter the Grasmere Guides Race (which was run under the 'professional' code at the time) falsely under the name of W. Wilson just because he fancied running in the race.

Bill Smith died in September 2011 aged 75, having apparently fallen in a peat bog as he ran across Saddle Fell. His body was found by a walker, but in this remote area there was no mobile phone signal, so he eventually raised the alarm. A Mountain Rescue team returned the following day to recover his body by helicopter. Smith had been due to be a marshal at the Thieveley Pike race and friends became concerned when he didn't turn up. It is uncertain exactly when he died, and Lancashire Police said they believed he may have fallen into the bog and his body lain undiscovered for up to three weeks.

The first *Fellrunner* magazine after Smith's death contained four full pages of tributes. It also had a list of the significant contributions he had made to the magazine, which covered (with commentary) another two full pages. As well as his classic tome *Stud marks on the summits*, he wrote numerous articles for many other journals. *Studmarks* contains 22 pages of finely crafted words specifically on the Bob Graham Round. He has also contributed several pivotal pieces to *The Fellrunner* magazine.

Roger Smith was editor of *The Great Outdoors* magazine. In 1979 he became the 117th member of the BG Club, completing his round in 23 hours 37 minutes. In a short report on his round in Cumbria magazine (issue 29) he noted that they 'were exceptionally lucky with the weather, which could not have been kinder.' The naturalist in him commented that the 'skylarks go on singing virtually all night.' A fuller account was published in *Climber* magazine and later appeared in an anthology, *The Winding Trail*, which Roger edited.

Roger Smith wrote the first version of the booklet *42 Peaks: the story of the Bob Graham Round* in 1982. It had a foreword by Harry Griffin, and a piece on the Bob Graham 24 Hour Club by Brian Covell. The booklet was reprinted in 1992. A new version appeared in 2005, now credited to Paddy Buckley and Roger Smith, and it has been reprinted twice since then.

Mike Sadula created a website[1] that provided inspiration to many. Unfortunately, Mike died on 3 March 2009 after a short illness. The Bob Graham 24 Hour Club has preserved the last-updated version of this site for posterity. In 2000 Sadula created an online survey to gather statistics about people's rounds. One interesting statistic was the percentage of people who took the various routes at Mickledore. It isn't clear how large the sample was, but his survey gave results of Broad Stand 60%, Lord's Rake 36%, and other (presumably Foxes Tarn) 4%.

The Bob Graham Club preserves a certain kudos associated with membership. Writing in *The Observer* Chris Brasher called it:

> the most exclusive club in the world because you cannot buy your way into it, you cannot join because something has happened to you; you can become a member only by accepting the challenge of those 42 peaks to be traversed inside 24 hours.

---

1 bobgrahamround.co.uk

Chapter 16

Not all who try succeed

There are many ways of getting things wrong on the Bob Graham Round. The following examples illustrate just some of them, and are taken from reports written by those brave enough to acknowledge having failed, in some cases explaining why. The following stories shouldn't really be considered failures, more as learning experiences. Some taught the participants what they needed to know to come back and complete the challenge; some didn't. In all cases, there is probably a lesson either learnt or to be learnt.

One particular 'failure with style' was that of **Pete Dawes,** who noted in an interview in the Autumn 1976 issue of *The Fellrunner* that he 'once set out from Dunmail Raise to go to Wasdale at mid-day prior to doing the Bob Graham to reconnoitre the route and on arriving at Wasdale decided to continue to Honister and on to Keswick. By this time it was gone midnight and I didn't feel like eating food and eventually after quite a sit in the car decided to continue over Skiddaw, Calva and Blencathra to Threlkeld but on starting to climb Calva realised that with the lack of food I was out of energy and I kept falling over in the heather and had to keep resting and recovering to reach Blencathra. After breakfast at Threlkeld I felt all right again but thought I had done enough for one day.' To be fair to Pete Dawes, he had NOT actually set out to do the Bob Graham Round.

Sometimes, however, a casual approach can produce an unplanned round. **Chris Brasher** tried the Bob Graham Round a couple of times, without success. In his regular column in *The Observer* in 1997, Brasher described his first attempt at the age of 49 (in 1977). He set off from Keswick with Paddy Buckley and George Rhodes. He started at night, being paced by Joss Naylor, and was mysteriously joined by a 'Charlie', who was holidaying in the Lakes with his family. At Dunmail Raise Paddy Buckley retired, and Joss had to leave them as he had to catch a train to London because he was having lunch with Muhammad Ali. Ken Ledward, Frank Milner and Boyd Millen took over as pacers, all being BGR completers. Charlie was still there too. The BGR spirit is shown when it came to climbing Broad Stand: 'Terry Thorpe and his wife, who gave up city life to manage the campsite in Wasdale, had climbed 3000 feet in the dawn to fix us a rope – a long hard trudge to give us a few seconds of safety'. After a break for a massage at Wasdale, Brasher continued up Yewbarrow, but was so ill when he met Stan Bradshaw at the summit he abandoned and dropped down to Joss's farm. George Rhodes carried on, paced by Bradshaw and Millen to finish in 23 hours 9 minutes. The story concludes: 'And Charlie? He gave up pacing at Wasdale and became a contender, taking off at great speed with our fittest pacer, Chris Brad . . . finishing strongly through the lanes to Keswick. "Just an hour's jog up Skiddaw," he had said to his wife and now he was back in Keswick 21 hours 57 minutes later'. It was **Charlie Ramsay**, who was obviously very fit, but hadn't expected to be doing a round while on holiday. A year later (1978) Charlie established the Charlie Ramsay Round, which is generally regarded as an even tougher challenge than the BGR.

Peter Travis was a reasonable standard fell runner, an excellent poet, and coincidentally also the author of a book called *The Round* (a novel based on the Bob Graham Round). He had a go at the BGR at the age of 51, and 'failed miserably on the first attempt', as he put it. 'The second attempt was better and I got round three sections, but found myself out of time due to some early navigational errors.' That didn't stop him trying again, but sadly a third attempt also failed.

Others expecting you to fail can often be a great motivation to succeed. **George Brass** was one of the early great performers on the fells, having a seemingly unflappable ability to navigate and continue progressing in the foulest weather conditions. He was memorably the only finisher in the Lake District Mountain Trial in 1962. Harry Griffin reported in the *Lancashire Evening Post* that, 'All other competitors, drenched to the skin by the incessant driving rain, buffeted and frozen by the cold gusty winds and lost half the time in thick mist, had retired'. Those retiring included Joe Hand, Eric Beard and Joss Naylor. Joss was lacking in protective gear when he cramped badly, and was reckoned to have possibly been in serious danger of exposure if several other competitors hadn't come across him and assisted him. George Brass came in to the finish carrying his left shoe, which rocks had ripped to bits throughout the event, and which had been a useless encumbrance for the last mile or so.

A few years later George Brass was attempting a round, and was out on a foul night (in 1974). Bill Smith was pacing him, and reported in an appreciation of him in *The Fellrunner* that 'climbing Fairfield in pouring rain, wild winds, thick mist and darkness, we met another 42 Peaks aspirant – a highly experienced fellsman – on his way down to Dunmail. "Are you carrying on?" he asked in passing, at which George growled, "Does he think we're going to pack it in?" Coming at such an hour and in such conditions, this comment completely summed up for me George's typically indomitable spirit'. The wind had been so strong along the Helvellyn ridge that George Brass was literally blown off his feet descending from White Side. He didn't pack it in though, and battled round to become the 19th BGR completer.

The definition of winter when referring to challenges like the BGR has already been discussed. Obviously the weather on any particular day, and the underfoot conditions, are going to have a considerable influence on the outcome. This is well illustrated by an unsuccessful winter round reported by Martin Stone in the February 1996 issue of *The Fellrunner,* which I think gives a feel for what a winter challenge can turn into. On 28 December 1995 **Trevor Dibben** set out at 4.30am on a solo anti-clockwise round in conditions of near complete snow cover.

It was a beautiful night. Trevor was equipped to cope with severe weather but this did require quite a heavy sack. He arrived at Wasdale on schedule to find that his support team were having severe problems with frozen gas, fuel and water, in temperatures as low as -15 degrees Centigrade. Trevor carried on, adding a small ice axe to the contents of his sack and made slow progress onto Scafell. By now a breeze had developed and his camelback of water was frozen by the summit. Lord's Rake was snow-filled but not too difficult and the ground wasn't too bad as far as Bowfell. It was impossible to find any running water and so Trevor had no prospect of a drink for five hours. The snow deepened and became a very dry energy-sapping powder as he approached the Langdales. To seal the fate of the attempt, the high pressure weather area was slipping eastwards and at dusk a full gale with white-out took hold as Trevor was around Thunacar Knott. It was no time to be on the fells and he set a course to pass High Raise and ran for his life, dropping to the relative safety of Calf Crag. Trevor said that he felt like 'the wind was picking the cold off the snow and throwing it at you.' By now the cold had penetrated his neoprene socks and after 15 hours it was time to call it a day at Dunmail. Trevor described it as quite an exhilarating finish to the attempt and there was no way he could be disappointed with the result. Although he thought that he had escaped unscathed, some frost-nip blisters developed on his feet throughout the next 24 hours.

Dibben concluded that he might have been better off going clockwise; but it is debatable in those conditions if it would have made any difference. In the end he was safe, and could look back on a rewarding if also frustrating experience. In passing, I remember well my own Lord's Rake snow experience, where a group of us naively started up the rake in deep snow in just walking boots and a couple of us nearly came a cropper.

Three separate attempts were planned for 21 December 1985. That day turned out to fall during a period of torrential rain and all were doomed to fail. **Martin Stone** noted in his history of winter rounds (in Feb 1994's *Fellrunner*) that he and Stan Bradshaw Jr 'had a meeting with their big Clayton support team, sheltering from the rain in the loos in Keswick and decided to forget the BG in favour of a good night in the pub'. **Graham Webster** reached the summit of Skiddaw but was blown straight back down to Keswick. The late **Steve Parr**, who was renowned for his strength and tenacity, battled for eight hours in storm-force winds and rain running anti-clockwise, but reached only three summits before retiring at Wasdale. That night Keswick High Street was flooded to a serious depth.

But don't think it is just bad weather than can stop people from completing. It is possible to have weather that is *too* good. Someone to suffer in this way was **Alan Heaton**. In 1995, on the 35th anniversary of his first Bob Graham Round attempt, he set off on a round at the age of 67. Heatwave conditions prevailed, which in the past hadn't troubled him unduly, but on this occasion lack of water over the Langdales caused him to suffer dizzy spells, forcing him to retire at Dunmail. If you are thinking that 67 is no age to be doing a BGR, then give credit to **Dave Sleath** who in 2012, at the age of 68,[1] completed a round in 23 hours 59 minutes – which is indeed cutting the timing fine.

One of the less celebrated members of the Bland clan is **Chris Bland** – Billy's cousin. In 1976 Chris failed on the famous round that Billy, David and Anthony Bland completed. All Billy said to me was that 'Chris was first to start struggling because he was always going to be the weakest of us'. Not to be outdone, Chris trained for a year and came back to succeed the following

---

1 Ranulph Fiennes completed the Marathon des Sables at the age of 71 in April 2015. It is 'a gruelling multi-stage adventure through a formidable landscape in one of the world's most inhospitable climates – the Sahara desert'.

year. On the last weekend in June he completed his round, with Jean Dawes. That same weekend Stan Bradshaw did it, aged 65, and Harry Walker and Bob Whitfield also completed, with Pete Walkington doing a repeat round. A pointer to the dominance of the Bland family during one period of the fell scene in the Lakes is the fact that in Keswick AC's own club championships in 1977 Chris Bland was 7th, and every person in front of him was a Bland.

As well as being secretary of the Fell Runners Association for a while, **Mike Rose** was a reasonable standard fell runner himself. The story of his two attempts at the BGR is surely a measure of his perseverance as much as anything else. After helping several others on their rounds he was persuaded to attempt a full round himself in 1982. In an appreciation of him that appeared in the October 2003 *Fellrunner* magazine, written by several who knew him, his attempts are described as follows: 'The first attempt saw him run out of time after 60 miles, with only the Skiddaw group of hills to complete. We all thought he'd totally flipped when he announced outside the Britannia the next lunchtime that he was coming back the following Saturday – it is customary to recover for three or four weeks (or preferably a winter!) before having another go. All went well for 65 miles or so until Mike slowed over the final hills; it was pointed out to him rather firmly that none of his pacers was keen to be back in Keswick for the third weekend in a row and the last ounce of effort saw him back to the Moot Hall with nine minutes to spare.'

Bob Wightman runs a website[1] that has a fund of information of use to BGR aspirants. He completed his own round in May 2005, and has a report of it on the site. There are also reports on his two previous failures, which took place in June and July 2004. On the first he bailed out at Wasdale, going clockwise, saying he was 'in the early stages of hypothermia and I was still cold 12 hours later when I got home and went to bed'. In

---

1 http://bobwightman.co.uk/run/bob_graham.php

addition, he was losing time against his schedule, concluding that 'much of the time lost was down to navigation on the night-time section: it was nearly impossible to tell if you were on the path or not. Also moving at night with only a fuzzy circle of light proved to be somewhat disorientating.' On the second try (set for the next full moon) he went clockwise again, on what he described as a more lightweight attempt. Once again the weather proved the critical factor, and he abandoned coming off Helvellyn. Wightman's analysis of this second attempt was that: 'yet again the weather conspired against us – just bad luck and eternal optimism. Having breaks mid-sections to take food and water certainly helped as I find that I just cannot get large amounts of food down my neck at the road crossings. The pace was very easy, if Hall's Fell had not been so slippery and the batteries in Ali's torch not faded we would have been well up on schedule without really trying.'

Snapshots such as these vividly illustrate some of the things that can go wrong. Earlier in my retelling of successful rounds, there were many incidents that *might* have led to non-completion, but were surmounted. The BGR is a mighty rocky road. If you want to read a more detailed example of achievement over (perceived) failure then a good place to start is the two long articles by **Allan Greenwood** in *The Fellrunner*,[1] the first recounting his two failed bids in 2005, on the second occasion by 23 minutes, and the second article telling of redemption with a completion a few weeks later.

---

1   In the Feb 2006 and June 2006 issues of the magazine.

Endnote

We have come full circle, as a round demands; finally, we return to another 42 at 42 round. Nothing exceptional about the time for this one, but it is by someone who has been influential in this story and who has certainly been instrumental in encouraging others into the sport, and particularly to try challenges like the Bob Graham Round. While he was not a record breaker in BG terms, **Adrian Belton** has a superb *palmares* which shows his formidable achievements as an endurance athlete. These include records for the South Wales Traverse, the Irish Traverse, and the Paddy Buckley and Charlie Ramsay rounds (the latter of which still stands).

As well as these exploits, Belton has been very generous with his help to other contenders, on both standard and extended BG Rounds. His own five Rounds include a fast 18:14 with Mark McDermott in 1987, and the third of his Big Three rounds was done jointly with Helene Diamantides, helping her to a new ladies' record of 19:11 in 1989. He also formed a formidable partnership with Mark McDermott over the years, which included being runners up and winning the KIMM in 1990 and 1991, being second together in the first Dragon's Back race in 1992 and supporting Mark on his 76 Peaks 24 hour record in 1988.

Having established contact with Adrian we agreed to meet at St Pancras International Station one day when he was working in London. (Adrian is Chief Executive of the Construction Industry Training Board). He proved to have an excellent recall of his exploits, going way back to 1981. This was supplemented by his collection of minutely recorded 'splits' charts, and also the written reports by himself and others who he had supported on rounds, which he had helpfully brought along. Some of these he kindly allowed me to borrow and make notes from. Over a coffee and chocolate we ranged widely over the subject of UK endurance challenges, with him pointing out how he was the first (and only?) person to do the Big Four Challenges in one 12-month period.

Adrian Belton is a man of Yorkshire. He was at school in Sheffield, and enjoyed cross-country there. At that time Seb Coe was at school just down the road, at Tapton. 'I might have run against him at school, my sister knew his sister very well,' he said. Running became part of Adrian's life, and he also got into orienteering through a teacher at school. He was Yorkshire schools orienteering champion, then went to Durham University and was selected for the British U23 orienteering team. 'At University I was training with Hugh Symonds (who I later helped on his long run), and the former National marathon coach Alan Storey was there. I did a load of training in the morning in the cold, and that got me a basic fitness.' After university he carried on orienteering, but also started getting into longer events like the Karrimor (KIMM). By the early 1980s he was more into fell running and long distance events.

Adrian went into banking, working for Barclays from 1977 through to 2000. He lived in Royston for much of that time, as it was the furthest north he could get, while still commuting to London. 'Therfield Heath was very hilly and you could get away north quickly', he explained. 'Meanwhile I had to affiliate to a club for fell races, so it was MDC, as my parents live in

South Wales. I relocated with Barclays to Knutsford, and moved to Macclesfield in 1991, by which time most of my big epics were over.' For the last 10 years he has been working in the public sector. As Chief Executive of the CITB he divides his time between Sheffield and London.

Assuming there had been a progression through orienteering, road running and then on to fell running, I asked Adrian how he had developed as an athlete. 'Yeeesss, but not really that logically,' he replied. 'Road was only a way of getting speed. I have won various cross-country marathons such as the Three Forts and Punchbowl races. I thought I needed to get a road time so did the first ever London Marathon and was around 250th in 2:38. I still have the souvenirs.' He liked racing, and would race sometimes twice a week, and trained every day. 'Being in Royston I couldn't do so many fell races. I used to train on my own and then do some Munro bagging. I had friends in the North already.'

In 1985 Adrian had the idea of doing a BGR. One of the people who inspired him to have a go was Chris Hirst, a noted orienteer. 'He was a year or two younger than me, and was British Champion,' said Adrian. 'Chris had a go and failed, and I think eventually did it. I thought if it is that tough, it was something I would like to have a go at. My then wife Valerie, and one other friend from Royston, set out to do it. We had prepped for a couple of years, and had been up and down the motorway, and up and down the hills. Pacing out every bit, schedules galore.' [*which he helpfully showed me to explain timings*] Adrian was the only one who actually finished. 'I had a choice towards the end, do I stop and wait for the others and not do it, or do I crack on in the time left to do Great Calva and Skiddaw, and I did it just in time, 23:51. I thought it was only fair to the pacers who had given up their weekend that someone did it.'

Adrian commented again on his massive racing programme. 'I did a marathon a week after a round on one occasion, and also went orienteering for three days and did one of the records on the fourth day.' Reflecting on that round afterwards, Adrian knew he could do better. 'I went back in 1986 to help John Simpson and Havard Prosser, who were neighbours in Royston, and who I used to train with. I set off as a pacer, but they had to split and there weren't enough pacers to go round. So, I stayed with Havard all the way, which I hadn't intended to.'

Now being familiar with the challenge, Adrian came back with Mark McDermott to support him in 1987. 'At that stage there was a group of us, Mark McDermott, Martin Stone, Andrew Addis and Rex Stickland. Mark Rigby was coming on the scene, and Mark Elsegood (who was revving up to do his big Munros effort),' he noted. 'We knew each other well, and I think there was a situation of egging each other one to progressively harder and faster records. Martin Stone was pioneering many of these. On Mark McDermott's round Andrew Addis couldn't quite keep up towards the end, and Mark and I finished strongly, with Andrew a few minutes later. It was good conditions, all in daylight.'

He then wondered whether the four big rounds could be done in a year. The South Wales Traverse was just being initiated, and so was the Paddy Buckley, and the Charlie Ramsay had not long been instigated. I doubt if many had thought of doing it, but Adrian was wondering who was going to be the first person to do those three plus the Bob Graham Round within one year. 'I was still in the south, and did my recceing in Scotland by getting the shuttle up from Heathrow to Glasgow and being picked up. I would spend a lot of time in May up there, Munro bashing and doing the Scottish islands yacht race, followed by the Jura race.' That was laying down the fitness, and typically Scottish weather would be good then.

He then started thinking what was the best you could you do in 24 hours in Scotland. 'Mark and the others were cleaning up in the Lake District, and I didn't think I was as fast as them. I did the big three in 28 days in 1989 [*no-one had done them all in the same year before*], and when I did the South Wales Traverse the next spring it was the first time anyone had done the big four in the space of 12 months, and some were extended rounds too. I think Helene Diamantides (who was my then girlfriend) and I agreed to do the last one together and call it quits. She broke my Ramsay record the same weekend as I was doing the extended Paddy Buckley. She had broken my Buckley record the week before, setting a new overall record. She set a new Ramsay record, which I then took out, so we agreed to do the third one together.'

They were both very fit, and Adrian reckons Helene knew she could set a record. 'It was just one of those entertaining days out. We had Martin Stone's brother [*Paul*] as a pacer. He was a fighter pilot and very fit, but we had to carry his rucksack later on, I remember that.'

Adrian paired up for the Dragon's Back race with Mark McDermott in 1992. Martin Stone and Helene Diamantides won it, but Adrian felt he and Mark could have beaten them. 'We were leading till about two hours to go,' he said. 'It was a five-day event. They won the first, we won the second, they won the third, and we won the fourth. So, we set off in the lead on the last day. Kept it, then lost it, and took it back when they got lost. By then I had been suffering from shin splits most of the day. I was reduced to a hobble and they overtook us on the last stretch. I should have been taking Nurofen!'

We discussed food and drink on long endurance events. Both Adrian Belton and Mark McDermott used to have a reputation for demolishing food without it touching the sides. 'Gels and energy bars weren't about, so we had rice pudding and real food as much as possible, and water and Staminade to drink. I liked honey butties with sultanas in actually.' Adrian's approach to how to use support points changed over time. 'In the first round it was 20 minutes, fresh socks, feet in hot tub of water, be fed things, put on a fresh top,' he noted, pointing out that sometimes that meant that he started off stiff each time. 'So later I got down to very little rest, a minute or two, not even sitting down, eating on the run and trying to keep moving.'

I asked Adrian about Mark McDermott, who he had paced

for quite a bit of his extended record. 'It was mind-blowing, and we had a celebratory breakfast afterwards. There is no question he did it. Thorough preparation, but living near Macclesfield he was not part of the Lake District circuit.'

Adrian's own organisation level was spectacular. When he decided to try to complete the ascent in one day of the four highest mountains of the countries of Scotland, England, Wales and Northern Ireland (originally he wanted to include Snaefell on the Isle of Man) he enlisted the help of a good friend, John Bateson, who owned a twin-engined plane (John was also his skipper on Three Peak Yacht Races) to travel between them. 'We, that is Mark Elsegood and I, cycled to the mountains in order to run them,' he said. 'So, that meant each of the four mountains from sea level under our own steam on one day – which we did in 1993.'

When asked which of his many achievements he was most proud of, Adrian nominated the 28 Munros in 1991 [*this was in effect an extended Ramsay Round, completed in 23:57*], because it was against pretty desperate odds. 'It was in June and we had summer and winter weather on adjacent days. I was sunburnt on the first day and my beard was frosted over on the second day. I still reckon 30 in a day is possible.'

Adrian never really tried for an extended BGR record. Around 1992/3 he got a bad inflammation of the achilles tendon. A specialist reckoned surgery would be too intrusive. 'So I had to pursue a combination of physio, anti-inflammatory pills, and cutting my shoes. The heel stiffened, and I would try and it would stiffen again, so I moved to cycling and Duathlon. The Dragon's Back shin splints put me back a bit too, I was on crutches for ages. Ironically I had the operation last year, done by a Bob Graham aspirant. The heel is fine now and I am getting back into running.'

When asked what ambitions he had now he is back running, he replied, 'My wife Helen and I are just planning nice days out in the mountains. We recently went up Toubkal in the High Atlas in Morocco. I have beasted my body, have set records,

been there, done that and don't feel I need to go there again.' I
finally asked Adrian why he went back to do the BGR at the age
of 42. 'That was helping a friend, Steve Williams, who wanted
to do it on his 40th birthday, and it was a kind of memorial to
the original 1932 round.'

So, on 5 June 1998 Adrian Belton decided to attempt his fifth
BG Round, being the same age as Bob Graham was when he
set the original mark. Adrian says he was a 'spent force' (his
description), aged 42 and a father of three. As he put it to me,
he had had 'several years of domestic life, and many more of
having previously wrecked my body doing long distance mountain challenges.' In his own notes he described the day:

Training had been months of sleepless nights, changing
nappies, cradling babies, and pushing prams. Certainly no
running, and definitely no recceing. The summer of discon-
tent of 1989, when my trusted pacers threatened to 'run to
rule' in protest at my unreasonable schedules and attempts,
was clearly not forgotten.

First they fixed the weather, clag, rain, thunder and lightning. So, no views, too cold to stop, and no rests. Then they
shoved me up Broad Stand as water ran off the rock down
into my upstretched arm sleeves. To cap it all, just as it looked
as if I might get round in good time to enjoy a pint before
closing time, I got led off the route on Kirk Fell into greasy
boulder fields, rain lashing down, chill factor rising with my
spare clothes in a 'lost in the mist' pacer's rucksack.

We stayed in style in the Stakis Lodore on Friday, allowing
our rooms to be 'hot bedded' by grateful pacers not used to
such luxury (nor the interruption of a surprised chambermaid
finding a succession of different men in the same bed!). It was
a clearish night up onto Skiddaw and, marvel of marvels, a
heather-free descent off Great Calva. Clipping a slight amount
of time off a generous 22 hrs 30 mins schedule, the pacers
were noticeably labouring up the early hills. By Dunmail the
gathering ghouls in the lee of the weather hastened us up onto

Steel Fell in lightning-quick time, and a fresh crew stepped up the pace and the banter.

Yewbarrow was as bad as always, and the weather deteriorated even further. Hot soup was needed at Honister, but by some final twist of fate the clag lifted and the first views of the day occurred as we came off Robinson. Midges in the valley hastened a rapid trot back to Keswick, to arrive just a few minutes before closing time.

Recovery was swift, but within minutes of getting home, rough and tumble with the children soon exposes the overworked limbs. 'Well, why did you do it Daddy?'. Silence. Oh the age of innocence.

Adrian's finishing time for his round was 22 hours 57 minutes. It says something about the respect he was held in that his supporters for this relatively low-key attempt included Mark Hartell, Mark McDermott and Martin Stone. His account, and the fact that he chose to do it in the circumstances, encapsulates many of the themes that have run through this book and says a lot about the pull of the Bob Graham Round.

I will conclude with two quotes from Fred Rogerson.[1] First, when describing what he felt when thinking about the Bob Graham Round, he said: 'Memorable days with companions worthy of the occasion. The reward – a handshake and possibly a celebratory drink.'

Fred Rogerson's second quote also gives a nicely rounded view of the place of Bob Graham and his eponymous round in the pantheon of endurance challenges. Rogerson felt that [*this was said in 1995*]: 'Bob Graham has now got the recognition he should have got many, many years ago. What he did in 1932 was an epic of this century, and I am delighted that so many people have followed in his footsteps. They had around them on the day the people they wanted around them, just as Bob

---

1   From the soundtrack of the film documentary *It's Bob's Round*.

had in 1932. The majority of them have gone on to do harder things, which they wouldn't have done if they hadn't got the Bob Graham Round under their belts, and they have a standard and a yardstick of their physical ability which they have obtained by doing the Bob Graham Round.'

I hope this book, bringing together accounts of successful and unsuccessful rounds, running friendships, records and traditions, has gone some way towards consolidating the recognition accorded to Bob Graham, and will also record for posterity some of the feats, and feelings, of those 'following in Bob Graham's footsteps'.

References

Researching this book involved a lot of background reading. The books and other sources that proved especially useful are listed below. Much of the factual matter included here has been assimilated from three main sources. Many reports of early attempts on the round are available in Fred Rogerson's massive compilation *History and Records of Notable Fell Walks, 1864–1972, Within the Lake District*. Other reports are to be found in the FRA digital archives of *The Fellrunner* magazine. The chapter on early long rounds relies heavily on material published on Bob Wightman's website (http://bobwightman. co.uk/run/bob_graham.php). Where information is to be found in magazines, newspapers, academic journals, or other media, then the specific reference is included within the footnotes.

Books
Askwith, Richard. *Feet in the Clouds,* Aurum Press, 2004
Baddeley's *Lake District,* Ward, Lock and Co, 1964
Bott, George. *Keswick. The story of a Lake District Town,* Bookcase, 2005
Chilton, S. *It's a hill, get over it,* Sandstone Press, 2013
Griffin, A.H. *In Mountain Lakeland,* Crowood Press, 1991
Hoys, Dudley. *English Lake Country,* Batsford, 1969
Hutchinson, William. *History of Cumberland (1793–1797)*
Jones and Milburn, *Cumbrian Rock,* Pic Publications, 1988
Palmer, W.T., *In Lakeland Dells and Fells,* Chatto and Windus, 1903

Smith, Bill. *Stud marks on the Summits*, SKG Publications, 1985
Symonds, Hugh. *Running High*, Hayloft, 2004

Booklets
Buckley, P. and Smith, R. *42 Peaks*, Hayloft, 2012
Rogerson, F. *History and Records of Notable Fell Walks, 1864–1972, Within the Lake District*, unpublished manuscript

Appendix

Fastest BG Rounds

1	Billy Bland	13 hrs 53 mins	1982
2	Mark Hartell	14 hrs 54 mins	1999
3	Stuart Bland	14 hrs 56 mins	1982
4	Mark Palmer	14 hrs 59 mins	2011
5	Andrew Schofield	17 hrs 01 mins	2003
6	Steve Birkinshaw	17 hrs 09 mins	2005
7	Simon Bourne	17 hrs 20 mins	2006
8	Chris Near	17 hrs 23 mins	2010
9	Morgan Donnelly	17 hrs 24 mins	2005
10	Richard Mellon	17 hrs 38 mins	2010
11	Geoff Clucas	17 hrs 40 mins	1989
12	Mike Nicholson	17 hrs 45 mins	1977
13	Neil Wrigley	17 hrs 48 mins	1997
14=	Mike Johnson	17 hrs 49 mins	2009
14=	Ian Charlton	17 hrs 49 mins	1983
16	Steve Parr	17 hrs 58 mins	1981

Lake District 24 Hour Fell Record (Men)

Bob Graham	1932	42 Peaks	23 hrs 39 mins
Alan Heaton	1960	42 Peaks	22 hrs 18 mins
Ken Heaton	1961	51 Peaks	22 hrs 13 mins
Alan Heaton	1962	54 Peaks	23 hrs 48 mins
Eric Beard	1963	56 Peaks	23 hrs 35 mins
Alan Heaton	1965	60 Peaks	23 hrs 34 mins
Joss Naylor	1971	61 Peaks	23 hrs 37 mins

Joss Naylor	1972	63 Peaks	23 hrs 35 mins
Joss Naylor	1975	72 Peaks	23 hrs 11 mins
Mark McDermott	1988	76 Peaks	23 hrs 26 mins
Mark Hartell[1]	1997	77 Peaks	23 hrs 47 mins

Lake District 24 Hour Fell Record (Women)

Jean Dawes	1977	42 Peaks	23 hrs 37 mins
Anne-Marie Grindley	1978	42 Peaks	21 hrs 05 mins
Ros Coats	1979	42 Peaks	20 hrs 31 mins
Anne-Marie Grindley	1979	58 Peaks	23 hrs 20 mins
Anne Stentiford	1994	62 Peaks	23 hrs 17 mins
Nicky Spinks	2011	64 Peaks	23 hrs 15 mins

---

1   One distinction that Mark Hartell does have is to be by far the fastest of those who have set 24 hour fell records. He has a fastest round of 14:54, with Mark McDermott (with 18:14) the only other of the men on this list under 22 hours. For the women Nicky Spinks has a fastest time of 18:12, and Anne Stentiford a fastest time of 18:49.

Index

Notes: Some early walkers are known only by their surnames. These are indicated in the index accordingly, e.g. 'Gibbs (early walker)'. For principal summits such as Skiddaw, Helvellyn and the Scafells, only significant references have been included. There are many other passing references in the text.